IRON MAIDEN

Thirty Years Of The Beast

Iron Maiden - Thirty Years Of The Beast
The Unauthorised Biography

by Paul Stenning

A CHROME DREAMS PUBLICATION

First Edition 2006

Published by Chrome Dreams
PO BOX 230, New Malden , Surrey
KT3 6YY, UK
books@chromedreams.co.uk

WWW.CHROMEDREAMS.CO.UK

ISBN 1 84240 361 3

Editor Cathy Johnstone
Editorial Assistant Jake Kennedy
Front cover design Jon Storey
Layout design Marek Krzysztof Niedziewicz

Printed and bound in Great Britain by William Clowes Ltd, Beccles, Suffolk

IRON MAIDEN

Thirty Years Of The Beast

The Unauthorised Biography

Paul Stenning

*This book is dedicated to my wonderful wife Isla
and of course, Tommy Vance R.I.P. 1941-2005*

Acknowledgements

The following people were invaluable in the help given to me in producing this ultimate Maiden tome. I am particularly indebted to the following individuals who are all very nice men and supremely helpful, cheers to:

Steve 'Loopy' Newhouse, Neal Kay, Roy Z, Derek Riggs, Chris Dale, Tony Moore, George Matsagouras, Keith Wilfort.

Thank you to the following for also contributing valued time and effort:

Paul Di'Anno, Janick Gers, Maurice Coyne, Dave Lights, CJ Wildheart, Jase Edwards, Bill Leisegang, Barry Fitzgerald, Chris Aylmer, Dave Pattenden, Lauren Roberts, Jeff Hateley, Tony Platt, Baktash Cyrus Houshangi, Jon Hinchcliffe, Dennis Stratton, Samir Puri, Marco Gamba, Vinicius Renner Lampert, Steffen Rogne, Smiler, William Luff, Jonathan Selzer, Michelle Gregson, Brian H. Martens, Oscar Guerra.

Oh and thanks to the dickhead who originally got me into the band, no thanks for the bullying afterwards though – you know who you are!

The publishers wish to thank Joe Geesin for his generous assistance in the production of this book.

Photographs courtesy of:

Front Cover: Life, Back Cover: Redferns
Inside Photos: Redferns, REX

Record covers courtesy of EMI
Posters and Programmes courtesy of Iron Maiden.

Lyrics courtesy of Zomba Music Publishing Ltd.

Music author and journalist Paul Stenning is a writer specialising in the genres of Rock and Heavy Metal. He is currently a regular contributor to the hallowed pages of *Metal Hammer*, *Terrorizer, Record Collector* and *Metal Maniacs*, and has previously written for countless other publications and websites. He has interviewed numerous bands and artists from those genres including Iron Maiden, AC/DC, Alice Cooper, Judas Priest, Meatloaf and a host of other top names.

His previous books include the only available work on Guns N' Roses, *The Band That Time Forgot; AC/DC - Two Sides To Every Glory* and *My Chemical Romance - Something Wicked This Way Comes*.

Paul Stenning lives in Manchester with his wife Isla and can be contacted at czechzebra@yahoo.com.

Prologue

I would certainly not be the person I am today without the existence of Iron Maiden – hell I'm not sure I'd even be alive! If you are reading this book as a fan, the greatest heavy metallers of all time will undoubtedly hold equal significance within your own personal truth. For me the band were important as the first heavy metal outfit I ever heard, having previously been exposed almost exclusively to pop such as Michael Jackson, Pet Shop Boys and Go West. Hearing Piece Of Mind *for the first time was a shock to the system to say the least. Suddenly life changed, and all for the better. The sound of loud guitars, implausibly high shrieking vocals and catchy choruses was 'the future' as far as I was concerned, and apparently I was not alone in this view.*

Iron Maiden were not the first heavy metal band, but what an introduction! The Maiden initiation paved a path to every other heavy metal band the universe had to offer, there to be discovered like a metallic family tree. At the time all I knew was Piece Of Mind *and it was the greatest thing I had ever heard in my life. In the following weeks I ran around with Walkman headphones strapped to my ears, replaying the track incessantly and screaming along with the lyrics, while imagining just how amazing the people who created this impenetrable sound must be.*

Maiden has the unique effect of making the listener feel as if he or she is being played to exclusively as an individual, and you immediately feel at one with the music. On entering the Maiden Kingdom, it is unusual for anyone to want to leave. I know there are literally millions of people like me, who discovered the band at a young age and who were helped through some very tough times thanks to the Iron Maiden back catalogue. Yet frequently there are new listeners coming through, eager to be at one with the Maiden phenomenon.

Maiden has never been a band to write 'grunge' type lyrics, where the listener feels a partner to their pain – they didn't need to. There is something intrinsic in Maiden's sound that simply makes you feel better, as if they understand you totally and their lyrics (whatever the subject) resonate with honesty and realism. There is no hardship that cannot be lessened by blasting out ten tons of molten metal on a loud stereo, and no better band than Iron Maiden to blast it. They probably don't know it, but this heavy rock fan, now well into adulthood, along with countless others would have found life to be a lesser experience without the existence of The Maiden. Here's to each one of them and their music, for without it, we are small.

Paul Stenning, May 2006

Introduction

Oh well, wherever, wherever you are,
Iron Maiden's gonna get you, no matter how far.

'Iron Maiden' - Iron Maiden

When one considers the words heavy metal, a number of images instantly spring to mind. Many facets define the genre but whether you picture long hair and tight trousers or deafening over-amplified electric guitars, the chances are, when you think of bands in the field, Iron Maiden would be one of the first which spring to mind.

Over three decades this group has managed to keep its image fresh in the public eye. This is the rarest of metal phenomenon, a traditional heavy metal ensemble that actually makes the pop charts in numerous countries, with every new album or single release. As much as the conservative establishment would like Maiden to disappear it simply refuses to, and by sheer virtue of its staying power has become all but accepted as an institution, at last 'allowed' to grace the areas usually reserved for pop acts.

Iron Maiden has travelled beyond its popular 80s metal status without fading away, unlike many of its peers. In turn, those bands who have managed to prevail, such as Metallica, would not even exist without their Maiden predecessors. The Brits have influenced other musicians since the late 70s and remarkably continue to do so to this day. Even now there are young fans who know little of Maiden's exploits in the early years, becoming hooked on the band thanks to 2003's *Dance Of Death* LP. This is just one way in which Steve Harris and company have carved a spectacular and unique career for themselves. They have an ability to evolve with the times, without losing their essence or striving to be overly 'current', always retaining a sharp song-writing edge regardless of the type material they are creating.

From its crude young days as a fledgling NWOBHM (New Wave Of British Heavy Metal) outfit, often mistaken for a punk group, to a multi-million selling, arena filling global spectacle, Iron Maiden has seen and done everything. Its tremendous success stems primarily from its iconic bass player and leader, Steve Harris, better known as 'Arry. His vision, and intense drive meant Maiden was never likely to find itself simply 'on a par' with its fellow NWOBHM peddlers. The plan was always for his setup to give the fans something extra, added verve in performance, greater creativity in the song writing and guaranteed 100 per cent dedication. Where local acts of the time were struggling to write more than a few decent songs, Harris was always ten-steps ahead, pondering how he could enliven the stage show and create new and innovative sounds. He envisioned everything from song writing to presentation, from the musicians who would play in the group, to the mascot and the logo that would represent it.

With such strong mental focus, Harris merely stuck to his guns, ploughing through a succession of members that weren't quite right, before eventually settling on a line up that would record the first Maiden record proper. From then on, despite changes of singer, drummer and guitarist over coming years, Maiden would increase its fan base from show to show, album to album, a feat which has continued right up to the present day.

Heavy metal is nothing without Iron Maiden and a metal fan who fails to acknowledge Maiden as king of its genre is probably not worth his weight in leather. There is an infallibility regarding Steve Harris and his cohorts. Like King Midas, Harris undoubtedly has the golden touch and despite approaching his fiftieth year, shows no signs of slowing down.

There are many reasons why this down to earth English metal act has survived countless shifts in public taste, and ever evolving line-up changes. For all the information readily available on the band and its members, it is still largely an enigma, often superficially covered with a few throwaway references to loud rock music and spandex.

This book aims to delve into the Maiden camp that little bit deeper than previous works on the group. For every review of an album by them, there is an untold story, a tale that has waited for some years to be revealed. This collection is the result of a teenage obsession that has lingered for some twenty years. For many, once Iron Maiden enters your life, it becomes a part of your make up and is virtually impossible to shake off. Instead, fans become collectors, collectors become obsessives and obsessed collectors and fans can end up going to extremes, even to the extent of writing a book such as this.

This is no ordinary rock biography, but then Iron Maiden is no ordinary outfit. Where in times past it has received a basic history retelling, the time has come to underline its place in metal history with a fitting tome which encompasses more information than any fan could possibly already know.

Not only is Maiden's history thoroughly examined in every minute detail, there is also in-depth analysis and coverage of the major players in the story, be they roadies or ex-members. Though Iron Maiden evolved from one man, its roots and branches extend deep and wide, beyond Steve Harris, and many along the way have helped Maiden to become an institution in rock music. This story covers everything from the identifiable mascot Eddie to the striking cover paintings of official artist Derek Riggs, and features every aspect in-between. For young and old, novice or expert, *30 Years Of The Beast* encapsulates all you could possibly want when reading of the one and only Iron Maiden.

Fly on your way, like an eagle,
Fly as high as the sun.

'Flight Of Icarus' - Iron Maiden

Chapter 1
Birth Of The Beast

"Steve was both driven and creatively ruthless. I quickly saw that he knew exactly what he wanted and would not suffer fools gladly. He didn't see the band as dependent on any one person (well, except for himself of course). Iron Maiden was always far more precious as a band than any of the individual members." Tony Moore

When Stephen Percy Harris spilled into the world on March 12th 1956 in Leytonstone, Greater London, there would have been little indication that the newborn 'Arry would later be positioned at the forefront of the British heavy metal movement. A month before Harris' birth Elvis Presley had only just entered the American charts for the first time, setting a precedent for 'dangerous' rock n' roll for years to come. As Steve Harris grew up and progressed through adolescence there was scant evidence of his future musical prowess. Along with three sisters, he was raised primarily by his mother, while his father worked away for long periods as a truck driver.

Harris was obsessed with sport, specifically football as a young boy, and by 1972 when he finished his schooling at Leyton County High School, he was offered a trial by his favourite football team West Ham United.

The club had been formed from a merging of the Thames Ironworks and Shipbuilding Company Ltd. and, coincidentally, had originally been nicknamed 'The Irons'. Only in 1900 was the team renamed West Ham United once the club became a limited company with their nickname also changing to 'The Hammers'. West Ham's most memorable period came in the 1960s, a decade in which they managed to win the F.A. Cup, the Charity Shield and the European Cup Winners Cup. They were also League Cup Finalists in 1966 and enjoyed the honour, in the same year, of providing three players to England's World Cup winning side. Of all the players involved in the World Cup final against West Germany, perhaps the three most significant were the three immortal West Ham players – Geoff Hurst, Bobby Moore and Martin Peters.

By the time Steve Harris joined his favourite club, the Hammers were in a somewhat less respectable position, and it wasn't until 1975-6 that they enjoyed another trophy heyday – winning both the European Cup

Winners Cup and F.A. Cup in that period. By this time however, Harris was concentrating on music.

"I was on their books for about eight months," Harris would later say, "and at that time I was playing every day of the week between West Ham, my Saturday and Sunday clubs, and school. I played Saturday afternoons for Melbourne Sports Reserves and on Sundays for Beaumont Youth, which is where I got 'discovered' by a famous West Ham scout called Wally Serpa. I couldn't believe it when I heard West Ham were interested. It was great, but fourteen is the wrong age really because all I wanted to do was start having a few beers and meet a few birds – which doesn't mix with playing football. They want you in bed early and all that stuff. In a sense it disillusioned me because I thought, 'if I can't be dedicated to the club I really love then what's it all about?' It did me in a bit, really. If it had been a couple of years later it maybe would've been a different story."

Harris' love of West Ham was fanatical, but as far as a career in the game was concerned, he gradually came to the realisation that a future in music could perhaps offer a less stringent lifestyle. A friend of his named Pete Dale had peeked his interest in music. Initially Steve considered the likes of Genesis, Jethro Tull and Black Sabbath "weird", but after borrowing a few albums from Dale he began to grow into the music, while coming to the realisation that a musical career route would allow him to "still drink beers and see birds." And so it was in 1972 that Steve settled on learning an instrument, at the relatively advanced age of sixteen.

"Like many others, I started by learning the guitar," he says. "I even spent a few years learning the classical guitar, then I gave up because I got bored of it. In fact, I wanted to play the bass, and I had been told that in order to do that I absolutely needed to learn the bass chords on an acoustic guitar. When you think of it, this is pretty stupid, and I know now that you can play the bass without wasting your time like I wasted mine. As soon as I started playing with a band, I gave up the acoustic guitar and I focused exclusively on the bass. Sometimes I think it's better when you start late because you get too many preconceived ideas, especially if you get someone teaching you when you're a kid. I think it's wrong to get too many of those kind of ideas in the first place."

The influences for Harris' bass studies were wide and varied. It was no surprise that in a golden era for rock he focused on such prominent musicians as Chris Squire of Yes and The Who's John Entwistle. There was also Wishbone Ash's Martin Turner and, more obscurely,

Rinus Gerritsen from Golden Earring whose style had a major impact on the young Harris. He would later often credit Golden Earring as steering much of his upfront image.

Harris did not take lessons, preferring to teach himself from records. "I used to listen to early Free, early Sabbath, stuff like that. I liked some of the Free bass lines, fairly simple, but really nice technique." It has always been a natural progression for a true and honest musician to write his own material and Steve was no different. In fact he had written his first song, titled 'Burning Ambition' when he was just 16. This track would later appear as an Iron Maiden b-side on their 1980 debut single 'Running Free'.

It was at this point Steve began the first vestiges of a real band. "When I first started playing we used to muck about in my house. I used to have a couple of guys coming over from school, just sort of messing about," he explains. "This guy used to play guitar, and he was a lot better on guitar than I was on bass at the time, and I used to just try and jam in with him. Then we decided, 'Ah, well, we've got to get a drummer!' So we got this guy; anyway, he had this kit. He was pretty useless, but we didn't really know at the time. We thought he was alright, but as we started to progress and get a bit better, we realised he wasn't any good, and we sacked him."

Actually, as Steve admitted, the rest of the band "wasn't very good" at that time either, and they were predominantly playing cover tunes. "They were doing more rock-boogie sort of stuff, like Savoy Brown, early Fleetwood Mac. I wasn't really advocating the sort of stuff they were playing. I just thought, 'Well, it's good experience for me.' I played about sixteen gigs with them."

Although this band has gone down in the annals of Iron Maiden history as a serious and exciting group – and with a name like Gypsy's Kiss they were bound to be remembered, if for that alone. The reality however was rather a different story, as Harris was the first to acknowledge, and he soon moved on to join a more mature troupe known as Smiler. The other members of this outfit were older, so Steve figured he would learn a lot, "Which I did. I think I was about eighteen and they were twenty-six, which I thought was really old at the time! Only problem was, when I started writing my own songs, they didn't want to play them because they thought there were too many time changes and that sort of thing. So I figured, 'alright,' and I just left to form Iron Maiden."

The main reason Steve's songs did not sit well with Smiler was the simple fact that he was ascribing to the progressive rock ethic, and according to Harris the remainder of the band were against experimentation, themselves preferring a kind of "rockabilly" sound. By Christmas 1975 Steve had formed the very first line up of Iron Maiden with Paul Day on vocals, two guitarists, Terry Rance and Dave Sullivan and drummer Ron Rebel.

An 'iron maiden' was a medieval torture device and this matched Harris' vision for a nasty heavy rock band. However he was not the first to coin the name. Five years previously there had been an early 'doom' group by the same name (originally they had called themselves Growth and then BUM). However, for their debut album, *Maiden Voyage,* the Essex four-piece was to be known as Iron Maiden. It is intriguing to note that they hailed from the same county as Steve Harris, and also their most famous song 'Ballad of Martha Kent' featured harmonies very similar to 'Heaven Can Wait' (a later Harris/Maiden track).

"We were doing pubs and clubs on the weekends," Harris says of his early Maiden gigs. "Then we'd go take time off of work, call in sick or something, that was the usual thing, to go up to clubs in the north of England." The day job for Harris at that time, was as an architectural draftsman, a sideline 'career' which lasted for about five years. But the ultimate goal was always to play in a band full time. Though it was clear Harris disliked the punk movement (later linked to Maiden), at the time he formed Iron Maiden there was in fact no punk scene to speak of, so as he explains, "I didn't start the band as any kind of crusade against punk. I couldn't have because Maiden began in 1975, before all that, doing East End pubs like The Ruskin Arms in East Ham and The Bridge House in Canning Town. It was when Led Zeppelin and Deep Purple were finishing – a lot of the influences came from them, the twin guitars from Wishbone Ash and Thin Lizzy, the time changes from Yes and Jethro Tull. We wanted to get all the ingredients in there and come up with something different."

For that they needed a prominent front man, and though Day was a decent singer, he lacked true stage charisma. Steve 'Loopy' Newhouse, who knew both Day and Harris from the early days, recalls: "Paul Mario Day, as he now prefers, was a member of the group of kids that hung around together in Leyton, but I didn't meet him until a few years later. He was older than us, and married. He was also a biker, so most of us were a bit wary of him to start with, but once I got to know him, we became very close. I didn't know that Paul was a singer in a band, until one night he pulled up on his bike and told me and a guy called Trevor Green, that he was doing a gig at the Cart and Horses in Stratford, and would we like to go and see them. We said ok. Trevor Green wasn't into rock music as much as me, but we went and saw Iron Maiden for the first time. Apart from Paul Mario Day and Steve Harris, I'm not really sure of the line up. I seem to think Dave Murray was on guitar, but I may be completely wrong. And I think the drummer might have been Ron somebody or other, but again I could be wrong. I don't remember much about the night, apart from the fact they were loud, and because there were only a few people there, Paul had plenty of room to run around in."

Come May of 1976 Day was the first to utter the immortal words "Iron Maiden's... gonna get you... no matter how far" at the Cart & Horses Tavern at Maryland Point, Stratford, England. The line quickly became part of their signature tune 'Iron Maiden'.

David Michael Murray, another local, born on December 23rd, 1958 in Edmonton, London, joined Maiden in mid 1976, as Harris noted Rance and Sullivan were merely rhythm guitarists, incapable of playing lead guitar. When Murray appeared on the scene the other two guitarists coupled together and gave Steve an ultimatum, "it's Murray or us." Steve opted for Murray, the cheeky faced guitarist who would later be known as 'Moonface'. Born of Scottish and Irish descent, Murray was a keen football fan like Harris, though the team he followed was West Ham's London rivals Tottenham Hotspur. The Murray family were very poor; Dave's mother worked as a cleaner and his father was disabled. They also moved around frequently, resulting in Murray attending a dozen different schools before finally finishing his formal education, aged sixteen. Neal Kay who would later play an important role in Maiden's career says of Murray, "Davey is one of life's all-time nice guys and unlike many nice guys has reaped the rewards and finished first. He has a great temperament and appreciates all he has. There is more to him than his on-stage persona suggests. He can be determined when he needs to be, and has several interests outside of music."

As the punk scene, led by the Sex Pistols, took a hold of the British youth it began to affect the honest toil of the heavy rock outfit Steve Harris had assembled. "After a year or so we weren't getting gigs any more," he exclaimed. "Then we did hate punk because we felt pissed off that these guys just picked up a guitar, jumped around a bit and because of this so-called 'energy' they got the publicity and they got the work, but they couldn't play and we could. I went to the Roxy once because we were offered a gig there and I'll never forget it because there were geezers spitting all over each other! Well we had quite a hardcore following and we knew if we went down there it would be all off: ructions."

As Murray joined the Maiden fray, his presence coincided with the departure of Paul Day and the arrival of Dennis Wilcock. The latter was more of a performer than a singer, but at least he brought a more theatrical aspect to the band as Steve would later reference. "We had smoke machines, bubble machines, all home made – bung a bit of dry ice in a kettle, that sort of thing. Then Dennis Wilcock started us thinking. He had this stunt where he waved this sword about, then slashed the blade across his mouth and blood would come pouring out. Of course it wasn't real, but a couple of girls did faint right in front of him once – the Stars & Stripes Club, Ramsgate, I'll never forget it. Still he looked a bit daft to be honest. So we came up with the first Eddie The 'Ead, this horrible mask which stood at the back of the stage. We rigged up this pump we got out of a fish tank and at a given moment it would spit buckets of blood all over the drummer."

Future Maiden fan club secretary Keith Wilfort recalls his Maiden initiation. "I first came into contact with Iron Maiden in May 1976. Some friends from work and I were driving around looking for somewhere to go for a drink and as we drove by The Cart and Horses Pub in Stratford, East London, we heard some rather good music coming out and so we decided to stop in and check it out. When we got there, the band were half way through playing 'Transylvania' so we stayed around for the rest of the show. It was memorable due to the fact that at the end a fight broke out between two punters and also one of my friends, who was wearing a new white jacket, got spattered with fake blood during 'Iron Maiden'. Den Wilcock the singer used to put blood capsules in his mouth and during the climax to 'Iron Maiden' would run a sword through his mouth and spit the 'blood' out. The line up at that time was Steve, Den Wilcock, Bob Sawyer and Dave Murray with Ron Rebel on drums. We liked what we saw and went back the next week and gradually over the next few months got to know the band. We went to other gigs they played in and around London and became familiar faces. We'd buy them drinks and vice versa and sometimes give them lifts to and from gigs. I sort of became the official number one fan; I'd get T-shirts printed with designs signifying Maiden song titles and the band catchphrases."

The lesser ability of many punk musicians did not steer Harris towards playing more straightforward rock. On the contrary, he became even firmer in his love for vast, expansive music with multiple time changes and a true progressive feel, and this led him into seeking a keyboard player. By early 1977 the line-up had shifted again, with Thunderstick taking over from Rebel, Terry Wapram replacing Murray and keyboardist Tony Moore joining the fray.

"I scanned the *Melody Maker* ads for any bands in London that were looking for players," Moore remembers. "I think this was sometime during the early summer of 1977. I saw an advert that said something like 'Keyboard/Synth player needed for Lone Star style band'. I called the number and think it was Steve that I spoke to first. He explained that Iron Maiden wanted a line up a bit like (the original) Lone Star who had a hit in the 70s with a song called 'Bells Of Berlin'. The formula they established was dual lead guitar and synth player with a rock foundation, and that was what the newest incarnation of Maiden was inspired by. They were holding auditions at a rehearsal room called Scarf just behind Mile End station in the East End of London. The band rehearsed in the evening because everyone had a day job. Steve had a company van, very useful for carrying gear around in."

Moore notes that even during this early 'version' of the band, with Steve Harris at the tender age of nineteen, there was a determination and desire from the outset. "Steve had always been a man with a dream and a passion," Moore states. "His drive was compelling and his long wavy hair flicked around his shoulders as he played. With a bass rig that dominated the room and a Fender Precision Bass that he played with a plectrum, he was always pushing and directing what should happen. We used to rehearse at least once or twice a week. Steve was a stickler for professionalism and seemed very loyal to those around him."

Moore recalls of Dennis Wilcock: "He wore a kind of sheepskin leather bulky USA airforce style jacket. His long, blonde curly hair had tight ringlets in it and his eyes bulged a little, making his face both dramatic and unusual. He was very animated in the way he talked and acted. Dennis would, on the surface, appear to be the main character in the band. He was loud, and flamboyant and everyone would talk about his stage antics and what a great front man he was. Even though Steve purposefully steered from behind, I think he allowed the energy to be focused through Dennis. I was always a little quieter around Dennis as his personality tended to dominate the room and I was still feeling a little provincial, taking my time to fit in and lose some of my West Country naivety."

Talking of his audition, the keyboardist explains, "I remember them starting the first song and the volume, power and tightness was both frightening and exhilarating in equal measure. The jump from silence to giant power chords and thundering drums made my heart jump. I started to try and find my way into the song, listening for the riffs, identifying chords, looking for space to add my part. Alternating between tweaking the synth to produce ethereal sounds, vamping on the piano and attempting to follow the intricate guitar melody lines that Terry was throwing out with effortless ease. I am not sure how long it all lasted or how many songs we played, but fairly quickly Steve and Dennis came out and asked me if I wanted to join the band. I was over the moon. I didn't think I had done a particularly great job, but I HAD got on with everyone really well, and my attitude has always been very positive and professional. I agreed and that was it, I was in the band!"

Moore has a refreshing viewpoint on the direction of the Iron Maiden material. Coming from a less rock-oriented background than the others he observed the Maiden style as follows. "I think Steve saw this as an opportunity for a new wave of British rock music that was dynamic and fresh and impossible to ignore. During rehearsals he always wanted everything to be played as fast as possible. It was as though he had absorbed the spirit of punk and could instinctively see WHY speed appealed to people. It made the heart beat faster when you heard it. Combine this with exemplary musicianship; anthemic rock themes with cinematic lyrics and the result would be both groundbreaking and yet familiar. I could see that Steve's vision was clear and focussed and I was happy and inspired to follow him. Even though the bands music was not the kind of thing I had played or really listened to before, I got on with Steve very well as we swapped stories of the great gigs we'd seen and how we would be a part of the new generation of bands whose shows were legendary."

Dave Murray's departure from Iron Maiden as Moore joined, followed an argument after a gig at the Bridge House, during which Dennis Wilcock punched Murray. This resulted in the reserved guitarist's decision to call it a day with the Maiden, going on to join his long time guitarist friend, Adrian Smith, in a band called Urchin. This had been an ongoing outfit since 1974, having formed from the remnants of Evil Ways, which had previously featured Murray.

Maurice Coyne, Smith's original partner in Urchin describes the band set up; "Urchin became the name of the band after we got the record deal. Our management decided that we should change the name to something more 'catchy' and came up with Urchin. I'm sure they had a long term plan to make us dress up like extras from *Oliver*! So I never really joined Urchin, it was just a name change. I don't think we ever thought of anyone as the leader but Adrian was the main songwriter – although bassist Alan Levett, David Hall (vocals) and I wrote too – and, after Dave left, took on lead vocals as well. There was no doubt that, at that point, Adrian was the main focus of the band with all the responsibility that came with being the front man. It was always clear to me that Adrian was 'special'.

He's a really talented guy and a fantastic guitar player. In those days I was probably, technically the better guitarist but he always had a great feel to his playing and that's not something you can learn.

"I think the two best memories are when we all went camping in Cornwall during the summer of '76. There was a heat wave that year and the weather was amazing. We all slept in the van, got drunk a lot and had an amazing time.

"From a playing point of view, I can remember a gig at East London College in Whitechapel, where we played to a packed house of around 2,000. We played out of our skins and got called back for five encores. It was just a magical night – one to tell your grandchildren about.

"The worst memories are the first time we played the Marquee and Dave (the vocalist) turned up one minute before we were due on stage. It was such a big night for us and to have to deal with all that tension was terrible. That was the beginning of the end for Dave. The other bad memory is of the night I left the band. I'd been soul searching for weeks and finally decided to leave. Telling the guys, who were my best mates, was really hard. Luckily, we all remained good friends and are still in touch."

Speaking of how he joined Urchin, Coyne says, "A guy I worked with told me that his friend's band were looking for a guitarist because the one they had was leaving and put me in touch with the bass player, John Hoye. I went down for a jam with John and Adrian and Dave Murray, the guitarist who was leaving, turned up. At that stage the band was called Stone Free (Dave was a big Hendrix fan). I remember Dave pulling out all the stops – playing with his teeth, etc. He was a very extrovert player for such a quiet guy! Stone Free kept going for a few weeks longer – I can remember going to see them play in a talent contest in a pub – but then Dave finally decided to leave and we got together as a band.

"We used to rehearse in a school hall on Monday evenings and our first gig was at a school dance. We were all petrified but it went really well, as far as I can remember. A few months later, we decided that Peter (the drummer) was not right for us and we put an ad in *Melody Maker*. Barry (Purkis who replaced Peter as drummer) turned up with his brother and blew us away. He thought he was rubbish but he was a breath of fresh air after Peter. We soon started gigging at local pubs and the rest is history.

"We really were a band of brothers – not only the musicians but also Dave, Terry and Tom who were our road crew. I don't remember any big arguments and we were very democratic about songs, etc. It was great playing in local pubs and building a following. We learnt how to be a band by playing in sweaty boozers three or 4 nights a week for £25 a night!"

Dave Murray's replacement in Iron Maiden, Terry Wapram lasted only a few months, and soon Murray was back in the band. Wapram insisted he could only work with an organist/keyboardist, but Maiden decided after just one gig that a keyboard player was not right for Iron Maiden. In Thunderstick, Maiden had found not only a solid, hard-hitting drummer but also a flamboyant character who sported a bondage mask!

"The first band I had was the bedroom band," Thunderstick, aka Barry Purkis, says of his early musical education, "which was 'Phalanx' and we were trying to be, sort of, progressive rock. We would play at schools and colleges and stuff like that. You know, nothing big at all. Ninety per-cent of the time it was stuff that we put together ourselves, to try and self promote. Then, when I was 17, I left home and I went to Sicily and moved in with a band that had been going since the 60s, a band called The Primitives.

"Come 1974 I was in Sicily. I came back, I joined a folk rock band that was like Steeleye Span. They'd never had drums until then, they'd had congas, so I was the first drummer to come in with them and we ended up sounding like Gong, that very weird and wonderful kind of stuff. The band was called Oz. I then moved on to Iron Maiden.

"With Maiden the set-up seemed to be a lot better. You know, they were getting their own PA, they had their own truck and Steve Harris was very directional with what he wanted. He used to come to my house and we'd sit in the bedroom going over the bass and drum parts and stuff like that. That was it. Then they just phoned me up and said 'yeah, you've got the gig' so I started playing with them.

"Some rehearsals sounded great, absolutely great, I've got some on reel-to-reel at home; they're probably worth a bit. We've got the whole set with 'Sanctuary', 'Prowler' and 'Wrathchild', 'Iron Maiden', all of the early stuff."

Thunderstick only lasted around eight months in Maiden but his impact was certainly felt and ironically he would go on to play with Maiden's future (and most revered) vocalist Bruce Dickinson, in Samson. He explains how he ended up losing his place in Iron Maiden; "I was married for eight years and I was having an affair at the time with this beautiful woman who had just told her husband that I was having an affair with her. My wife had just found out. All three were at the gig. I had just bought a brand new drum kit, a Gretsch, and I'd never played it before, not even to rehearse on it. I literally took delivery of it that afternoon of the gig with Iron Maiden. So it took me a little while in the sound check to kind of set it up and try it out. And, yes, I did drop something. It wasn't acid or anything like that, it was a barbiturate, it was a downer, a Valium or something like that. I was so on edge that whole gig, because of the circumstances of my wife standing there, right next to her is my girlfriend that I'm screwing at the time and her husband and my new drum kit... I was used to the other kit and every time I'd go around it there wouldn't be a tom-tom there."

Harris thought his drummer was just a sloppy player and so Doug Sampson was enlisted as his replacement. By this time, not only had Harris' own playing improved tenfold, he was also writing songs that were to remain in the Maiden live set for years to come. Considering his youth and revolving band partners, Harris was putting together very strong material and the East End fans were beginning to take notice of this ambitious rock outfit.

Maiden really hit the jackpot when they acquired Paul Di'Anno who had previously sung for the obscure outfit Bird Of Prey. Steve 'Loopy' Newhouse says of Di'Anno, "Paul and I used to hang about in the same crowd when we were kids in Leyton, London. We also went to the same school, George Mitchell High School for boys. I can't really remember how we actually met, but it must have been around 1970-ish. Paul was a year younger than me, but I think we became instant friends and stayed best friends for many years. He was quite a cool character, with wide musical tastes, from Queen to Bob Marley and even Emerson, Lake and Palmer. It was actually a guy called Trevor Searle who named me Loopy. That was a few years later. Prior to singing with Maiden, Paul had sung in a couple of dodgy punk bands, including Rock Candy, who were one of the few who actually made it out of rehearsals and onto the pub circuit."

Rock Candy were a more serious band than Bird Of Prey. Newhouse describes the set-up; "They were based in the Romford area during the mid 70s, with Paul on vocals, Nigel Foster on guitar, Rob Cunningham on drums, and Martin Waites on bass. Martin was told his voice wasn't strong enough, so they got Paul in to do the job. How they met in the first place is anybody's guess. I wasn't there that day. After spending several months rehearsing in a concrete bunker in the middle of a potato field at Bonzers Farm in Romford, we arrived there one Sunday afternoon to find the bands gear had been stolen from the bunker. The band tried to carry on and even did one gig, at the Three Rabbits, Manor Park, East London, but by then the writing was pretty much on the wall, and they called it a day shortly after."

Steve Harris and Paul Di'Anno forged an important union, which began somewhat predictably in a pub. "It was the Red Lion, in North London," Harris remembers, "In fact, I had a mate, who knew that I was looking for a new singer for the band. At that time, we were a three-piece: Dave, Doug Sampson and myself. So, he introduced Paul to me and he said, 'I'd really love to sing, but I have no experience whatsoever'. And I told him that I didn't either and that we could rehearse together anyway. So he came down there and we played a few covers, like Purple's 'Lady Double Dealer', or some songs by Black Sabbath or Led Zeppelin. Then we started playing our own songs, 'Iron Maiden' and 'Prowler', and it worked out really well. We were convinced that Paul was the singer we needed."

Ironically, Di'Anno was more versed in the punk style of singing and though tremendously adaptable as a vocalist, had not previously sung in a heavy metal band. But Di'Anno recalls that at his audition for Maiden he realised his "voice fitted metal perfectly and that, although I'd never sung this kind of music before, I was the one Maiden needed to become huge. And also Steve's incredible confidence in his music and in his band convinced me to accept the job right away, without asking myself any questions. After I joined Maiden, I became a metal disciple and I blended completely into this scene. I loved the way of life and the attitude that went with it. I started enjoying every moment of my life as a metal fan and I threw away – literally! – my old punk records in order to prove that I was the new King of heavy metal! Meeting Steve Harris changed my life in more ways than one and I'll be forever grateful to him."

'Loopy' Newhouse remembers the day Maiden and Di'Anno first joined together; "Paul was my best mate," he says. "We went everywhere together. It was a warm summers day in 1977 and we were going to see some band play at the Red Lion in Leytonstone. We met up with a couple of guys from Rock Candy, including Trevor Searle. We had already heard that Maiden were looking for a new singer, and it just so happened that Steve Harris was there to see this band as well. Trevor knew Steve, and introduced him to Paul. They chatted for a while, and Paul was offered an audition for that following week. Paul had no problem convincing Iron Maiden that he was good enough for the job, and shortly came round to tell me all about it. I had helped Rock Candy with their equipment, so I had an idea of what was needed – Humper and General Dogsbody! If you have those qualities mate, you're in. So that was it. Every rehearsal, I was there to hump the equipment up the stairs, set it up, get ear damage, take it apart, and take it back down the stairs again. Later on in life (with Maiden) although we all got the equipment in and out of studios or gigs, I started working closely with Dougie Sampson, and became his drum roadie. My job was to set up the kit, clean it when necessary, and generally look after Doug – drinks on stage, fag before the encore, etc."

For Steve Harris the new look Iron Maiden was the definitive line-up and he truly thought there would be no more changes. In Dave Murray he had the perfect guitarist to play the increasingly complex material he was composing. And Doug Sampson seemed more natural and down to earth than the eccentric and unpredictable Thunderstick.

'Loopy' Newhouse also recalls, "As well as being a blinding front man, Paul also had another talent which the band always found useful. When travelling out of town to do gigs, prior to being signed, the band would travel around, and sleep in a converted van. The problem with this, however, was that it tended to get extremely cold in the van, and the band can recall mornings where they would wake up with a layer of frost on them! Paul, however, had a certain way with the ladies, and would usually manage to pull, and then persuade the girl in question to allow a couple of his fellow band member's to crash on her floor!"

It didn't seem to matter that Di'Anno was not schooled in the rudiments of heavy rock. His voice certainly suited the material and to Harris that was the most important thing. "Basically, I wasn't a heavy metal fan," Di'Anno confesses, "but I have to admit that, after I saw Maiden play for the first time, I started to take some interest in this kind of music. So I started to go see other bands on stage, to buy loads of records so I could have a good collection. Before I joined Maiden, I used to listen to The Small Faces and punk. I think that the only hard rock bands I liked were Thin Lizzy and UFO. Afterwards I even found out that Steve also loved these two bands. In fact, Steve always wore those tight, black-and-white stripy trousers 'cause Pete Way of UFO was famous and wore the same ones. He thought it was great, so he nicked the idea from Pete and made that stripy spandex even more famous. Steve Harris invited me to audition for the band, and I more or less realised that Maiden had the potential to become a successful international act, provided that they found the right line-up and mostly the right front man. Maiden had had other singers before, but none of them had either the voice or the personality required to make the band a world-class success."

Di'Anno and Maiden rehearsed for a solid 6 months before attempting their first gig together. Previously the line-up of Maiden for that particular week would play a gig regardless of how well drilled the members were. But with the 'definitive' line-up Harris knew to take his time and settle on the right way to present the new look outfit.

Eventually Di'Anno was ready for his first gig with Maiden at the Cart & Horses in Stratford. "Great memories!" Di'Anno says of his live debut with the band. "I remember the confidence I had that, from now on, the band could make it big because I was the singer, and the pride I had from it. I was very young and very self-confident, but I was also confident in Steve's abilities. I remember being on stage at the Cart & Horses, watching him and thinking, 'Here we are! We're gonna become the greatest metal band on the planet!' The reaction from the audience was incredible and I remember many fans coming over to tell me that they were going to tell their mates to come to our next gigs, something that had never happened to me before. I think that that night we got £15! From then on, Steve started reinvesting all our earnings into the band to make it go further. With hindsight, I realise how much, so early in our career, he was involved and going for it. I remember that the same night, at the Cart & Horses, two different birds – in the very same pub – gave me a blowjob in the toilets; that's when I realised that something different and exciting was happening in my life."

Young, good looking and lean, Di'Anno would be a magnet for the females in the crowd, though in those days there weren't many! And despite the singer's penchant for partying he was more than capable of being serious come show time. Besides Steve Harris was in control of the managerial side of things, booking gigs himself, promoting the band and writing the bulk of the material.

"We had to be well organised," Steve says. "We started doing our own t-shirts, a couple of hundred at a time. The kids liked them because they were like an 'Up Yours' to the people who put metal down all the time. We travelled all over the country to get gigs. Aberdeen and Blackpool over a weekend and back to work on Monday. We fixed up this big old Austin van we called the Green Goddess, with space for the gear and nine bunks in the back for the band and the crew – who were mates, we couldn't pay them. We would sleep outside the gig and wake up in the morning with frost on the blankets."

At first Maiden's rise through the pub ranks was hardly meteoric and the early gigs were not paying exorbitant sums. The fee was usually £25 with a few beers thrown in if you were lucky. "It was a matter of chipping in your day job money," Dave Murray remembers. "Steve borrowed £3,000 off his aunt to keep us going. Those early days in the pubs and clubs were good fun. You'd turn up about seven o'clock and have a few pints with your mates and you'd be carrying your little carrier bag with your stage gear in. You'd go into the toilet to get changed and there'd be people taking the piss. It's pretty much the same now, but we don't get changed in the bogs."

Following numerous line-up changes there was to be one more vital switch, occuring again in the guitar department. After the quick coming and going of both Paul Cairns and Paul Todd, 'Loopy' Newhouse remembers who came next. "There was a bloke called Tony Parsons who nearly became the band's second guitarist. He also had a Marshall stack, an excellent Gibson Flying V and was a really nice guy. If only he could have got over the fact that he was not Michael Schenker then he might have done better. It's a pity, because he came so close to being Maiden's fifth member. He even did a couple of gigs with the band." But Parsons was not to last, and his replacement was the blues-rock oriented Dennis Stratton.

By now, despite their ever-evolving line-up Maiden, was becoming an East End institution. They frequented every well-known rock pub and things were starting to hot up by the day. A new venture had been created by a collection of DJs in Kingsbury. Come 1975 the Heavy Metal Soundhouse (or the Bandwagon as it was also known) was in operation. Previous to that, from 1970 onwards the disco/night club had been better known as a place where young folks could boogie down to Rose Royce and The Fatback Band tunes. But following the success of a resident Sunday night rock band, Bethnal, it became known as an experimental all-rock club night. This went down a treat and 'London's Only Heavy Rock Disco' was born.

By 1975 the venue was the home of one Neal Kay, a veteran DJ who would ultimately lead the Bandwagon to worldwide recognition. Kay was as bolshy as he was enigmatic and with his long shaggy mane and walrus moustache he was the perfect visual accompaniment to a night of rocking songs.

"I walked into the Bandwagon one Wednesday night in September 1975, to answer a call from the stage in search of a 'Presenter of Rock'," says Kay. "I confess that I had absolutely no idea where treading that path would lead, or of the incredibly colourful and diverse characters that would subsequently surround me at all levels of my life in rock n' roll from both sides of that stage! It has taken me almost until now, when life finds me in my late middle age, to realise and understand fully just how important those far-off times have been to all who grew up with, became a part of, or were touched by the magical Soundhouse Years.

"I left school with one O level at sixteen and a half," Kay reminisces on his early life, "and I saw an advert in a British newspaper for a British DJ to go to West Berlin and I got the job so I went. I drove over land with a transit van full of gear. I went with my soon to be first wife and she had been hired at the same place as a dancer. We had to work from eight pm to six am the next morning, six nights a week, it was tough. Strippers would come off stage and leave their g-strings on my boom stands!"

This was Kay's first professional taste of DJ-ing but he had good grounding. "I won the National Youth Club Championships for three years running back in the mid 60s – Alan Freeman, good ol' 'Fluff', presented the awards." he remembers. "They wouldn't let me go for it anymore because they got fed up with me winning. Then between 1966 and 1969 I was a DJ in the West End."

By mid-1976 punk exploded across the UK and changed the hitherto unblemished classic rock scene. As a bastion of professional, quality music Kay was not enamoured with the unwholesome punk scene. "Punk was my enemy, I wanted to destroy it even then, because they were destroying real music," he says unabashed. "They couldn't sing, they couldn't write they couldn't do fuck all except gob, spit and curse and I don't approve of that onstage. That is impure, it's not real music, it's not classic rock. Somehow punk got in to the mainstream, the suit and tie guys thought they could make a quick buck out of it I suppose, but it wasn't for the music it was for the fashion. I loathed Johnny Rotten more than any one character and I loathe his manager even more, shameful bastard, someone should shoot him!"

Thankfully it wasn't long before a new troupe of musicians started to wrestle the limelight back to pure rock. Iron Maiden had started to feature in the regular music weekly *Sounds* under a new term: The New Wave Of British Heavy Metal (known as NWOBHM for short). Effectively this was a gathering of many underground youngsters writing and releasing the odd single of hard rock. The genre has often mistakenly been accredited as the merging of hard rock and punk. The reason punk is often referenced lies in the fact that many of the bands were of a small scale, promoting themselves by playing pubs and clubs, with organisation very much of a DIY nature. And equally, there were countless bands who would have benefited from a few guitar lessons. As with punk, the emergence of a simple new form of rock meant accomplished musicianship was not required. But in truth those kinds of bands were well under the radar and only latterly emerged as having been part of the NWOBHM scene.

Neal Kay did not put "shit bands" on at the Bandwagon, he says today. Only groups who were competent or at least brought the punters in would get a shot. The audience at the Bandwagon was wild and untamed but they were serious about music. Bands who had the capacity only of the punk upstarts were given short shrift. Partly because of this marker of quality, Neal Kay managed to rope in the one reporter who was to be pivotal in the development of the NWOBHM and Iron Maiden.

"Geoff Barton was the first journalist who came to the Bandwagon," Kay remembers. "He did a double centre page spread in *Sounds*. It was actually called 'Would You Believe it: A Survivor's Report From A Heavy Metal Disco', those were his exact words. He was the one who put the Soundhouse on the map and I knew that I was going to help these bands, lift the whole movement.

"I kept on and on at Geoff, saying 'Come on, come and see something unusual' and in the end he came. He made the place an international name. *Sounds* printed the weekly chart of everybody's requests and this went out around the world and from there came all the demo tapes and letters etc."

Kay was always the consummate professional, aiming to take bands beyond pub level. Cleverer than the run of the mill DJ, he found new ways to promote the Bandwagon. With a fair amount of gumption he developed the idea of bringing in famous American rockers to put his venue on the map. "I thought of having bands and artists make personal appearances," he explains. "I managed to pull one off with CBS and Epic. I got Ted Nugent and his whole band to do a personal appearance at the Bandwagon on a Tuesday night and they all fucking came, the whole band and half of CBS with them. The crack was to get the music papers down to cover it. They didn't get paid. It had never been done before. And it was amazing to see these international rock stars coming to a place in Kingsbury. We started making it more like a social club, we were getting people from all over Britain. But once I started to put bands on Maiden were always repeat guests, they were *so* well loved."

Though there were ultimately thousands of British bands who could be loosely termed NWOBHM, the man who was largly responsible for the success of the scene is adamant it was never quite the movement people imagined. Neal Kay recalls; "Out of the hundreds of nominated so called NWOBHM bands, in my view there were only three that ever were going anywhere, maybe four. Maiden is one, Praying Mantis was the near miss. If they had done what was asked of them back then… I stood on my stage at the Bandwagon negotiating this out between the members of Praying Mantis and Peter Mensch and Cliff Burnstein. They came to me looking for a band to take back to America after the success of Maiden. For a week they were begging Tino (Troy, guitars/vocals) to get a front man, get a keyboard player and they would take them to America and I know they would have been bigger than Maiden because their music had a more radio friendly sound. And it was only after that they found the next best thing and that was Def Leppard. They came down to play my Music Machine show when one of them was only fourteen and a half. And I suppose in a way, Diamond Head might have been number four but their songs were not good enough for international 50,000 seater arenas. You needed more than they had."

Paul Di'Anno was also unimpressed by the so-called NWOBHM movement. "Maiden wasn't part of any movement whatsoever," he says. "And then, all of the sudden, we saw all those bands appearing and trying to copy us because we were generating a lot of interest and they wanted to make the most of the scene that Maiden – well, Steve – had created. The only band that I could relate to Maiden, if we have to talk about the NWOBHM, was Samson. 'Cause Paul Samson used to play before the same audiences as we did, at the same time, and he opened many doors for us. At that time, a band like Praying Mantis used to make me laugh 'cause I considered that they were doing crap, even if they were sometimes opening for us."

Kay reveals the business thinking which allowed certain bands to play at the Bandwagon; "There were a lot of so called NWOBHM bands who played at the Wagon but that was because they were good for business, you have to temper one with the other. But as far as those I would actually help, well I was probably very rude and caught up in my own ego. It seemed at that time that my club was the only one in the world that was making a stand against punk and was reaching out across the world through the music papers of the day. I used to listen to every demo tape that came my way."

Indeed he did and eventually there would be one particular band that stood out – namely Iron Maiden. Steve Harris would later say, "'Prowler' is a very special song for us. When we made *The Soundhouse Tapes* we took the actual tape to Neal Kay. He used to have a heavy metal chart, which was compiled from record requests and printed in *Sounds*. 'Prowler' got to be number one just from the requests for the demo tape. That's why we had the tape made into a record, because so many kids were asking us how they could get hold of the demo tapes. It was just a demo. It only cost us about $400 to make the whole thing. It really wasn't great quality."

"Maiden were one of those bands who came to me with a demo tape in very early '79, that's how it first started," recalls Kay. "It was Steve who came to me one night and I was so rude to him. I didn't know who he was, they were just a small band from East London. And in Steve's usual manner, he approached me. No ego, just very quiet. He put a tape in my hand and said, "ere mate give this a listen will you', and I turned round and said, 'yeah you and half the country, when I'm ready I will' and I forever hate myself for that.

"I took it home and I couldn't stop bloody well playing it. I thought 'fucking hell, what's going on here?' I had Goosebumps all over my arms, and I was head banging up and down the lounge and throwing myself about. I thought this is it, this is really happening. So I phoned Steve up and said 'Hey, you've dropped this tape off with me. I'm going to tell you something now, you are going to be real big, real famous and incredibly rich – you've got everything it takes'. And he laughed. And then of course I said the same thing on the back of *The Soundhouse Tapes* EP which carried my sleeve notes."

Though Maiden had taken an important step in making their first demo, it didn't automatically guarantee them an audience, certainly not from prospective record labels. As Kay confirms, "I remember taking the tape round to the record companies and everything, getting laughed out the door. CBS and A&M both thought I was crazy. You know these people just couldn't hear a fucking thing. And that was really annoying considering the amount of work I'd done with them. Rod came along in the end, the two of us used to attack the companies then."

At the end of 1979 Maiden met with the one man who would help them transcend their humble pub rock roots. Rod Smallwood of the MAM agency saw the band playing one night at the well-known pub venue The Windsor Castle. Quite out of character for Harris, he'd had a falling out with the group on the night Smallwood first came to see them and didn't actually perform. Although Smallwood persisted, at the next gig Paul Di'Anno was arrested for carrying a knife just before the band was due to play. Thus, Smallwood's first look at the Iron Maiden act came with Steve Harris on vocals for a few minutes and an otherwise instrumental set. Quite surreal!

As Harris recalls; "At the time, Rod Smallwood was managing Cockney Rebel, but he was looking for something else due to some tensions within the band. He even wanted to quit the business. After he got our first tape, he came to check us out at a pub gig we were doing in London. The problem was that, that night, Paul had been arrested by the police because he was carrying a knife. So, we had to play the gig almost completely instrumental, and I was singing on a couple of songs. Rod told us that he'd come back to see us with the singer, and that he'd make a decision only afterwards. So, we got Paul out of jail and we started rehearsing seriously, because I hadn't forgotten what was promised to me. The next time, Rod did come back and saw the full band on stage, and decided he was going to manage us. That was a few months before we signed with EMI."

Smallwood's coming on board led to Maiden's first real fan club, with Keith Wilfort responsible for the initial version of the organisation. "I was twenty-three." Wilfort recalls, "We created Iron Maiden FC and I'd take care of the fan mail, merchandise and any non-secretarial duties and the occasional bit of bookkeeping and looking after the office while Rod was away with the band. Before I started working with Maiden I was a Clerical Officer with British Telecom. It was a steady job, but when the offer to work for Iron Maiden came along, I figured it was too good an opportunity to pass up, that if I didn't go for it, I might regret it. My family and friends warned me, that I could be making a mistake, but I always knew from day one that Maiden would be huge someday. The speed of it took all of us by surprise. So began an amazing seventeen years!

"In 1979 when they signed with Rod Smallwood as their manager, they told him about me and I went for a meeting at his office in Knightsbridge," Wilfort continues. "He asked me if I'd like to answer the fan mail and sell T-shirts and later *The Soundhouse Tapes* at concerts and mail order from home. It would be part-time but that one day it could be permanent. Eventually in August 1980, I started working for Rod and the band full time."

Steve Harris was still working his day job and he recalls the moment things with Maiden became more serious. "From 1975 to 1979, we never had any management," the bassist explains. "So I was doing everything in the evenings when I was available because, like all the others, I had a day job to survive. Then, as the band was getting more and more organised, I was getting phone calls at the office, and I had to explain all this to my bosses in the company where I was working. Eventually, they allowed me to use the telephone for private calls. I was a clerk, writing up various documents, and my bosses were amused by the fact that there was a rocker in their study; they used to call it the 'Bomber Harris Enterprise'. But it became rapidly hard to manage and, when Rod Smallwood arrived, things got much better."

"It was more of a team situation," Wilfort remembers. "Everyone had their specific areas of concern but we would all help each other as needed. I became more of a link between all the separate departments. So I was still involved in lots of things just not to the same degree. One day I'd be answering fan mail, or helping the Tour and Production Managers,

I could be entering accounts info into a computer, taking and collecting stuff from the band's homes, running errands etc."

Keith describes Rod Smallwood as "An amazing person. He's not as fearsome as legend has it (as long as you stay on his good side) and he has mellowed out over the years, but the right person for a manager. He knows when to be tough, when to ease off, but will always find a way to get the job done. He lives and breathes Maiden. A typical Yorkshire man who really defines the phrase 'self made man'."

And Neal Kay sums up his personality with this anecdote: "In their early days before they got their deal, Steve introduced me to Rod at the Bandwagon. I remember taking Rod to a rugby match on the back of my motorcycle. He used to be a member of either the Wasps or the Harlequins, I can't remember which. But we got there late and the only way we could get in was through some players entrance and the match had started, and Rod said, 'come on follow me' and we were bloody running up the touchline with half of one of the teams following us! But Rod has that determination and totally blinkered belief in Iron Maiden so that absolute determination ran right through the team. It's like 'shit or bust'. Rod sold his house for Maiden, he actually sold his house! I mean, how much more belief could you possibly put behind your band than that?"

There was a partner in Smallwood's eventual Sanctuary Management empire, a man named Andy Taylor. "More of a Dr Jekyll to Rod's Mr Hyde," is how Keith Wilfort describes Taylor's input. "He and Rod are like 'good cop/bad cop' when it comes to negotiating and setting up deals. Andy knows the financial aspect inside and out. To many he appears the archetypal corporate businessman but he is not solely motivated by the bottom line at the expense of people." Taylor would mostly be a background figure in the career of Maiden, with Smallwood taking on the chief responsibility of managing the band.

But of course, it was Steve Harris who had really pushed Maiden to the stage of vying for record company attention. Without his songs the band would simply not have been anywhere near ready to sign for a label. According to Neal Kay; "Steve really is 'Mr Iron Maiden!' He has been called tyrannical and single-minded in his devotion to Maiden, which has sometimes cost him much. However, without his driving force and belief in the dream, there would not be an Iron Maiden now. Steve is strictly no nonsense. He is loyal to acquaintances and employees, but you have to do your job or it's goodbye – no hard feelings. I'm glad to have known him personally and professionally."

In October 1979 Iron Maiden played a series of free concerts at The Swan, in Hammersmith, London in the hope of attracting major record labels. One such company was Chrysalis Records who attended one of the gigs but declined to sign the band as they "weren't sure" how far they could go. Fortunately Maiden had bigger fish to fry as by the end of the month they had inked a deal with EMI records, an association that was to last some three decades. There has long been a rumour that EMI were actually in town to view local band Angelwitch but chose Maiden instead, though no-one connected with Maiden can confirm this as truth.

"There was a bit of a buzz about us at the time," Steve says. "There were actually a few companies who came out to see us. In fact, I think we got turned down by CBS and A&M. Even though we were playing pubs at the time, we had all these fans from the East London area who would follow us around all over the place. When we would play in East London, none of the record companies would come out to see us, they only hung out in central and West London. East London was like the wilderness, so they would never venture over there."

In the space of three years Steve Harris had transformed his band from a bunch of pub rockers with a revolving door policy, honing their skills along the way and creating a new organisation in the process, with the help of Rod Smallwood: Iron Maiden Inc.

Urchin's Maurice Coyne admits today, "I must say that when I first saw Maiden in about 1976 at the Cart & Horses in Stratford I didn't think that they would one day be one of the biggest bands on the planet! Until Maiden took off in about 1978/79, Urchin were a much bigger band. Maiden were playing the sort of gigs we'd been doing three years previously, whereas Urchin had a recording contract and were playing name venues, colleges, etc. Strange how things work out."

DIGGING DEEPER WITH TONY MOORE

Tony Moore is perhaps the greatest enigma of the Iron Maiden timeline, not least because he was employed as a keyboard player at a very early stage with the band and yet Maiden did not fully utilise a keyboardist until some years later. Therefore it's somewhat of an anomaly that Tony Moore hooked up with the band who would eventually become a heavy metal colossus. Tony explains his history and more about his time with the band as follows:

"I grew up in Bristol where I had always had my own band even at school (Bristol Grammar School), wrote the songs and played keyboards and guitar. The band was called Quantum and we did all the usual school gigs as well as lots of little pubs and clubs. We played a set that combined covers like 'Wall Street Shuffle' (10CC) 'Hi Fly' (John Miles) 'Maxwells Silver Hammer' (The Beatles) along with songs that I had written.

"In 1973/74 I remember being given a ticket to go and see Genesis. I had never heard of this band before, and I wasn't all that keen to go, but my friend insisted.

We sat up in the Gods, the very back of the top most circle seats at the Bristol Hippodrome. The rake of the seating was so steep that I almost got vertigo just sitting there.

"The stage was fascinating. Everything was painted white and the keyboards resembled something like a model city. Big bulky shapes, all in white, with no brand markings and weird lights shining through. I became fascinated with what was going to happen. And then they started with Watcher of The Skies, a track from *Foxtrot*. The sound of mellotron and organ made the building shake, it was awe-inspiring. From the moment they began 'til the final encore ('The Knife') I was transfixed. It was magical and inspirational and unlike anything I had EVER seen in my life before. I had an epiphany and knew that more than ever before, music and performance were what I wanted more than anything in my life. Peter Gabriel was magnetic and hypnotising with so much gentle charisma and the band were so amazing. From that moment on I wanted to BE Genesis and The Beatles at the same time! I began to embrace more and more progressive rock music. Yes, Pink Floyd, Supertramp, Greenslade, Argent, basically anything with great melody and musicality and passion.

"The first music I remember, and that I loved, was The Beatles. My Mother had their records and played them all the time. My Mum had been a ballet dancer and my father, a classically trained pianist and tenor. It was a very Bohemian household and, aside from pop music, I grew up listening to my dad playing Mozart, Beethoven, Rachmaninoff – and more – on our piano at home. His powerful voice used to reverberate around the house as he sang the classic Neapolitan Love songs of Italy. He didn't write music and could only play with the sheet music in front of him. I, on the other hand couldn't read music but loved to compose at the piano from an early age.

"From the Beatles I then began to get into T Rex, David Bowie, Alice Cooper and the whole Glam/Pop thing. At the end of 1976 I bought a small Korg synthesiser that I used with my old classic Wurlitzer piano.

I was trying to recreate Tony Banks (from Genesis) lines and experiment with sounds. The keyboard itself was nothing very spectacular. A Korg Micro Preset. I had longed for a Mini Moog or ARP Odyssey, but those instruments were out of my price range.

"Bristol was a very nice, middle class town with a music heritage that jumped between pub rock/blues and heavy dub reggae, nothing very original or challenging – or melodic enough for my tastes – and musicians seemed to feel comfortable there and never travelled very far."

THE MAIDEN EXPERIENCE

"I loaded the car up in the morning with all my equipment and my girlfriend at the time, Sally Johnson. I had been to London a few times before by train – it was always so exciting to arrive in London, see the music stores with vast arrays of guitars, drums and keyboards and films that were released so far ahead of regional cinemas etc. This was the first time I had actually driven up and it was a very thrilling day. I somehow managed to navigate my way through central London and find the obscure location that the band had arranged for auditions.

There were two or three rehearsal rooms on the top of a warehouse in a courtyard off a little back street. Sally and I made our way upstairs, found the band and introduced ourselves. Just being there was quite overwhelming in some ways. It is hard to describe just how it felt in those days, to come from a place where everything seemed so amateur. In Bristol we rehearsed in my parents' house, enlisting various mums and dads to ferry our equipment from gig to gig. But this was *London*, the metropolis, the capital. I had never even been in a proper rehearsal room before. This smelt of rock and roll, stale smoke and hot amplifiers. The PA was dark and mysteriously massive in each corner and the array of guitar stacks and bass amps with their glowing valves and red neon lights, was fascinating.

"After I was offered a position in the band full time, Sally and I sat in the car to talk it over. This was my chance to move to London, it was daunting yet it was everything I had ever dreamed of. The music was very different, both from what I listened to and also what I had ever played before. However the energy was great and I have always loved a challenge, something that would push me and extend my skills.

"The weird irony of it all, was that I found myself living in the same road and about a quarter of a mile away from Terry Wapram. So I used to drive him to rehearsals on the other side of London. I seem to recall that Terry couldn't actually drive anyway, so it was good for both of us to be so close. The trip from Kilburn to Mile End was always through rush hour traffic and took forever. We passed the time talking about Maiden and gigs, and guitars and, well a little of everything. Terry seemed very laid back and so 'London'. The more I got to know him the more his vocabulary and vocal mannerisms would make me smile. I liked Terry a lot, he had a soft and friendly air about him and he was a very accomplished guitar player.

"We all used to chip in to pay for the rehearsals, Iron Maiden was very much a collective in that way. During the breaks we would go out to the corridor where the owner had stacked up some boxes of fizzy canned drinks that he had bought in bulk from some warehouse. We would get a Fanta or Coke and talk about songs (and tempos!) Already well established in the repertoire were songs such as 'Charlotte The Harlot' and 'Iron Maiden' that I began to find keyboard parts for.

"Although we used the rehearsal room PA, the band owned their own PA system and truck. This was driven by Vic, who I believe was originally from Malta. I was never sure of the background or connection between Vic and Steve but he seemed to fulfil the role of driver, sound engineer (at least during the rehearsals), roadie, stage manager, minder and friend. His odd cockney accent would fill the room as he made suggestions about songs, and running orders and gigs.

"The other regular character that was always at rehearsals was Dave Lights. And as his name would imply, he looked after the lighting rig. This lighting rig actually consisted of a few coloured spotlights on the floor and a bank of switches that I think he had got from an electrical shop and would normally be found controlling domestic illumination. These were the bookends to Iron Maiden, providing support, encouragement and muscle power when needed

"In many ways, I was a little frustrated with my role in the band because so much of the music was based on riffs and lines and, to my mind there weren't really parts for a keyboard – or rather *my* keyboard playing – to fit in. My musical taste was far more Catholic and song based. I generally felt comfortable with more established chord structures. That's not to say I didn't enjoy what I was doing, I think it just felt a little alien to me and I was trying to work out where I could fit in.

"We worked solidly through the summer, polishing up the older songs whilst working on newer material. I remember Terry and I going over to Steve's Grandmother's house to work on a new tune. It was a piece called 'Phantom Of The Opera'. Steve's vivid imagination could see how titles of books and films created inspiration *and* were half way into the public psyche giving them a head start to get into people's consciousness.

There was a middle section that Steve, Terry and I laboured over to try and make fit. This was the height of the London Pub Rock era. Pubs were the breeding ground for acts to develop and win their audience, and for some, they were also a good source of income. People would go out to see bands and many groups had a loyal following and made good money without ever needing a record deal or hit single. London bands were usually very road hardened and tight. In fact, to be called tight was a real compliment. It showed an almost military precision and understanding of roles within a band. It was impressive and entertaining. In fact, in the cold light of day, a lot of the bands didn't have very good songs or lyrics, but in the heat of the moment and with the volume of big sound systems, the arrangements and playing could really make you enjoy the band enormously.

"Sometimes Steve and I and his girlfriend would go out and see our contemporaries. It was partly social and partly to keep an eye on the competition. We often visited the Brecknock Arms just north of Camden and would see groups like The Helicopters (very tight) and Urchin. This latter band had Dave Murray playing guitar and he had played with Steve in the past. We always used to get on really well with Dave and I know that Steve valued his guitar playing very highly.

"In order to begin the PR campaign for the new line up, it was decided that we should get a photo shoot done. Iron Maiden had always built their reputation on being an East End band, even though Steve was actually the only one who presently lived there. The Blind Beggars pub was chosen as a place that epitomised the East End's tough reputation (Ronnie Kray, one of the infamous Kray Twins had killed a man in there).

With style (?) and humour a friend of the band was co-opted into playing the part of a blind beggar, whose role was to be kicked around by the band outside the pub. I think it was early on a Sunday morning that we actually did this and I turned up in my favourite Oxford Bags. These were massive white canvas trousers with a three-button waist-band and were as wide at the top as they were at the bottoms. Had they been six inches shorter and finished off with tartan I could have passed for a member of The Bay City Rollers. It wasn't terribly rock and roll, in fact, it wasn't really rock and roll at all, but my wardrobe hadn't been born out of a history of pub rock and heavy metal.

"Soon it was time for our first gig, November at The Bridge House in Canning Town. This was pretty much a homecoming gig for the band and there was great expectation for the show. We arrived in the afternoon to get set up and the stage was wide and shallow, located at one side of the pub. I was stage left and the band ranged out next to me."

Sources:

Paul Stenning Interviews
http://www.bookofhours.net/samson/
Kerrang! #396
*http://www.maidenfans.com/imc/?url=album06_sit/interviews06_*
sit&lang=eng&link=albums
Gerry Kelly and Mark Blake http://www.hmsoundhouse.com/hmsound-
house/default.htm

Chapter 2
The Good, The Band And The Ugly

"I have to admit that I found their music a bit tough to stomach. Many people say that they lost touch with their roots after the first albums. I don't think so 'cause they've had a fantastic career. If I'd stayed, Maiden would have made me a millionaire and money wouldn't be an issue anymore. But there's another side to the story: my son Jack, who's thirteen now, has always seen me play, ever since he was five. He often talks to me and tells me that if I'd stayed in the band we'd have a large house and nice cars. So I tell him, 'Certainly, but if I'd stayed, you'd probably have never been born.' We have to be happy with what we have most precious in life." Dennis Stratton

In late 1979 EMI hit upon the idea of issuing an album of various unsigned metal bands. At Neal Kay's suggestion they called it *Metal For Muthas* and it was to be Iron Maiden's first official vinyl appearance. The tracks selected to showcase the band were 'Wrathchild' and 'Sanctuary'. The cover art was distinctly crude and tacky, as were most of the bands appearing on the compilation. It didn't take a metal expert to see Iron Maiden was head and shoulders above the competition. Names who would disappear sooner rather than later (at least in popularity) flooded the album: Toad The Wet Sprocket, Praying Mantis, Sledgehammer and Ethel The Frog. There were at least appearances for Samson and Angelwitch who in fairness were closer to the real deal. But still, Maiden was undoubtedly in a completely different league.

The collection brought them further attention all over the world and it was at this time EMI realised they might be onto a winner with this band. Little did they know just how popular Maiden would become.

The band was quickly asked to choose a single, to be their first on the EMI label. They went with 'Running Free', and recorded Steve's first ever song for posterity on the b-side. Maiden proved just how hard they had plugged their material in the preceding years, by promptly selling 10,000 copies in the first week alone. This meant the single hit the UK charts at number 44, a phenomenal achievement for a new band who actually wrote their own material, and played it live.

The live aspect was to be the source of much consternation with the producers of Britain's most popular weekly music TV show. *Top Of The*

Pops thought it would be a good idea to rope Maiden into the studio to 'perform' their blistering new single, the only problem being that bands appearing on the show always mimed, mimicking playing their real instruments and lip-synching to the song. Maiden was having none of this however, and protested loudly, giving the simple ultimatum: either we play live or we don't appear at all. *Top Of The Pops* relented and Maiden became only the second band in the history of the show to insist on performing its song in real time. The only other band to previously put their foot down in this way was The Who, which said a lot.

The idea of Maiden on *Top Of The Pops* was still almost a contradiction in terms and despite permission to plug in, the band was not happy with the weak acoustics, claiming that it sounded as if someone was broadcasting the song through a tin can. Nevertheless all true music fans appreciated this stand, and the rendition was good enough to cause anticipation for the full album.

However before this could be recorded a couple of changes were to take place. Doug Sampson could not handle the pressure of more gigs and increasing popularity – he easily became exhausted when touring and as soon as Steve Harris realised he could be a liability (and especially with a tour with Judas Priest on the horizon), Sampson was sacked.

His replacement was Clive Burr, an experienced drummer who had already paid his dues in one NWOBHM prospect, Samson. Keith Wilfort describes Burr as "a nice bloke, a practical joker and very good drummer who could have been one of the greats had he not been sidetracked along the way by rock and roll excesses and a series of domestic problems in 1982. His contribution to Maiden is sometimes falsely underrated."

Indeed Burr would go on to secure a prominent place in the hearts of many Maiden fans as the real rock of their early albums. There was no doubt Burr was a great technical drummer with supreme flair and though it can often be difficult to recognise a change in drummer, with Maiden Burr's presence did change the face of their debut album.

Joining the ranks at about the same time was yet another new guitarist, Dennis Stratton. Another London boy, Stratton was just the perfect personality for the band at that time. He had played in a number of local bands, including the strangely named Remus Down Boulevard.

"We used to live in the same area," Stratton says of his old colleagues. "Maiden were looking for a new guitar player at the time. That was just before they recorded their first album. They wanted somebody who could play the harmonies, and who also had some experience in the studio. At that time, I was working near Stratford and I saw Steve's girlfriend who told me that a telegram from Rod Smallwood was waiting for me at my place. Sure enough, when I got home my wife told me that a telegram had arrived. The message said, 'Dear Dennis, please call Rod Smallwood at the following number...' The next day, I met Steve, Dave Murray and Rod in a pub near to the Marquee. Rod told me that Steve wanted me to join Maiden. They gave me a tape so I could learn the songs. The first song I played when I got back home was 'Phantom Of The Opera', with all those harmonies. I thought to myself, 'Well, not bad at all...' When I arrived at the studio, I understood that they were also looking for a new drummer. I told them to try out Johnny Richardson, but the poor bloke was ill and he gave up after 30 minutes, he was knackered. Some time later, I saw Clive Burr in a local pub – we knew each other 'cause he was playing the same venues as RDB – I told him I was rehearsing with Maiden and that they were looking for a drummer. The next day, he came along with me. The rest is history..."

With Burr and Stratton in place, the band went straight into Hollywood Studios to record the LP that would become *Iron Maiden*. Though it sounded exotic the studio was actually in the less glamorous surrounds of Clapham, but Maiden more than made up for the small town location with bundles of star quality. "When I joined Maiden, they didn't have so many harmonies on the guitars," Stratton says. "As I was nuts about harmonies, I sat in a corner of the studio and I added some here and there, like for instance on 'Running Free' and 'Phantom Of The Opera'. Many parts were right for them so I put loads in there. When we recorded, I spent quite a lot of time working on these harmonies, but they weren't all kept in the end. During the 'Phantom Of The Opera' sessions, Paul did the vocals and I recorded up to four different harmonies to complement his voice. When Rod went into the cubicle to listen to the result, he shouted, 'It sounds like fucking Queen!' and he left. Half of Paul's vocals were taken out. We also had to re-record 'Running Free' in order to have a different mix 'cause the song was supposed to be aired on the radio. It was the same with 'Women In Uniform'."

One thing Maiden had in its favour was the nature of its song writing process. With Steve Harris being the most prominent writer, the material was composed first and foremost on his bass, giving the songs a unique sound, which distinguished them from the other metal bands. "Some I write with a main bass riff and work out the melody on top of it," Harris explains. "Some songs begin with a strong melody line and I work out the music behind it. I pretty much work everything out on the bass, the actual riffs and the harmonies. 'Running Free' came together when I put a riff to the main drum beat by Doug Sampson."

It is no surprise therefore that the band's first single begins with a chugging bass riff along with a galloping drumbeat. The tale of a rock n' roll drifter, the song is perfectly presented by Paul Di'Anno and, despite the prominent bass accompaniment, there are plenty of spaces for Murray and Stratton to throw their flourishing guitar licks into the picture.

Six string heroics are especially apparent on the opening song, 'Prowler' which was of course, already a well-known Maiden track. 'Prowler' is dark, energetic and, most importantly, was vastly different to anything else currently available in the rock market. There are hints here, and at a couple of other points on the LP, of the speedy time changes and fretboard frenetics the band would later become more familiar with. But essentially the debut album is all about strong songs. It is not hard to see just how special Maiden were in 1980, as almost 30 years on, *Iron Maiden* still buzzes with an intense energy and passion.

1980 was actually a significant year for heavy metal, but most acclaimed albums of that year were by well-known bands, with releases from Motorhead (*Ace Of Spades*), Judas Priest (*British Steel*), AC/DC (*Back In Black*), Black Sabbath (*Heaven And Hell*) and Scorpions (*Animal Magnetism*). The only other comparatively new band to compete with Maiden that year were their perennial peers Def Leppard – the Sheffield quintet who also released their debut album, the comparatively polished *On Through The Night*. But there was no disputing the fact that in Iron Maiden lay a new group with extreme desire and enthusiasm and with more tricks up its sleeves than most magicians.

The *Iron Maiden* album displays its diversity from the outset. After 'Prowler' comes 'Remember Tomorrow', a virtual power ballad that really could not be pinned down to any one genre. It then goes on almost to invent a new one with 'Phantom of the Opera' in particular. A completely outrageous, awe-inspiring riff begins one of the most intricate songs the band would ever record. There were few, if any, who could compete with this kind of virtuoso guitar work in the first year of the 80s. Not until a good five years later would the technical, soulless bravado of instrumental whizzkids be a factor in the heavy metal scene. Steve Harris pre-dated the lot of them, and what's more he actually penned great songs with memorable melodies. 'Phantom Of The Opera' was never just about *that* riff, but 7:20 minutes worth of all sorts of clever interplay, bruising vocal lines, harmonious singing and guitar work. Not surprisingly, at the time Steve Harris felt it was his best song to date. There were certainly nods in the general direction of Steve's progressive rock favourites, but still, the track is particularly inventive, highly demonstrative and a definite highlight of the first album.

Up next was even more proof of Maiden's musical ability, and another sole Harris credit. The instrumental 'Transylvania' was proof that Maiden had gone into its gut instinct. Initially assembled as a regular song with a full set of lyrics, on hearing it played without the words, the band decided to leave it that way. And it is now quite difficult to imagine vocals over the top of this piece of galloping guitar wizardry! This is followed by another plaintive track in 'Strange World', with Maiden taking its foot off the pedal and easing into first gear with this rather unlikely number – a strange song, with shades of Black Sabbath in their most melancholy moments (see 'Changes' or 'Planet Caravan' for instance). So what better way for Maiden to offset this soft charm than with a song about a prostitute! The fictitious 'Charlotte The Harlot' is an anomaly, a song written solely by Dave Murray and meant for Paul Di'Anno's vocals. Sure it's heavy, verging on hard rock, but with a definite punk overtone to the chorus. Yet, as always with Maiden, there's a section other bands would never dream of throwing in. The breakdown of the song gives Di'Anno another chance to show off his vocal prowess, initially bursting with emotion, before ripping back into harsh mode towards the climax. Closing the album is the obligatory 'Iron Maiden'. "As long as I can remember we've closed our set with this song," Steve said. "It's quite simple. The bass line is fairly straight forward as is the drumming. But the guitar is over the top with harmony, and the bass is descending behind it. I think this makes it pretty special."

It certainly is special, and equally memorable with a bass line reminiscent of one of Harris' heroes, the Yes four stringer, Chris Squire. It was fairly out of character for the band at the time but over the years it became moulded into something titanic, a far more 'heavy metal' style number. Yet, even in 1980 it closed the album in style and was another demonstration of Maiden's assorted talents. Unfortunately the single released, and one of the band's best-known numbers at this point, 'Sanctuary', was not on the British version of the album. This was rather strange given there were only eight songs without it, plenty of room to squeeze in a veritable classic. Around the rest of the world however, those who had never seen a Maiden gig could console themselves with one of their strongest songs to date.

The one aspect of this immortal album clearly not up to standard from the outset was the production. The relatively obscure Will Malone presided over the material and despite the fact that production techniques were not anything like as sophisticated then as they are today, other albums of the time managed to sound a lot bulkier than *Iron Maiden*. This is hardly surprising, however, when we learn that Malone was mostly responsible for pop bands and artists of the decade, such as Neneh Cherry's 1989 album *Raw Like Sushi*.

Iron Maiden was released on April 14th 1980 and went straight into the UK top 20 album chart. The day itself was memorable for all concerned with the band, as Paul Di'Anno recalls; "I remember it very very well 'cause my mother hit her head pretty badly on that day and she even had to go to the doctor's! For the release of the album, EMI had put all those posters in the shopping centres of London and on the main streets. My mum was shopping in Walthamstow and found herself face-to-face with one of those massive posters, and she was so shocked, both by the picture and by the fact that her son was becoming someone, that she walked straight into a lamppost! Luckily enough, the doctor told her that she had nothing serious. As for me, I knew which week the album was going to be released and I went to several shops in London to see if the album was really there... and also, let's face it, in the secret hope that someone would recognise me! That week remains one of the best memories of my early career."

In August 1980, mega rock stars Kiss invited Maiden to open for them at a series of concerts for the next two months. In contrast to many of their peers, Kiss were apparently the proverbial nice guys and wonderful hosts to Maiden. It was clear they respected the British group and to their credit they were intent on choosing a strong, upcoming young act to open for them and weren't in the least fazed by the favourable reaction Maiden received. "We were ready to fight and become popular in the UK, but we didn't think we could make it big outside of the country," Steve told Philippe Touchard of Maiden's rise in popularity, undoubtedly in part thanks to the Kiss tour. "We'd gone through such hard times just to be known in London, that our aim was only to break through in the UK. When we heard that the album was selling very well in Europe, then in the States, we thought it was all a dream."

"The guys from Kiss were wonderful, especially Gene (Simmons) who was looking after my money, which isn't exactly my strong point," explains Di'Anno. "In fact, he was keeping my dough and was giving me the strict minimum when I really needed it, which prevented me from blowing it on rubbish. Gene has treated me like a son, he taught me what to do and not to do. We started the tour as support for Kiss and, all of a sudden, we became very popular. So, it was Kiss that looked like an opening act. It was also during this tour that Dennis Stratton's fate was sealed." Stratton remembers, "After we came back from Oslo where we were opening for Kiss, we filmed the video clip of this song at the Rainbow Theatre. When the shoot started, I didn't understand why no single camera was on me. I understood some time later, though." By October Maiden's debut album guitarist had left the band. The reasons given were many and varied, but both Stratton and the rest of the band were in agreement that it was for the best. "Dennis didn't follow the evolution of the band," Steve claimed, by way of explanation. "He never understood that, once the album was released, success was close at hand and we needed to work even harder. He thought we were still at the level where we played in clubs and pubs, hence the split."

Paul Di'Anno explains in greater detail the reason why Stratton could never have lasted; "Dennis had a fantastic pop voice and should have become a pop/rock singer – he loved this soft style. Before he joined Maiden, I used to go often to the Cart & Horses and watch him play with his former band, Wedgwood: he was then an excellent singer and seemed to be more comfortable there than as a member of Iron Maiden. Dennis has never really been part of the metal world and he's never accepted this universe. He was really into pop and he wanted to have three-voice harmonies in Maiden, or crap like that. But Steve never gave in. We even had to force Dennis to wear a leather jacket, which he hated, and we tried to get him to act 'metal'! Steve and Dennis had a few ding-dongs" Di'Anno further elaborates, "because he didn't like the metal gear and was only listening to Pop music. He really pissed Steve off during the Kiss tour when, in Spain, he started complaining that he had to wear denim and leather – he used to call that the 'Cunt Kit'. Steve was doing his nut and I think that this is when he realised that he had to get rid of Dennis. During the whole time he was in the band, we had to pretend that he was one of ours, which was an outright lie 'cause he only liked the Beach Boys and the Eagles."

Not surprisingly, Dennis holds a different view as to the exact nature of the reasons for his departure; "When I joined the band, I gave one of my first interviews and I told the journalist that I was sorry not to be able to answer some of his questions 'cause I didn't know Maiden very well yet and I wasn't a die-hard fan of their music," he says. "Steve interrupted the interview and told me that I couldn't say things like that. I quickly realised who was the boss. It was like going back to my school days... Then, during the *Metal For Muthas* tour with Praying Mantis, Paul started acting like a rock star: he demanded that he had his own dressing room and didn't want to talk to anyone. I was getting along pretty well with the Troy brothers from Praying Mantis and I often shared my hotel room with Dave Lights. Rod wasn't too keen to see me hang out with musicians from other bands 'cause he wanted to create some kind of exclusive kinship between us.

"The icing on the cake remains the story about the Walkman: one day I was knackered and my head was about to explode after a gig. I only wanted one thing: to relax. I was listening to 'Soldier Of Fortune' by Whitesnake, a pretty quiet and melodic song, when Rod came into my room and started to shout at me, telling me that I wasn't supposed to listen to that kind of music. I told him that if I was to listen to Motörhead twenty-four hours a day, my head was going to explode. He then told me that I shouldn't be in the band if I was listening to that kind of music. It was absolutely ridiculous. And he didn't stop there: during the Kiss tour, I got on really well with Paul Stanley and Gene Simmons. On my birthday, in Stockholm, they invited me to the restaurant. Rod simply blew his top: he came over and started shouting and screaming – no-one else but Steve was allowed to mingle with Kiss. I've done enough tours to know that you can't remain constantly with the same people. Rod wanted to isolate us and force us to stay all the time together, but that couldn't work. I met him four years later in Los Angeles and he was better, he'd realised it himself 'cause he'd gone through it with the rest of the band."

The choice of a replacement for Stratton came easily to the group. They needed a guitarist well versed in the East End customs and equally a player who would not clash with Dave Murray. For the blonde bombshell Maiden-ite the choice was easy, his old mate from school and then Urchin, Adrian Smith. The band hoped Smith would join. At first he declined and their second choice was actually Girl guitarist Phil Collen, who would later join Def Leppard. Thankfully Smith relented and said 'yes', forging a union between himself and Dave Murray that would last for many years to come.

Talking of Smith, whose nickname is 'H', Keith Wilfort says, "H is a very nice person to know. He too goes a lot deeper than people give him credit for. In many ways he can be compared to George Harrison's role within The Beatles (except Adrian writes more). He can often take a while to make up his mind, wanting to explore all avenues before committing to something, hence one of his nick names Willhe o' Wonthe? His musical contributions and song-writing abilities are invaluable and out of all the Maiden guitarists he's the most technically gifted player. He appears to be disinterested and quiet on stage, but he is the glue that holds the sound together. He also has a wicked sense of humour." Wilfort's comments confirm Smith's reputation as easy going and Mr Nice Guy. "We just really seemed to hit it off and had lots in common. I tended to get on well with everyone really but Adrian stands out."

Another factor that contributed to Maiden's success was their easily identifiable artwork. The cover for *Iron Maiden* was unlike anything else in the metal world at the time – a glaring monster (known as Eddie) on a dark, dingy street staring straight at the viewer. The man responsible was Derek Riggs, who explains how the association came about. "They got in contact with me. I was working as a freelance illustrator in London designing record covers and the occasional book cover and their manager saw some posters of some pictures I did for some Jazz records and he asked to see my portfolio. I invented the character of Eddie. Eddie came before Maiden. I designed Eddie as a specimen artwork for my portfolio one and a half years before Iron Maiden even had a recording contract. It was in my portfolio that long before the manager asked to see my work and before I met the band."Originally the character of Eddie was known as 'Electric Matthew'. "I used to give my pictures silly names," says Riggs, "and that first Iron Maiden picture was called 'Electric Matthew Says Hello' but there was no story behind it I just painted it."

There was also the unmistakeable Iron Maiden logo, designed by Steve. The lettering style was inspired by the movie *The Man Who Fell To Earth* starring David Bowie. Steve was often verbal in his praise of Rigg's work, stating that his contribution was, "very important, his painting is so good. Who's to say, we could have got another really good artist, would it have been Eddie? It's fate, I suppose." The immediacy of the impact Iron Maiden had on the world of heavy metal could also be described as destiny. By the end of the year, the band had not only released a stellar studio album, they had also put out their first video. In December 1980 they issued *Live At The Rainbow*, which was their entire set at the Rainbow Theatre in London. It was a credible homecoming show with a reaction that displayed just how far Maiden had come already. "That was the first major set of Maiden, and all our friends and families were there," Paul Di'Anno recalls. "That was the first concert my Mum attended. We knew then, from the audience's reaction that night, and then that of the press a bit later, that we were heading in the right direction. I personally consider that everything really started with this show."

Steve 'Loopy' Newhouse, speaking today, describes the moment Maiden outgrew their humble origins. "At the start I didn't know what to expect, but once I got used to the songs, and the people making the music, there was always a chance that they could go on to bigger things. The big break came when the band were asked to play at the Music Machine, in Camden. From then it was obvious. Maiden was second on the bill to Samson, featuring one Bruce Dickinson on vocals. Most of the audience on the night were Maiden fans, so by the time Samson took the stage the place was half empty. The other act on the night was a south London band called Angelwitch, a Sabbath-esque metal outfit, now sadly defunct. Iron Maiden was easily the best band of the night. The proof is in the pudding, as they say."

Despite their increasing popularity and status, there were no big changes in the outlook of the Maiden camp, as 'Loopy' confirms, "Each and every member of the band was exactly the same as when we all first met. There were no egos. There wasn't time for all that. We gigged all over the country, and travelled hundreds of miles at a time to do it. I was extremely proud to be involved with such a great bunch of people."

THE DEEPER MEANING OF EDDIE

"There is no message. I made Eddie as the end result of learning to create symbols with pictures. I was studying symbolism and how to make a picture that could be read. Pictures that could get a concept across." So says Derek Riggs of the birth of the 'Eddie' style. "I was painting in a surreal kind of way – not in a horror style at all. Eddie was created in the late 1970's during the punk rock boom and he was made as a symbol of the ideas of the time that the youth were being wasted by society. Eddie works because I did it properly and people identified with him. I never started out to draw scary stuff, that's just the way that one picture turned out to look, and I got kind of stuck with it. Sometimes I think God is taking the piss."

Derek would soon become known not only for Eddie, but also his trademark symbol, which graced every future Iron Maiden cover. "The first symbol I used had some meanings which are outlined below," he explains, "the little gold one I use now is just a back to front letter D, and a letter R side by side inside a circle and has no meaning beyond the fact that I got fed up with the bullshit and felt like a change. The original symbol comes from the Jewish mystical path called the holy qabalah (or kabbalah), they are from a diagram called the tree of life which consists of ten such circles, representing different concepts or states of being, called sephirot. The big circle at the top represents God, or the fundamental generative power of the universe, the two beneath represent opposing forces or concepts. In one instance they can represent male and female (archetypal male and female as two aspects of the creative force, one is energy and the other is structure. Energy without structure just evaporates, structure without energy is too restrictive to do anything) and therefore the balance of opposites.

"The arrow is the direction of the flow of energy from God to earth, or the flow of inspiration from the unmanifest world (subconscious mind) to the material world. Also the arrow points to the chasm or barrier between God and the world or between the unmanifest and manifest aspects of reality, which cannot be crossed. For a better understanding of this refer to the book *The Mystical Qabalah* by Eliphas Levi."

Sources:

Paul Stenning Interviews
Rock Hard Magazine Hors Sériis #1
www.praying-mantis.com
Enough Magazine 2001

Chapter 3
Killer Behind You

"We always believe that a song is a short story and then you pick some-thing from within the lyric that describes the song. Lyrics are important... though not the most important thing. I would say the music and the melo-dies of the vocal lines are the most important. However, having said that, the lyrics shouldn't just be a load of old crap." Steve Harris

Adrian Smith would only have four months experience as part of Iron Maiden before being thrust into action on their second studio album. "It took him quite a while to settle in," Steve remembers, "and it also took both he and Dave a long time to get the right guitar sounds. Even on our second world tour, they were still changing equipment at various intervals to get the sound they were looking for because they're both perfectionists when it comes to sound." Thankfully for the two guitarists they were able to concentrate exclusively on their playing, since the album, released on February 2nd 1981, was to be the only LP where Steve Harris laid claim to every song writing credit (with the exception of one joint effort – with Paul Di'Anno – the title track 'Killers'). Perhaps because of this monop-oly on the musical style, *Killers* was a very personal album for Steve and it also ranked as something of a wildcard recording, and certainly not a staunch favourite with Maiden fans. Few of the songs from the album were chosen for later live performances, with only 'Wrathchild' and the title track providing long lasting enjoyment for many fans, the remainder being less catchy and straightforward than much of the material from the debut album

But it should be taken into account that it was a difficult time for the band members, who were still finding their feet both musically and per-sonally. Smith was very much a new face in the group and to add to this, Paul Di'Anno's attitude was becoming problematic in more ways than one. Not only was his partying becoming increasingly more important than singing in the band, but also he now seemed incapable of or disinter-ested in contributing much in the way of musical ideas. This left Steve in an unenviable position – though he would see *Killers* through with Paul, he knew in the back of his mind, even before a note of the 1981 opus was recorded, that Di'Anno would have to go.

In the end Di'Anno made it easier for the band by quitting before he was pushed, but the rot had unquestionably set in way before *Killers* was released. "The worst memory I have of the band is when the atmosphere changed," Di'Anno says today. "When Rod, Steve and Dave took over control. I thought the band was going to remain democratic, as was the case in the beginning. But on the other hand, as it was Steve who'd founded the band, it maybe was inevitable. He sometimes said things that divided Maiden a bit and I'd felt uneasy several times. But, to be honest, that's about it: I never really had bad times with the band. And when I left, I forgot about it, it wasn't important to me."

It was inevitable, with Steve's single mindedness and determination that he was only going to do what was right for Maiden. No-one member, aside from himself, was more important than the collective and though things were indeed changing and becoming more business like, Di'Anno was not helping himself with his behaviour. If anything he was subconsciously sealing his own fate by acting just to please himself most of the time. With hindsight the singer can admit, "Now that we're older and wiser, I can look back onto the past and realise that I was sometimes a right cunt. Steve must have wanted to kill me quite often. I had a big gob, I was a cocky young bastard who'd screw every bird passing by, who'd get on everybody's nerves and who'd always say the wrong things... In Steve's shoes, I would have probably hired a hit man! I was up to the most stupid things, like getting arrested by the old bill just before a gig. I'd find myself banged up in a cell while Maiden was on stage, waiting for me. Once, Steve had to sing instead of me – he's got a horrible voice! – 'cause I'd been arrested for carrying a knife. Rod Smallwood managed to bail me out and I could sing the last two songs of the set. But when you're very young and you're faced with such success as quickly as that, it does your head in and I really went berserk big time, 'cause everything was crazy right from the start. 'Nightmare', that is the right word to describe what Steve must have experienced with me 'cause he's a lovable geezer, really laid back, fully involved in his music and all aspects of Maiden, and he had to put up with this fucking monster from outer space called Paul Di'Anno. In fact, Steve always managed to cope with my craziness...'cause he always had control over everything."

Despite the troubles with Di'Anno, *Killers*, although no classic compared to the future 'greats', continued Maiden's pursuit of metal glory and kept interest ticking over for the next year. Maiden even changed tack for the running order, building into the album an instrumental track 'The Ides of March'. "We used to play that through the P.A. before we went on," said Steve. "Then we went right into 'Wrathchild'. 'Wrathchild' was originally on *Metal for Muthas*. That was before we had a record contract. The version on this record is pretty different. A lot of people asked us why we didn't put it on the first album. But we felt because it was on *Metal For Muthas* we didn't want to put it on the first album. By the time we did *Killers* we weren't happy with that version so we wanted to record it properly."

Credit for the track should go at least in part to Thunderstick who already laid claim to a number called 'Thunderburst', distinctly similar to, and clearly inspiring 'The Ides Of March'. "Yes, it was," says the man himself. "I came up with a drum pattern that did that constant rolling. I would have ideas and Steve would then transpose that, because I don't play guitar. It was the same with Samson... I'm unable to pick a guitar up and show my idea, I have to sit there and go 'du-du du-du du, no that's the wrong note' and we'd go through it like that. So that's how it came about. And I had a drum pattern and I was trying to explain the chords to go down on the drum pattern cause the whole thing goes around the drum pattern. I think we played it a couple of times with 'Iron Maiden' as an opening track. Just an intro, it was a throwaway thing, not really a track. The story behind that was that after we'd recorded *Head On* and they'd recorded *Killers* Clive Burr went round to Paul's house to listen to the new Samson album and in turn took the new *Killers* album with him. So Paul put on side one and they were 'Yeah, it's great stuff,' turned it over and up came 'Thunderburst' and Clive nearly fell of his seat and went 'Fuck, that's 'The Ides Of March'. Paul was like 'What the hell is he talking about?' So anyway, to cut a long story short, I got summoned to EMI and there was Rod Smallwood and Steve Harris sitting there and a lawyer, solicitor, and an EMI representative and just me. So what was decided in the end was that Steve Harris would share 50-50 the publishing rights on the Samson version of it, but I never got Sweet F.A. on the Iron Maiden version."

The song is certainly heavy on percussion and given Harris does not play drums, surely some credit should go to the drummer. Regardless, Clive Burr does a fantastic job of holding the track together before the band launches into 'Wrathchild'. Now this is pure Steve Harris, a bass driven monster with a spitting vocal by Di'Anno. A fury driven rock n' roll number, 'Wrathchild' would remain in Maiden's set for years to come. Short and snappy, this track proved Maiden was still capable of finding the form they'd exuded on *Iron Maiden*, and includes a glorious scream from Di'Anno which was not too far removed from his eventual successor. But the real jewel in the *Killers* crown is the pumped up slamming rage of

'Murders In The Rue Morgue', based on Edgar Allen Poe's short story of the same name. Featuring one of Di'Anno's best performances in an Iron Maiden shirt, the song is speedy and immediately catchy, and a raucous update on a spate of '70s rock bands that stated their piece in short, sharp bursts of energy. It was also the kind of track Paul Di'Anno could really attack, and in this respect he and Iron Maiden were perfectly suited.

Steve felt that along with the title cut, 'Murders In The Rue Morgue' was the best song on the record. "The first album really sounded like a first album," the bassist commented. "With *Killers* we started to sound more like Maiden. It was the first album where we felt some satisfaction as far as the sound of the album went. 'Killers' and 'Murders In The Rue Morgue' stand out because they are great live favourites." (Which begs the question as to why the band did not play it live more often later in their career).

'Genghis Khan' is more in line with the future Maiden style, though the epic nature of the song could arguably have benefited from a beefier production. "Originally it was written to depict the feeling and sound of Genghis Khan's army going into battle," explained Steve. The band felt a vocal melody would clutter an already frantic song, and thus it was left as an instrumental.

'Innocent Exile' features a cute Steve Harris bass line and it is no surprise to learn that this was actually a song from the earlier days of the band. It does not quite have the Maiden stamp they would eventually come to be known for and in some ways stands out as being very different from the rest of the *Killers* material. Nevertheless it includes some clever vocal phrasing from Di'Anno and of course, the requisite guitar breaks. The title track is a well-drilled affair featuring numerous switching sections and a soaring scream from Paul at the beginning. Lyrically the song is quite fittingly about a serial killer and suits both Maiden's approach and Paul's voice. In fact it is a surprise that Maiden does not have more tracks of this nature, eerie and drowned in minor chords.

'Prodigal Son' is another highlight showcasing Paul Di'Anno's voice, which here shows greater adaptability than he is later given credit for. The track itself is on the lighter side of the Maiden armoury, much like 'Remember Tomorrow' or 'Strange World'. Many aspects of the 1981 album could have belonged in the mid '70, such was the overall style and sound found on *Killers*. Martin Birch had not deliberately set out to make a retro sounding album but he had managed it, a factor which in some ways held the negative connotation that the group was unable to recapture their signature sound so well displayed on *Iron Maiden*. *Killers* was therefore viewed by some as a strange progressive move, and by others as something of a step backwards in time.

Only the likes of 'Purgatory' seemed able to relate to the previous Maiden pattern and standard, and this song was actually a pre-existing number, originally titled 'Floating', from the band's earlier days. The chorus is in the vein of an archetypal Maiden classic and was rightly issued as a single. 'Twilight Zone', also chosen as a single for the band, could easily have been included on the album, but for some reason, in Britain was left off.

'Drifter' ends the album with another bass flourish and a Di'Anno scream. Combining many of the different bases covered in previous *Killers* material, the track quickly became a live favourite, with a great breakdown section perfect for crowd participation. *Killers* is essentially the creation of one man and it is testament to Steve Harris that, despite single-handedly composing 95% of the album, he had managed to produce a highly diversified piece of work, always with something to go back and rediscover. It is also certainly worth owning as part of a rich kaleidoscope of Maiden colours. Although *Killers* could never be described as one-dimensional or boring, it smacks of a group not quite yet firing on all cylinders, still searching for their definitive sound and, in truth, it is poorer for the lack of collaboration with other band members – the benefits of which would be seen with the future contributions of Adrian Smith and Di'Anno's eventual replacement that would add spice to the band's capabilities.

The experience certainly helped the band collectively, now with two full LPs and a wealth of classy matèrial to its name, as well as positively effecting individual members. Even Paul Di'Anno was grateful to producer Martin Birch for his influence. "He pushed me to do things that I didn't think I was capable of," the vocalist later stated. "At the time, I didn't have any recording experience and Martin was my first 'real' teacher, he made me realise how I should or shouldn't use my voice. I was young and I thought I knew it all, but in fact, I knew fuck all, and Martin made me aware of it. He was a real inspiration to me and he'll always have a special place in my heart. And he was really good at transforming what we'd do 'well' into something 'great'. Even today, I remember a lot of his advice and I still apply what he taught me."

As was necessary, Iron Maiden would need to tour their butts off to make *Killers* a success and they did this by playing 125 concerts in six months. Despite several fantastic shows and a general feeling of attaining success on the back of *Killers*, which had gone into the UK charts and reached number twelve, problems persisted with Di'Anno which fully came to light during the 1981 tour. Steve Harris' tour diary from this time notes:

'Saturday Morning, 8am. Arrived at Heathrow – me and Clive meet rest of the lads including Ross Halfin, only to find that Adrian (bearing a close resemblance to Stan Laurel this morning) has left his passport at home (daft bleeder, now he has to wait for it to arrive and will miss the flight and have to get a later one) and Paul is still out of his brains from the previous night as usual.'

Paul would excuse himself to the band but really he was skating on such thin ice it was only a matter of weeks before he would have been sacked. "I must admit, we had thought about it but we didn't want him to go really because the band was doing well," admitted Steve later. "I thought we had a settled line-up. He was pretty unsettled in himself and I don't think he wanted to go the whole hog with it and that was causing problems on stage because some nights he'd be into it and some nights he wouldn't. We knew that if we didn't split with him, the band would go downhill. There's no real blame, but I just think he was silly to himself in a way because I feel he's got a lot of talent and he was throwing it away. Although in a way, I don't think the band would have done as well with him as a front man, maybe we were outgrowing him and it was a sad thing when he went."

Keith Wilfort says today, "Paul's departure was not really a surprise. He had become a liability, not taking care of his voice and getting too involved with the rock and roll lifestyle. The band had to cancel shows or go on without Paul. It was also clear that his heart really wasn't in it musically, although he never held back on stage. I was sorry to see him go as he was a really great guy, but it was clear the band could not progress with things as they were."

Di'Anno remained unrepentant about his behaviour for many years and equally to this day believes he was at least 30% responsible for the success of Maiden in the early years. When asked what he feels he brought to the band in those halcyon days he replies, "The voice. The attitude. The look. I'm not bigheaded, but Maiden looked like any other band on the planet, and me, I was the coolest front man since Elvis. My look allowed the band to stand out. And then, there was my voice... The voice of the singers in the other metal or hard rock bands was stereotyped, not mine. My vocals didn't sound like anybody else's – and it's still the case today – and when you heard me, you instantly knew it was Di'Anno. I've never sung high, those high-pitched girlie voices that were common in all hard rock bands. My voice had menace, aggression, soul. An unequalled sound.

"Let's say that the Maiden boys were lovely young people you could have introduced to your Nan. She would have loved them. But if she'd met me, she'd have died of a heart attack within a minute! The Maiden boys were musicians without an attitude, without an image, nothing – except they were the best Metal band in the country, but a band of nice blokes. They didn't have this spark until they met this nutcase called Paul Di'Anno. I brought them madness and an over-the-top aspect, all of this preventing them being like those numerous metal bands that remain stuck playing in pubs ad vitam æternam. Maiden was a great band, and I was a great front man, a front man that was different from all the others at that time, with a different look, without the compulsory long hair. I had this attitude 'cause I knew I was the best at the time, and I didn't give a fuck about what people thought of me. Iron Maiden may very well have been the best band at the time, but they needed an element to get out of the pub circuit. That element was me. And we helped each other. I was the Mike Tyson – when he was young and unbeatable! – of the metal scene, and, at that time, no-one could beat me."

Today however, Di'Anno feels differently, especially about leaving the band, which he admits was "totally irresponsible" and goes on to say "I suffered later on because of this decision. I was completely burned out, at the end of my tether, when the story came to an end. But at the same time, I felt invincible, I thought that nothing could stop me 'cause I was the voice and the front man of the metal band that was becoming the most important on the planet. At the time of the split, I couldn't have imagined that somebody would have the right abilities to replace me... But at that time, I was out of my head, and I became painfully aware that there was another excellent metal vocalist, Bruce Dickinson."

Neal Kay believes the problems with Paul were deep rooted and that he could never have stayed with the band for longer than he did. "Paul Di'Anno never did anything against me and I liked him when I met him initially," the DJ recalls. "But I soon realised Paul had a problem, with reality. When we went out on the first tour I still remember Paul telling people about his fleet of helicopters and every night that just got bigger and bigger, and a whole load of other bullshit stuff. Matters came to the first head I recall when we did the Mayfair in Newcastle. Paul went on stage with a pork pie hat; he was kind of into the Madness thing a lot back then. Or he liked to pretend he was into ska for some reason no-one ever knew. Everyone was telling him not to wear it, 'cos it ain't rock 'n' roll.

But worse was to follow, when he opened up he started talking about football.

"And I think he was talking about how West Ham were going to do the business over Newcastle. Stupid man, that did it. Something horrible happened that night – they had to leave the stage early, directly because of Paul's mouth. I had to finish the night off myself, as the DJ. Paul had a voice, but it was not good enough in my view to go the distance. It was nice enough but it was not a stadium voice that was going to survive, it wasn't powerful enough. And, because he was not professional in the way that he handled himself, eventually matters took a turn for the worse. Maiden needed the professionalism of somebody up front who would carry the flag forever and be controlled and professional enough to behave and look after his voice. And Paul just wasn't that character."

Just before they found a new vocalist, Maiden featured the talents of Paul Di'Anno on record one last time. In November 1981 the band issued a special treat for their fans and as a dedication to their Japanese followers, released four tracks recorded live there. *Maiden Japan* featured 'Running Free', 'Remember Tomorrow', 'Killers' and 'Innocent Exile'. The US and Brazilian releases contained a fifth track, 'Wrathchild'. The EP climbed as high as number forty-three in the UK charts and prompted mass fan adulation in Japan, as Steve recalled, "Everywhere we travelled, there were loads and loads of screaming girls. I mean, it was unbelievable, just screaming! Guys, as well, would run right down the road and start banging on the windows, it was absolutely ridiculous! I didn't think that sort of thing went on anymore, it's just the way they are; totally crazy!"

DI'ANNO: WHAT HAPPENED NEXT

Paul Di'Anno went on to become one of the most prolific musicians of his generation, recording with bands from many different areas of the globe. Some of his post Maiden material has, by his own admission, been sub par, but there is no doubt the vocalist always puts on great live performances and sings 'his' Maiden songs with great aplomb and enthusiasm.

Here is a comprehensive list of his most notable bands from 1982 to the present day.

LONE WOLF (1982 - 1984) – A 6-piece band in the vein of Whitesnake.

GOGMAGOG (1985) – NWOBHM supergroup, featuring Di'anno on vocals, Pete Willis (DEF LEPPARD) and Janick Gers (GILLAN) on guitars, Neil Murray (WHITESNAKE) on bass guitar, and Clive Burr on drums. Released a demo E.P. 'I Will Be There' in 1985.

DI'ANNO (1984 - May 1985) – Journey soundalikes. Released an album titled *Di'anno*, as well as a single from this album 'Heartuser' in 1984, on the FM Coast to Coast label (a division of Heavy Metal Records). They also released their second album, *Two Swimmers & A Bag Of Jockies* in 1984.

PAUL DI'ANNO'S BATTLEZONE (1986 - 1987) – Recorded *Fighting Back* in 1986 and *Children Of Madness* the following year. The drummer on the second album is Steve Hopgood of famed NWOBHM band Persian Risk.

KILLERS (Jan 1992 - present) – This project also features Steve Hopgood on drums and Nick Burr (brother of Clive) on guitars. The band has released several albums through the 90s and beyond.

PAUL DI'ANNO (1997 - present) – A mixed bag of original material with lots of guest musicians, live work – including Maiden tracks, and a multitude of cover songs

Paul has also appeared on many compilations and created several short-lived projects. He joined Praying Mantis for a live album, and was also at the helm for an obscure Japanese project in 1989. This included between fifteen and twenty members, with Dennis Stratton among them. It was exclusively for Japanese fans but did not seem to get off the ground after the one and only album, *Kaizoku*.

Sources:

Hard Rock Magazine #21
Enfer Magazine #42
Killers Tour Programme 1981
Rock Hard Magazine Hors Série #1
Rock Hard Magazine (France)
– Spécial Noël N°39, Décembre 2004
Guitare Magazine

Chapter 4
The Nature Of The Beast

"With Samson when you went on stage you didn't know what was gonna happen that night, whereas with Iron Maiden you know exactly what's gonna happen, at the beginning, in the middle and the end and all points in between. With Samson you never knew what was going to happen, it was on the edge of it all the time." Thunderstick

With Paul Di'Anno out of the picture, Iron Maiden had to focus on finding a singer who could do justice to their new material. First choice was a cult British performer known as Bruce Bruce, or Bruce Dickinson. Born Paul Bruce Dickinson on August 7th, 1958 he was the illegitimate son of two teenagers in Worksop. Initially Bruce was raised by his grandparents but after a while his father made enough money to pack him off to Oundle public school in Northamptonshire.

He loathed it. So much so, in fact, that he became head of the cadet force and made a habit of priming booby traps to disconcert his foes. "That was a classic case of parents wanting their kids to have everything they never had," Bruce told *Q* in 1991. "Some of it was good, loads to do, amateur dramatics, debating, but really it was the most illiberal place on the planet. Wacko! Mass floggings over minor practical jokes. Eventually I was expelled for pissing in the headmaster's dinner. Somebody informed on me. It was only half a cupful slipped into the frozen beans and I knew from biology that a bit of boiled urine wouldn't do him any harm. Ill judged though, I admit."

Expelled from Oundle, Dickinson was enrolled into a Catholic comprehensive school in Sheffield. It was every ex-public-schoolboy's dream as he later described; "It was brilliant. Everybody was, like, 'normal' and there were girls there – which freaked me out at first." Bruce left school aged eighteen with A-levels in English, History and Economics. He also joined the Territorial Army for a year. "Considering my education, I was supposed to take the exam to become an officer," he continued in *Q*. "But I strongly disliked officers and army men in general, so I went to London and registered at the university where I studied History for three years. During those three years, I reconsidered everything. It was the first time in my life that I really felt free. I spent the first year partying with my mates – we were pissed every night! At the

end of that year, I had put on twenty pounds! During that year, I let myself into all sorts of things: I got into politics with the students, I started playing rock n' roll, and I tried out all sorts of substances. Anything
coming my way was interesting to me, and I'd get into it systematically!
"At the end of that year, I decided it was time to calm down a bit. I looked
at myself in the mirror and I thought, 'I have to stop! No more beer, or I'll
end up dead!' I managed to keep away for months, not a drop of beer. In
the meantime, I got further involved in rock n' roll, playing with one band
or another."

During his time at college he met up with a fellow known as Noddy
White aka bass player Paul White who had a band called Speed. Though
musically they were naïve compared to other bands of the burgeoning
NWOBHM, their one and only release was to go on to become the holy
grail of NWOBHM collectibles once Bruce had found success with Iron
Maiden.

His ex band-mates would claim Bruce was merely a guest vocalist
'on loan' from Samson at the time. This was quite untrue seeing as Bruce
would not join Samson until some time later. Indeed Speed was as much
his band as anyone else who formed the remainder of the group. Together
they recorded the 'Man In The Street' single, which was a private, very
cheap pressing that featured 'On The Road' as the b-side. There was no
outer picture sleeve but there was an insert, which featured a rather strange
looking Dickinson complete (as was his custom in those days) with moustache.

Speaking of the Speed single Bruce revealed to Matthias Mader in
1997 that 'Man In The Street' was "a studio recording from when I was
still at college. The original Speed had already disbanded by that time,
but Noddy White asked me whether or not I'd come back and sing on
this number, which he intended to record with a couple of his mates. So
I agreed to help him out, and we even got as far as laying down a second
track. Back then we played Judas Priest and Stranglers songs alongside
our own material and toured in and around London in the late 70s. On a
couple of occasions we shared a stage with Angelwitch."

Though the single was crude sounding and clearly cheaply produced, it still fetches upwards of £300 from collectors. Bruce went on to
a group called Shots after replying to an advert in *Melody Maker* and was
also 'involved' with Xero in mid 1978. This period saw Dickinson finding
his feet both as a vocalist and performer.

He was determined to become a singer as his guitar work was
"dreadful." Drumming was initially his first love, and he feels he's a bet-

ter drummer than guitarist, but he switched to vocals early on since he "couldn't drive a car and couldn't afford a drum kit." Bill Leisegang, his guitar player in Xero says of Bruce's voice in the late 70s, "He was going for high screams and stuff, with quite an original and unusual approach (not so much Ian Gillan, more over the top). I don't think any of us were truly metal devotees at the time. We kind of got caught up in it as punk was dying out and new wave and new romantic wasn't for us. I guess our roots were all in 60s and 70's rock.

"He was a lovely guy, a wacky kind of guy," he says of Bruce's character. "I remember he used to wear strange clothes, big boxing boots and he was really into Arthur Brown. He was more theatrical than most of the heavy metal fraternity at the Marquee club."

Bruce was never actually officially in Xero, becoming an 'honorary member' of sorts without even realising it. Leisegang, who had also been in Shots, wanted to use an old Shots song (which Bruce had sung on, called 'Lone Wolf') for his new project Xero. In a rather naïve move, Xero released an EP of the songs 'Oh Baby' and 'Hold On' but also included 'Lone Wolf' as a 'bonus track' and advertised it as featuring the, by now, Iron Maiden vocalist, Bruce Dickinson. Once Rod Smallwood and co. found out about this release featuring Maiden's new singer but which they had not authorised, they brought swift legal action against Xero, forcing them to withdraw 'Lone Wolf' even though several hundred copies were already in circulation. Bruce himself, however did not even receive a copy of the single.

It had been while singing in Shots however that Bruce had sealed his own fate.

"I saw an ad in a local paper wanting a singer for recording," the vocalist later explained. "Together, we put down a song called 'Dracula' and called the band Shots. I was then working as the social secretary at the college, and Manfred Mann's Earth Band was going to play, so I put Shots down to play, and that's when the guys from Samson heard me sing."

Come 1979 Dickinson made his biggest career move to date and joined up with the British trio. Whilst still at college, Bruce was given a credit as appearing on the first Samson album, *Survivors*. Although this was not as singer – instead the cheeky chappy contributed harmonica and guitar parts – he was nevertheless credited as being vocalist and his time with Samson had begun.

The band was fleshed out by bass player Chris Aylmer, guitarist/ vocalist Paul Samson and initially Clive Burr. Aylmer told me of his initiation into rock music and how the first version of Samson was started.

"While still at school I started a band called The Moonshiners playing rock n' roll standards. The singer was a certain Ian Gillan! My family moved to the south coast and I joined an r n' b outfit called The Creatures who would play anywhere and everywhere – eight gigs in one week was a record! When I returned to London in the mid seventies I joined rock band Maya featuring Clive Burr on drums. He was an easygoing, friendly, nice chap. We had a lot of good times as a three piece. There was Gerry Sherwin on bass as I was still on lead guitar. Then I met Paul Samson at an audition for the Front Room Band and we hit it off immediately. Paul was playing with John McCoy and the infamous Roger Hunt (I did the sound for them on several occasions). When McCoy got the Gillan band job Paul coerced me into playing bass on the remaining gigs. I borrowed Gerry's bass and we continued the tour. When Roger left, Clive joined. I wanted to rename the band Samson but Paul thought it might be too egotistical – he was eventually talked into it."

Samson's first major coup was to enlist the services of Thunderstick, described by Aylmer as "a much heavier, more aggressive drummer" than Clive Burr. "We were the first band to have the first NWOBHM album out, *Survivors*, because up until then record companies had only been promoting and signing punk" the drummer recalls. "We had the first big major press thing in *Sounds* with all the fireworks and all that. We weren't trying to emulate Kiss at all but we had a roadie that was a pyromaniac, so that was that. He wanted to blow people up, so we just let him get on with it."

But the focus became the visually eye catching Barry Purkis who has also been known as Barry Graham. "I lived the life of Thunderstick which was really strange," he says, "because before you got into a town where you where playing or doing an interview I would garb up, put all the gear on, much like Kiss, so nobody saw you. I would go through periods of time where I wouldn't talk and the rest of the band would say, 'He's on a weird one at the moment, he's not talking, he's decided for the next three weeks that he's not gonna say anything, to cleanse his soul' and stuff like that. So I would do an interview with a guy, fully garbed up with the mask and all that and just look at him, just stare at him all the way through. They'd be asking me questions and I'd be going "...". It is very disconcerting I can assure you, it really is, but it's also just as disconcerting to be on the other side of the mask because you can't talk and you can't laugh. If somebody from the rest of the band makes a witty comment and you wanna laugh, you can't do it. You just gotta sit there. We used to have support bands that came out on tour with us and at the end of the tour they'd have people asking 'What does Thunderstick really look like?' and they'd say 'I haven't got a clue, I never saw him.'"

Such a mystique inevitably led to interest from girls as well as a band of somewhat unusual male fans. As Bruce would later refer to in an *NME* interview, Thunderstick could often chat up ladies by not talking at all, or in one case, just grunting. "It's true," says Thunderstick, today known as Purkis. "She wanted to fuck me with the mask on, basically. I pulled her, I fucked her and just sent her out of the window and that was it. Yes it is true. There are people out there like that, let's face it." There was also the time where the drummer set fire to a young girl's nightgown and threw her out of the window. "It was a ground floor window, it was alright, it wasn't very high. Nothing serious. That's the kind of life it was. Strange."

But Samson were not just about imagery or bizarre occurrences, they actually managed to create some wonderful music together and the members bonded personally behind the scenes. "Bruce and I had such similar taste in singers that we loved," says Thunderstick on a more serious note. "Paul would pooh-pooh these, he would hate them, he would go 'what a bunch of wankers! You like them? You like them?' What are you talking about?' And Bruce and I would be talking about people like Daevid Allen from Gong and Peter Hammill and the wonderful Arthur Brown and the vocal range that he has."

The attempts from Bruce to mimic this genius can be heard on all the Samson songs he fronted. And there is no doubting just what a band this was when on top of their game. Take a listen to their classic LP *Shock Tactics*, which featured the likes of 'Riding With The Angels' – a superb Deep Purple type number.

The previous album *Head On* was also considered something of a masterpiece. Happy with the unpredictability of the Samson set up, Bruce enjoyed himself so much during recordings for the album, he would later say he was amazed he recalls it at all.

"I remember recording it, I did the vocals with him," Thunderstick says. "And when we say drugs, we're talking about marijuana and hash, we're not talking heroin or the Guns 'n' Roses situation or we're not talking Mötley Crüe having to pull people back from the dead. We're talking about four guys sitting down over two or three joints before they start rehearsals, you know, that's all. And it was just strange. Bruce was really playful at that time and he wanted to get on. You could see he wanted to."

That is the main thing about Bruce, despite his party hard attitude, he could always do the business when required and it was inevitable he would shed the Samson skin if success eluded them.

Chris Aylmer describes Bruce as, "Self-determined, enthusiastic, hard working, talented. Sometimes he went too far and was seen as arrogant, but if you don't believe in yourself... He was always good at getting the crowd going and he had a bottomless bag of lyrics to hand when we were writing new material."

Unfortunately, despite the intriguing array of members in Samson and their frequently fantastic songs, not to mention the guitar wizardry of Paul Samson himself (and of course Mr Thunderstick), the band never received the respect they deserved. In fact you get the feeling this was a group who would never receive their due – they were destined to be cult favourites. It is intriguing, with hindsight, to consider the fact that only Bruce Dickinson would truly go on to receive worldwide recognition. "In the beginning it was chaos – the band went over the top in everything – whereas Maiden were much more organised," Aylmer reckons. "When we eventually got it together we were one of the most respected bands on the circuit but had lost ground to other acts. I wouldn't have missed it for the world."

"It hurts," says Thunderstick, of the Samson decline and lack of success. "I've got scrap books and there are rave reviews saying that 'this band is wonderful, it's what we need, it's a kick up the arse of anything before. It's got the energy of punk and the unpredictability.' That was always nice about it."

Collectively Samson resented the snatching of Bruce and the treatment they would later receive. Thunderstick believes Rod Smallwood had a 'grudge' against them, "Because there were all kinds of different things that happened, the 'Thunderburst / Ides of March' thing. And they completely omit from their stories things like when Doug Sampson left around Christmas after we'd finished the Metal Crusade tour with Iron Maiden supporting, and we were just about to go in and record *Head On* with Samson. Two days before Christmas Eve Steve Harris asked me if I wanted to rejoin the band. They just dismiss that completely, it doesn't even exist in the story. And the fact that I spent my whole Christmas deliberating – Thunderstick and Samson? or Barry Purkis, Barry Graham, whatever you want in Iron Maiden? What do I do? And I went and played with them (Maiden) the day after Boxing Day and Rod Smallwood sat there and we were just about to do 'Running Free'. Dennis Stratton was there and I remember Rod sitting there and saying to me 'this band's gonna be bigger than Led Zeppelin.' I thought 'it's really nice to be able to believe in your band to that extent but at that time, you know, 'bigger than Zeppelin'.

"I was still kind of committed to Samson because of the Thunderstick thing and the way that was taking off and I'd just got front cover of *Sounds* which was the topical magazine of the time, and they were looking for Barry Graham. They were also looking for somebody that was more like a solid player, because I was still playing within that *Head On* type of era, Neil Peart type of stuff. As soon as there was a break I'd go crazy on the drums and Steve Harris would go 'What?' so it was, like 'Thank you, but No.' We all agreed. It wasn't just saying, 'Oh, I'm not joining Iron Maiden' and it wasn't Steve saying 'Sorry Barry, we phoned you up, it was a mistake, it didn't work,' we agreed that I was going somewhere as Thunderstick. We were just about to start the second Samson album and they wanted somebody else. We were in the studio doing the second Samson album and John McCoy phoned up and went 'You'll never guess who just got the Iron Maiden gig' and I went 'Who?' and he went 'Clive Burr.' In fact, it got to a stage where I was gigging with Samson with 'Iron Maiden' written all over my drum cases and Clive was vice versa, he had 'Samson' all over his and he was in Iron Maiden. It's kind of weird. Then when they did the tours it was like stuff about riders where they nicked all our food one time and we went mad and trashed their dressing room and stuff like that. And Rod Smallwood is like an elephant, he doesn't forget those things... It's a bit unfortunate."

Shock Tactics proved to be Bruce Dickinson's last album with the mighty Samson, and at least it was a good representation of their talents and their diversity.

Regarding both Burr and Dickinson being stolen by Maiden, Chris Aylmer is reflective and accepting; "You always look at players in other bands 'cause you know what they can do," he states, "Better than putting an ad in and getting two hundred replies. Bruce was clearly the best singer around so they wanted him. Clive I'm not so sure."

Neal Kay explains from inside the Maiden camp how the capture of Bruce came about. "Steve rang me one night asking me what I thought about Bruce when he was still with Samson and I think I said something like, he's an awesome singer completely in the wrong place and Steve said to me, 'he's just an animal'. He was so classically misplaced in Samson it just wasn't true, what a waste of talent that was. You know, the band were going nowhere. It got to a stage where they did a gig at the Music Machine in which Samson headlined and Maiden were underneath them on the bill. My crowd, the Bandwagon crowd, were there and not one person applauded the whole of Samson's set. At the end of the night Paul came up to me and he said, 'you arranged that didn't you, you told them not to applaud me?' I just looked at him and said, 'Paul you're a nutcase, you're trying too hard mate. You'd rather blow them up with pyros than give them what they want. They don't want your stuff from twenty-five years ago, they want it modern now. And that's what Maiden gave them. And you're not doing it, you're an old blues guitar player and as much as you're a good guitarist you've lost it completely with what's happening today.

"And it's sad because Paul's gone now. And his wife and my wife were friends, we used to go over and see them in London. Paul was a happy chap he just didn't have a handle on the modern thing at the time. He couldn't have done it if he had wanted to because he couldn't see it. Bruce came down to one of my shows in Leytonstone and I think Steve had asked me to get Bruce to ring him. That was the start of Bruce joining."

"Steve Harris asked me to join Maiden," Bruce would later recall. "I already knew Steve before I joined Samson, and the first time I saw Iron Maiden rehearsing, I was immediately impressed by their music and mostly by Dave Murray. To me, he was a real 'Guitar-Hero' and his playing reminded me of Ritchie Blackmore's, who's my favourite guitar player. From then on, I was waiting for somebody to leave so I could replace him, 'cause I was crazy about that band. Then I joined Samson and, as it happens, we toured with Iron Maiden. I remember that, one night after a gig, I had a long conversation with Paul Di'Anno. He was asking me for advice, he wanted to know everything about my vocal technique, 'cause Iron Maiden was really starting to get big. They didn't have any album out and it was a good opportunity for them to open for Samson. "Then, two years later, we all found ourselves in the same studio. Iron Maiden were recording *Killers* at the Battery Studio and Samson were recording *Shock Tactics* at the Battery Studio I. So, we all lived together. Clive Burr used to come over often to watch us record, and I used to go and see Steve and the others. It's at that time that I realised that problems were starting to happen between Paul and the rest of the band." Aylmer admits that, at the time, Samson did harbour some resentment at the Maiden boys turning almost instantly huge while Samson seemed to be fading away.

"We lost a mega deal when Bruce left," he says. "On reflection a lot of it was our own fault – bad management, bad choices etc."

Sadly, though the Samson members would continue their rock assault for many years to come, they remained truly an underground act. Tragically, Paul Samson died of cancer aged forty-nine in 2002.

PAUL SAMSON AND THE NWOBHM AS REMEMBERED
BY CHRIS AYLMER

"Paul Samson grew up in a tough area of Southeast London. His first musical experiences were seeing bands like The Pretty Things in local pubs. Soon however he would come into contact with the musician who was to become such a major influence on his entire life – Jimi Hendrix.

"I first met Paul in 1976 at an audition for The Front Room Band. I was on guitar but we soon realised that we needed a bigger sound. We decided to audition in a local pub. People came and went but only one had the front to approach us. Paul marched up complaining that we'd told him the wrong place and insisting on several large drinks before he'd even discuss the band. Within a week he had totally taken over and, even stranger, we had become firm friends.

"Needless to say the band did nothing but our paths crossed at various London gigs. He eventually joined up with John McCoy and the infamous Roger Hunt in Scrapyard while I joined Maya with Clive Burr and Gerry Sherwin. On our days off we would sit in the Trattoria Mondello in Holborn devouring good cheap pasta washed down with copious amounts of Valpolicella. The main topic of conversation – after Hendrix of course – was that if we couldn't find the band we both wanted then we'd better form it ourselves. The chance came sooner than either of us expected. John McCoy got the Gillan band job and had to leave more or less immediately, so, rather than cancel the gigs, Paul informed me that I was the new bass player! I had done sound on a few occasions so I knew the set. I borrowed Gerry's bass and off we went. Paul's appetite for live work was such that we soon became one of the busiest bands on the circuit. Roger Hunt left and we got Clive Burr in. Even in the late 70s Paul was writing his own material. A lot of Hendrix influences but his love of blues showed through right from the start. He was also a great businessman. Realising that Samson needed to be heard by a wider audience he got us a management company who set up recording deals and major tours. Shortly afterwards he discovered a young university student singing in a local pub – Bruce Dickinson.

"I don't think it is an overstatement to say that Paul was the lynchpin of the New Wave of British Heavy Metal as it came to be known. Samson's management was responsible for most of the great gigs of the time. It was not unusual to see us with Iron Maiden, Angelwitch etc on the same bill on a regular basis. Sadly the management company turned out to be less than perfect and Samson lost ground to other acts.

"Paul's guitar playing never lost its freshness however. When all around were trying to fit as many notes as possible into every bar Paul just made sure that every note counted. Just go back to the Reading Festival of 1980 and listen to the gig broadcast on Radio One – surely the biggest sound of the entire weekend. When Bruce left most of us lost heart, but not Paul. He drafted in Nicky Moore and Samson took on a whole new lease of life. Paul always had ideas for new songs but would welcome other people's too so we developed as a team to produce *Before the Storm* and *Don't Get Mad* – the definitive Samson albums. When Samson finally came to a halt, Paul wasted no time in producing his own solo albums together with various blues projects.

In between bands our personal lives entwined and he eventually followed me up to Norwich where he set up his own studio. Samson as a band reformed with Nicky Moore and Thunderstick for some storming gigs notably the Wacken Festival and the Tokyo NWOBHM Reunion show. Paul was working on a new album when his illness was discovered. In typical fashion he refused to give in and continued to work to the very end.

"Paul Samson more than deserves his place in the pantheon of British guitar heroes. His style was truly original and, like Hendrix, he concentrated on feel rather than flashy effects or lightning fingering. His playing influenced a new generation of Heavy Metal bands and remains distinctive to this day. The rock world will be a poorer place without him. I miss him very much."

Sources:

Paul Stenning Interviews
Costa Zoulio, 5 February 1999 (Triple JJJ FM Radio).
http://www.bookofhours.net/samson/
http://www.paulsamson.co.uk/chrisobit.html
Q Magazine January 1991
NWOBHM Encyclopaedia – Malc Macmillan

Chapter 5
Run To The Tills!

"I dreamt for years about making albums and doing world tours. I'd fulfilled all my ambitions in one year." Bruce Dickinson

Steve Harris knew Bruce Dickinson was perfect for Iron Maiden and the audition Bruce attended would prove the bassist right. Not only did Bruce learn three times as many songs as he was asked, he also put in stellar performances on tracks the band were used to hearing Di'Anno sing. It was difficult to stamp authority on someone else's material, but Bruce, ever the consummate professional, managed it easily. When belting out the likes of 'Killers' he proved he could truly take Maiden to a new level with his adaptable voice and capable scream.

"Getting Bruce was a major coup and his demo just blew everyone away," Keith Wilfort recalls. "They had actually approached Bruce earlier, but he was still committed to the Samson cause. There was a lot of behind the scenes manoeuvrings going on before Bruce finally signed on the dotted line, but I'd say that was the single most important moment in Iron Maiden's history."

Bruce brought a new slant to the band both as a performer and as a person. He was and is, utterly unique. As Neal Kay says, "Bruce is an intellectual. He's highly intelligent. You sit down with Bruce and talk to him long enough and his mental power will destroy yours. I recall sitting down with him and his wife Paddy at Steve's one night and Bruce was on an acupuncture kick. And you feel so exhausted after talking with Bruce for a couple of hours that you just want to go to bed. The man has got the most intense eyes I've ever seen and his mental agility is awesome. He moves at the speed of light, which is probably why he's a good fencer. I understand his speed of mind because he flies great big aeroplanes professionally and you don't get into the right hand seat of a 757 unless you know what you're doing.

"He is an awesomely talented rock singer, but he is a whole lot more than that. He is an incredibly intense person, bright as a button. There is a lot of stupidity in him but then people who work hard, play hard. If you want to look at it another way, Battle Of Britain pilots would come home after a days killing and do the most ridiculous things, play stupid games like children. Dickinson is a great practical joker, he's very funny, when you are around him you need to have your wits about you."

Once Bruce was given the job he immediately joined Maiden to scream his lungs out for a couple of live shows in Europe. "At the end of 1981 we toured Italy, where I familiarised myself with Iron Maiden on stage," Bruce later said. "Then we came home to record the album, and we went out again for the European tour. From August 1981 until August 1982, I've never been so busy in my life. I didn't stop working." On November 15th Bruce played his first UK gig with Maiden at London's Rainbow Theatre.

With Dickinson in the ranks, the Harris/Smallwood partnership knew they had a real chance to push Maiden to a new level. Steve had long sought a higher calibre vocalist. It not only meant the group would have a more appropriate image (in truth, visually, Bruce was better suited to the band than Paul's more punk rooted look) but also that, for the first time, Harris could go completely wild with his song writing. He knew and would later attest that Bruce could sing 'anything'. His range was way beyond Paul Di'Anno's grit and workmanlike approach. Bruce was more the archetypal, classic heavy rock singer with an adaptable larynx and a truly awesome set of pipes. It is also arguable that Dickinson had more of a personable quality to his voice, meaning, all in all, he was utterly unique. With all due respect to Di'Anno, there were a million others who could match him for singing ability and his appeal was limited to only those who liked the straightforward gritty approach of punk or pub rock.

Bruce was clearly in a different league, and it was not something studied. He had simply developed his own voice as he had gone along, honing his skills to the point where he was able to contribute to a heavy metal landmark, and also go out on the road and support it for several months at a time. Unfortunately, due to a dispute with Samson's old label, GEM, Bruce was prohibited from penning any Iron Maiden material until 1983.

It was testament to Bruce's professionalism and Maiden's welcoming personalities that the newly assembled outfit could so instantly gel and not only compose a coherent set of songs, but write one of the greatest heavy metal albums of all time. Everything about the record known as *The Number Of The Beast* was perfect. The timing, the performances, the songs, the cover art and the promotion. And above all, Maiden released an album way ahead of its time. This was pure unadulterated metal at its most sophisticated and credit must go to Steve Harris for visualising Bruce Dickinson as the perfect front man for Maiden. Though Bruce's work with

Samson was impressive, it was on a different scale and style to his subsequent performances for Maiden. Quite how Harris knew Bruce could front such explosive heavy metal when he had previously only sung in a hard rock vein is unknown but he certainly got it right.

And so the band began work in early 1982, recording and mixing the album in just three and a half weeks. They had set aside 6 weeks but worked so quickly they were finished much earlier. "It was winter and we were at a studio in Willesden, in North London," Bruce remembers. "We got extremely pissed all of the time. The recording sessions used to go on until about four in the morning, and for the last three or four hours of that we'd play back what we'd done that day very loud and get drunk."

Whether their inebriation contributed to the events that accompanied the recording we don't know but, by all accounts, the sessions were eerie affairs. Lights went on and off on their own, equipment which had been working fine suddenly stopped. The gear was also responsible for making strange groaning noises – things were literally going bump in the night.

Perhaps the most curious anecdote, however, concerns Martin Birch's collision on the way to the studio one night when he smashed into another car. Fortunately, neither driver was hurt but, considering the name of the album they were recording was *The Number Of The Beast*, was it just a coincidence that not only was the other driver a man of the Catholic Church, but the repair bill, when presented to Birch, was for £666! Birch was taking no chances, and paid £1 more, just in case!

"Looking back, I'm not sure how we managed to actually record it," Bruce says today of the album. "The tape operator was a guy called Nigel Green, and he used to go out on what we called 'The Willesden Run' at about 1AM every night. There was some dodgy supermarket where you could get beer after hours and places to buy other things that helped you stay up late. It was sort of like a slalom for late night booze and chemicals! The first track we recorded was 'Run To The Hills.' We'd no idea how any of the stuff was going to come out, but when we played it back we freaked ourselves out. It was blindingly obvious that it was completely amazing."

The listening public would concur by making *The Number Of The Beast* one of the most successful heavy metal albums of all time. The record was perfectly weighted and expertly crafted. Though certain songs would often be overlooked, like 'Invaders' and the instrumental 'Gangland', this was purely because the remainder of the album was so enviable, with a gaggle of classic tracks from 'Children Of The Damned' to 'Hallowed Be Thy Name.' 'Invaders', the opener, is in many ways the perfect rock 'n' roll number to begin proceedings. The music is prime Iron Maiden, exercising twin guitar harmonies and a stellar upbeat riff. Perhaps the one down side to the song is the chorus, which is almost off key in its vocal/guitar combination.

But, for the song that would introduce fans to Bruce Dickinson, 'Invaders' was a sure indication of the direction the band were moving. Though written by Steve Harris the track is just the kind of material Bruce liked to dig his claws into, a story of the Viking invasions from an Anglo Saxon perspective. Immediately it was obvious Maiden had upped several gears with their new line-up, the Murray/Smith partnership in full force and a stronger production effort. But their maturity as songwriters was most in evidence on the second track, 'Children Of The Damned.' Though Harris would later say this song was not much different to earlier Maiden material that was played emotionally and with 'feeling' such as 'Strange World' or 'Remember Tomorrow', he was really doing a disservice to his new vocalist. There is no doubt whatsoever that 'Children Of The Damned' would have been a far messier song in the hands of Paul Di'Anno. It is not a criticism of the former Maiden vocalist to say he would not have been able to handle the intricate vocal style or the many changes and high, long lasting notes required for the song. Rather it is just testament to the style of Dickinson who was leaving listeners in no doubt as to who was now leading the Maiden crew.

Written by Steve Harris 'Children Of The Damned' (based on the movie of the same name) would become one of Maiden's most accomplished numbers – carrying the weight of an epic Harris tune, despite being relatively short at 4:34. Bruce pretty much nailed down every variant of his tremendous larynx, covering screams, melodies and a few woah-oh-oh's for good measure. These melodic flourishes were to pepper future Maiden material, and it was a sure sign the beast was establishing itself as a heavy metal institution.

The leap from *Killers* to *The Number Of The Beast* was immense. It wasn't just the addition of Bruce Dickinson that changed the whole outlook of the band but also the rapidly improving skills Steve Harris possessed as a songwriter. He had always hinted at being able to construct progressive epics with time changes aplenty, mimicking his idols. One only had to return to the likes of 'Phantom Of The Opera' for evidence of this. But never before had Harris cemented his influences in such a way as to pay homage, but equally strike out on his own as a separate entity with ideas not previously used in other bands. Whereby past material had been easily compared to the Harris heroes, here he was clearly building away from those influences whilst simultaneously reminding everyone they were still there.

It is incredibly difficult for a songwriter to tread new ground, especially when their chosen field has been so eloquently covered before. Harris couldn't hope to emulate or improve upon the Genesis back catalogue, but he certainly could wield those influences whilst carving out a niche for Iron Maiden. With their new album, that niche was well and truly carved. Though the genre was still heavy metal, this epic direction took the early work of Black Sabbath and magnified its splendour ten fold.

Talking of 'Children Of The Damned' Bruce even referenced the Birmingham doom masters, saying, "I have to make a full and frank confession that I was suffering from Black Sabbath-itis when I recorded that track, far too much 'Children Of The Sea' and all that stuff. Spotted by someone in the press at the time and vehemently denied by me, of course. I'd never listened to a track called 'Children Of The Sea' by Black Sabbath before I sang... ahem." Ozzy Osbourne might have been the Godfather of heavy metal but there would be no argument that the Oz could even hope to reach the notes to which Bruce ascended.

The album spat with an attitude still rooted in classic British rock but there were dazzling new depths being charted as well. Like an ardent explorer attempting to traverse a new country or continent, Steve Harris was travelling through the mists of musical history and writing new chapters as he went along.

'The Prisoner' is a particularly virile number, combining years of classic British televisual history with a penchant for hook-laden rock. Beginning with the voice of Patrick McGoohan, who had starred in the series of the same name, 'The Prisoner' was an ode to the cult programme. McGoohan was more than happy to lend his voice to the song and must have been secretly impressed a heavy metal band sought to pay homage to the series. This had been a somewhat eerie visual experience, and suited Maiden perfectly. At the start of the series (which he also helped write), McGoohan quits his job as an agent for the Secret Service. When he returns home he is gassed and wakes up in a setting known as The Village. Stripped of his identity the character known as Number Six realises everyone is assigned a number rather than a name. The higher up the ladder, the lower the number you are given and McGoohan soon learns Number One is in charge. It was a fantastic programme, utterly original and McGoohan played his role and expressed his character's confusion with military precision.

For the song it was no wonder the chorus was as snappy a one as Maiden had ever recorded, given it was a joint effort by Steve Harris and the commercially leaning Adrian Smith. The duo also wrote the updated story of Charlotte The Harlot with '22 Acacia Avenue,' an eerily melodic track which would become a future live favourite.

Opening side two was the title track, a song that was to land the group in hot water. Given the imagery of the front cover for the album, many presumed, wrongly, that 'The Number Of The Beast' was a satanic song. Its actual inspiration was a cross between a dream/nightmare Steve Harris had and the movie *Damien: Omen II*, the follow up to *The Omen*. It may have been ironic but not particularly amusing that a film as horrific and 'demonic' as this should simply be classed as entertainment yet when a heavy metal band take it as inspiration for a song and set suitably 'horrific' lyrics to it they are instantly branded Devil worshippers attempting to corrupt the youth of the day.

Much like Sabbath, the East End boys of Iron Maiden were reviled as evil creatures spewing heavy metal filth across the world, when in reality they were all down to earth guys who just liked to examine the dark side of life, or indeed fantasy. The chorus of the title track did not help, however, with the line *'666 the number of the beast, hell and fire was spawned to be released.'* The introduction of the song even referenced the renowned Satanist Aleister Crowley, another fact that was held up as 'evidence' of the band's demonic inclinations by the small-minded 'moral majority'.

The blood-curdling scream Bruce added to the song was not some form of satanic rite, rather a nod to The Who's track 'Won't Get Fooled Again.' It was not the first time Bruce had displayed his ability to emit this sort of wail. Samson's 'Blood Lust' from *Shock Tactics* featured a very similar approach by the vocalist.

'Run To The Hills', the song Maiden would come to be best known for, was certainly not their greatest, but it was their catchiest. With a thumping drum intro from Burr and almost silly guitar licks, the lyrics were equally outlandish. "It's about the American Indians," Bruce explained. "It's written from both sides of the picture. The first part is from the side of the Indians. The second part is from the side of the soldiers. I wanted to try and get the feeling of galloping horses. But when you play this one, be careful not to let it run away with you."

There is no doubting that the distinctly memorable chorus and the pounding rhythms of 'Run To The Hills' were indicative of Maiden's burgeoning song writing prowess at the time and also the pace of the song is highly appropriate for the subject, evoking images of Indians running across the plains. But in hindsight the use of this song as a single and the resulting eventual impression that this was their signature tune probably did Maiden more harm than good. This was the type of track the likes of *Top Of The Pops* producers and commercial magazine editors could lazily deride for being dumb heavy metal. Maiden would write songs which were equally bombastic, with sometimes brainless lyrics ('Can I Play With Madness' springs to mind) but 'Run To The Hills' was particularly memorable as it proved to be a favourite with their fans.

So much so in fact that Maiden could never drop the song from their live set, and thus anyone hoping to pour scorn on heavy metal always had the reliable and quite ludicrous 'Run To The Hills' to use as an example. Thankfully the band was also capable of penning a tune as remarkable as 'Hallowed Be Thy Name', which followed the rather throwaway 'Gangland' and closed the record in style. It also began a tradition whereby a Steve Harris epic would finish off the following 3 Iron Maiden albums.

Telling the tale of a man in his last hours before being taken to the gallows, 'Hallowed Be Thy Name' is a rather sombre affair. It was written with supreme accuracy, capturing the closing thoughts of a convict superbly, with a backing track that is equally solemn. This is a life's best performance from the entire band, with Dickinson particularly shining with his ability to enunciate several words in quick succession whilst never losing the emotion or feel of the song.

The breakdown instrumental section is arguably Maiden's best moment up to that time, with a searing backing beat and a multitude of scorching guitar parts. This is true heavy metal at its best and no-one could hope to come close. It would be justice to Steve Harris if the likes of 'Hallowed...' were the sort of songs that got released as singles. This track deserved to be top of every chart, but, as Harris would often muse, most people just did not appreciate long songs.

Quite rightly *The Number Of The Beast* stormed into charts the world over, staying at the top spot in the UK for two weeks. It also hit number thirty-three in America, staying in the Billboard Top 100 for eight months, easily outselling *Killers* in the process. As Keith Wilfort described, "*The Number Of The Beast* is the album that really set Maiden on their way and was a quantum leap ahead of the first two albums. It had such a powerful line up of material, and Bruce's voice was phenomenal."

Even Paul Di'Anno would admit, "I've always considered that Bruce didn't sing 'my' songs as well as I did, but I have to admit that he was, and still remains, a gigantic singer and there's no doubt that he was the best vocalist Maiden could ever find. My style was far too aggressive for the band and Bruce's softer, more operatic voice fitted perfectly with the direction Steve wanted to go. I think that the band's first album with Dickinson is fantastic and that nobody else could have done what he did with Iron Maiden since the release of this record, in a style that's his very own."

On the surface it seemed Maiden had conquered the world, but the reality was rather different, as Bruce Dickinson remembers; "The day the album went to number one in the UK charts, we were push-starting our bus on tour in Zurich, because the battery was flat. It was bloody freezing, but we were going, 'The album's number one! The album's number one!' So we had a number one album, we were on the road in Europe, and we were earning £100 a week! But that whole time was great. It was better than anything."

Lovingly titled 'The Beast On The Road' the tour for the album saw Maiden travel further round the globe than ever before. They even reached their fans in Australia for the first time ever, playing ten shows in the country, including four nights at a huge theatre in Sydney. "It was just a great time and I had a few lucky escapes," Bruce recalls. "I got persuaded to go rowing in Sydney harbour in a rubber boat and with a bottle of wine at night! And somebody mentioned when we were about fifty metres out, they went 'Shark!' and we thought yeah maybe we better come back in. But it was some great stuff."

The tour wasn't without other mishaps either, however. In Kings Cross in Sydney, Bruce had his drink spiked. "The thing was, it wasn't the spiking of the drink, but I was drinking half a pint of coffee! I was trying to be terribly straight, but the coffee had a bit of wizz in it. So I was up all night and half of the next day and I nearly lost my voice before the gig. I got a throat doctor in and I said 'Jesus! What's gone wrong?' and he said, 'Well, you know you've been up for like forty-eight hours!' I was like 'I can't help it!' I dunno, so they thought they were doing me a favour, put something in that would make me go a little faster, in the coffee, you know."

Worse was to come. During the American leg of their tour, in their very first performance of *The Number Of The Beast* in the States, Bruce was headbanging so much he injured his neck. He was forced to wear a collar, which could only be taken off while on stage (though you would think that was where he would have needed it most). Quite understandably Bruce was in a lot of pain and went through a babbling array of US doctors to try and rectify the problem. In response he was given a whole host of different medication including at one stage, horse tranquillisers! And it got even worse. Bruce was told he needed surgery by one money-grabbing quack who saw fit to charge $150 for a twenty minute consultation. Finally, a chiropractor fixed Bruce's neck, and the vocalist was to bang for some time to come.

Though Bruce always seemed to be involved in any action, there was usually enough incident to go round everyone in the band. This extended to the road crew on one particular occasion. Bill Barclay, the guitar roadie for Dave Murray was hit in the head by a firework and almost blinded by one crazed 'fan' at The Palladium in New York City. The common consensus is that several Maiden fans attacked the offending idiot after the gig and this resulted in a swift and merciless kicking!

The adverts for the Palladium show were also controversial and created a scene, which, it seems, has never been forgotten by some. In a move that was taken in good humour by most, the ads for the show featured Eddie holding aloft the head of Ozzy Osbourne. This was in reference to the recent stories that Ozzy had chewed on a bat's head (he also bit the wing off a pigeon and the head off a dove), thus ensuring his place in rock n' roll folklore and heavy metal trivia for all the wrong reasons.

Maiden's press release jibed that Eddie was a lover of bats and sought revenge on Ozzy for his bat biting antics. Osbourne's label boss Don Arden (who incidentally was the father of Sharon, Ozzy's wife) rang Rod Smallwood to complain, saying the advert was in "bad taste," and requesting it be withdrawn. Smallwood complied but must have been a little surprised, not to mention angry that such a request was made. Years later Maiden would again find themselves in conflict with the Osbournes. Perhaps the 1982 incident was indicative of the problem the other side had with Iron Maiden and their success. The world, in their eyes, was only big enough for one British heavy metal icon and that was Ozzy, not Eddie, Bruce, Steve or anyone else for that matter.

Come the summer of 1982, while Maiden were sunning themselves in every corner of the United States, a large volume of Christian fanatics had got wind of the Satanic imagery of *The Number Of The Beast* album cover, and its suitably Lucifer based lyrics. In Arkansas the religious bigotry hit its peak where scores of outraged parents burned heavy metal records, which included Black Sabbath and AC/DC LPs. Their 'point' was that if these records had to be released they should come with stickers, which warned of their "evil satanic nature." As ever, Maiden took such intense over-reaction in good spirits. "The Americans don't have the same sense of humour as the English or the French," Bruce said with some understatement, "and some of them took very seriously some of our lyrics with satanic undertones. Some religious lobbies demanded that stickers be applied on *The Number Of The Beast* album, warning people of the so-called satanic aspect of the lyrics! Many considered Eddie, our 'mascot,' as a dangerous character, even a subversive one. As for the reactions to the cover of our last album and the picture with the brain, that was pretty close to McCarthyism. Most of these lobbies are very rich, and they have ads on TV against Rock, condemning all those whose hair's not short, whereas all this isn't really serious."

McCarthyism, named after the US Republican Senator from 1947-1957 Joseph McCarthy, was known as a period of great suspicion. From 1950-1954 the American government was scouting the outbreak of Communism through the American Communist Party and its leaders. The 'witch hunts', as they came to be known, also extended to anyone considered to be a communist or have communist sympathies. The entire facts of the witch hunts are not known, but, as Bruce mentioned, Maiden's brief time in the heart of mainstream America was similar to those who had previously been shunned for their political beliefs.

Thankfully, most freethinking individuals saw through the accusations that heavy metal was to blame for virtually every problem of society in the developed world. Though Tipper Gore and her PMRC organisation would later successfully invent the 'Parental Advisory' sticker, if anything, the controversy behind heavy metal and its leaders and lyricists only helped to promote the bands.

But Iron Maiden didn't need much help in promoting their music, especially in their home country. Thanks to the success of *The Number Of The Beast* they were invited to perform at the annual Reading Festival. The only downside was the fact that they were in the middle of America at the time they were due to perform in the UK. This meant a 12,000 mile round trip just to appear at Reading. They travelled from El Paso, Texas to London and then to Los Angeles, California. Bruce would again be afflicted by the appearance of horse tranquillisers when he, along with Dave Lights, necked several tablets a few hours before having to board the plane to London. It took three days for the two to wake up properly. This didn't stop Bruce being "petrified with fear" at the prospect of playing at one of Europe's premier rock festivals. Thirty-six hours prior to the concert the singer completely lost his voice and began to wonder if he would make the gig at all. In the end he did make it but the fun wasn't over yet. Steve noticed his bass was taking precedence over the guitars for the first few numbers and then panicked when the bass seemed to cut out completely.

Adrian and Dave were both flustered, but, like true professionals, the group continued unabated and the crowd did not seem to realise the problems the band were experiencing. The show was a monumental success and helped raise Maiden's profile once again in their homeland.

Overall the 'Beast On The Road' tour was one of the largest international treks a rock band had ever undertaken. In just ten months the band played 179 concerts in sixteen countries and on four continents to well over a million people whilst travelling over 35,000 miles by air and 60,000 miles by road.

Everything was changing – Maiden's popularity was soaring and behind the scenes things were getting busier. "The band was on a crest of a wave following the album's success," says Keith Wilfort. "They were practically working around the clock. In 1980-'81, it had just been Rod and I in a basement office, but as things took off, we needed more people to take care of it all. The band took on a full-time Tour Manager and sound engineer. Accountants were brought on staff exclusively to handle the financial affairs of the band and of Sanctuary (still known as Smallwood Taylor Enterprises then). Andy Taylor, Rod's college buddy and a financial expert who had been more of a consultant, moved down to London and officially became a full-time, hands-on director. Tour merchandise was now in the hands of professional companies, Great Southern in the US and Bravado (Worldwide). The Fan Club membership quadrupled and hundreds of fan letters a week were arriving. Rod and Andy established their own merchandising company and extra people were taken on. By 1983 the merchandise and Fan Club matters were a full time operation with four people." Come 1983 Iron Maiden would need all the help they could get, for they were about to catapult to a status beyond their wildest expectations.

BILL LEISEGANG REMEMBERS BRUCE AND THE MAIDEN BOYS

PAUL STENNING: **Did you harbour any resentment at the Maiden boys going really** huge when Xero never found the same success?

BILL LEISEGANG: "I'm more interested in being creative with my guitar than being a superstar, although I wouldn't mind the cash! I still managed a career in music biz with lesser-known bands. I prefer working in the studio these days as it gets boring playing the same songs. I was playing in Rock in Rio with Nina Hagen in '85 and we were above Maiden on the billing, so that was a laugh. We went on just before Queen."

PS: What do you think of Maiden's music?

BL: "Attitude! Rough and ready but with a frantic and energetic vibe. They are truly a metal band, I remember they didn't sound so good at the Ruskin Arms!"

PS: Are you still in touch with Bruce?

BL: "I saw him at Rock in Rio in 1985. I had the feeling that the manager of Xero had succeeded in making people think I was dishonest and responsible for 'Lone Wolf' with Bruce appearing on our first single. The truth is we didn't have a clue 'til it was pressed up. We were gob smacked, as it did no-one any favours. Awful sound quality, the guy just edited it from an old, 2nd generation copy, demo cassette tape that was lying around."

Sources:

Paul Stenning Interviews
Costa Zoulio, 5 February 1999 (Triple JJJ FM Radio).
Q Magazine January 1991
NWOBHM Encyclopaedia – Malc Macmillan

Chapter 6
Fly With Your Boots On

"It's true that it's a band whose line-up changes quite a lot, which is a good thing in this case, as each newcomer brings a certain amount of freshness to each album. It's certain that Bruce Dickinson has improved the band as compared with Paul Di'Anno, who was isolated at the human level and who wasn't very productive. As for Piece Of Mind, *the contribution of Nicko McBrain was tremendous. He really is a great drummer."*
Martin Birch

1983 would come to be a crucial year for Iron Maiden. The boys knew they had to work harder than ever before to continue their momentum and solidify their place in the public eye. After *The Number Of The Beast* there was possibly nowhere to go other than down. When you release such a classic recording there are only two options: try in vain to revisit your glory or mark it down as history and do something different.

Luckily, the musical brain of Steve Harris was in tune with his business acumen and, as a result, the material that was to comprise Maiden's 1983 opus would follow the latter course and be something of a departure from *The Number Of The Beast*. Of course the band still featured Bruce on vocals and the singer was now fully ensconced in his role as chief fire breather. There was the reliable double act of Harris and Murray, always there, consistent and full of flair and then there was the additional benefit of having Adrian Smith, the quiet but immensely talented songwriter and guitarist who complimented the brimstone of the others so well.

Maiden was, however, about to change drummers. Clive Burr had decided long bouts of touring were not advisable anymore, although, ironically, he would end up being busier than ever before once he left the band.

Unless the member is the focal point of a band or a key songwriter, it is perhaps easier to replace a drummer than any other musician without losing much impact. Especially with Iron Maiden the drummer had never really taken part in the song writing, and Burr's replacement would continue this pattern.

The man in question was Michael McBrain, better known as Nicko, who came from French rockers Trust (interestingly, Burr jumped from Maiden *to* Trust). Even though he was yet to hit thirty, McBrain was a seasoned veteran of the rock scene having paid his dues as a session musician and notably he was also, at one stage, a part of the Pat Travers Band. Given McBrain's technical nous, it was suggested initially that the genial Londoner was merely a hired hand – a session musician simply lending his services until the full time replacement could be found.

Yet this was never an option for Maiden, and such rumourmongers should have known better. It was not in Steve Harris' plans to hire a drummer he was not 100% behind lest it damage the morale of the band, not to mention their momentum. On the contrary, the choice had to be made carefully, with the next few decades in mind. There was, therefore, nobody more suitable than the loveable, flat-nosed McBrain, who had made an impression on Maiden years before when Trust supported them.

"Brilliant drummer, raconteur, lunatic!" is how Keith Wilfort describes Nicko. "All these titles and more have been applied to Nicko, but as a person and friend he's one of the best. If it's rock n' roll, Nicko has been there, done it, read the book and watched the movie! He and Rod go back a long way, not that that ever stopped them having a good old-fashioned row from time to time. Nicko is always ready to voice an opinion and will stand up for what he believes is right, but, once its over there's no hard feelings."

This kind of outspokenness, coupled with a respect for his fellow man, was part of the reasoning behind bringing Nicko onboard. Equally, as a musician there is no-one more reliable than a seasoned session player. In fact, though hard rock and metal were Nicko's preferred tastes, the versatile rhythm-meister could turn his hand to most forms of music including jazz and blues. Such adaptability would actually make a sonic difference to Maiden and give them a stronger overall sound. There were no problems with Clive Burr's technique or style, but Nicko was certainly a harder hitter and, arguably, a better player technically. Whatever your opinion, it's clear the inclusion of the tall, lean blonde from Hackney pumped Maiden up further and the sound of the album which was to become *Piece Of Mind* was the better for his presence.

Though Bruce Dickinson would later state that Burr's drumming had started to suffer, he was quick to point out that this was due to personal problems Burr was experiencing at the time and that a line-up change was necessary. For the shy, retiring ex-Maiden member, it was easier to commit to Trust who were never as serious as Maiden.

Of course, it was not only the inclusion of McBrain that changed the face of the band. This was to be the first album where Bruce Dickinson was able to assist in the writing from the off. By now Maiden were comfortable with each other both as performers and writers, and each member knew the others' strengths, and their few weaknesses.

"In early January we went down to Jersey in the Channel Islands to start writing the new album," Steve said. "We took over a small hotel, set up the gear in the ballroom, installed pool, darts, table tennis, and some video games and got down to it for five weeks! Our new drummer, Nicko, fitted in great and is magic to work with. The new material is very much a band effort. Bruce was involved in the writing for the first time, and works really well with Adrian, and Dave came up with some magic riffs."

The chief songwriter was, as ever, Steve, but the emergence of Dickinson, who brought a completely different slant to proceedings, was certainly welcomed by Harris. *Piece Of Mind* would have been a vastly different type of album were it not for the Dickinson penned material and the quirky, underrated additions of Dave Murray and Adrian Smith.

Piece Of Mind has to go down predominantly as a Harris and Dickinson special however. This was Harris' baby but Dickinson complimented the bassist's inherent knack for intricate song craft with a more straightforward hard rock slant as well, of course, as his glorious vocals. 1983 was one of many peaks for Maiden, with Bruce in fine fettle as a singer and the hunger and unpredictability of youth still permeating the Brits' camp. Though they had already conquered vast sections of the world and swept across the metal media with almost universal acceptance and praise, they did not feel anywhere near finished. There was more ground to cover, first as songwriters and then as intrepid travellers, and everyone in the band was united, with their sights set on the group's common goals. It would be difficult to replicate the excitement Bruce's appointment had stirred at the end of 1981, but with the new line-up and resultant record in 1983, there was a natural enthusiasm behind the group and it translated perfectly onto record.

"We'd have problems if we were stuck with only one musical style," the singer felt. "But, as we write lyrics that mostly deal with fantasy, instead of having some political theme or other, we are quite free to do pretty much what we like. To me *Piece Of Mind* is the hardest album to listen to among the four we recorded. But we all think that's it's our best one so far."

Eventually *Piece Of Mind* would be considered one of Maiden's finest works, yet upon its release there was an element of doubt amongst some fans and certain reviewers, unsure of how to react to Maiden's 'new' direction. The album is a varied and cleverly sculpted metal opus, but, with its convoluted epics and introduction of new sounds and textures, it was always going to be an album that improved with time.

For some, the initial reaction was one of uncertainty. These songs, while not as instantly gratifying as say, 'Run To The Hills' or 'Number Of The Beast', were, crucially, much better and this is why, although the '83 work needed time to bed in the brain, when it did, fans were united in their approval for this ambitious recording.

And quite simply, as ever, no-one was releasing music anywhere near the stature or style of Iron Maiden. Heavy metal was really a genre otherwise devoid of Maiden's class and sophistication, so, although there was clearly no other genre which could hold them, this was a form of music that was often a shallow and dumb brand of rock. Though the usual criticisms were still applied to Maiden as to most metal bands – namely their 'Satanic' lyrics and their ugly mascot – they managed to carry off their version of the metal cliché with panache and guile, and nobody could match them.

There was no other album like *Piece Of Mind* in 1983, and the nearest anyone has ever come since is Iron Maiden themselves with their subsequent releases. How on earth could any singer compare to Bruce Dickinson? Was there a bass player as nifty around the fretboard and as thoroughly individual as Steve Harris? Were there any guitarists kidding themselves that they were really on the level of Adrian Smith and Dave Murray? Perhaps the one band who were remotely close to Maiden was New York's Manowar. They were vastly different in terms of style but the similarities included Joey DeMaio's upfront bass playing and the operatic vocal style of Eric Adams. Still, not even Manowar were really in the same class as Maiden.

There was a good reason why Maiden developed their incredible popularity and have attained such longevity. Simply, their releases with Bruce Dickinson are all amazing portraits of the heavy metal landscape, being varied, intense and entertaining, full of twists and turns. It was not simply about creating a couple of radio friendly tunes, and deceiving music fans into thinking the two decent tracks were representative of the album. With Maiden, as with most metal, radio was immaterial. This was music made for people who enjoyed an album from start to finish and got their money's worth with years of discovering new sounds upon the same album you'd played 100 times before. The songs you were playing on a regular basis were never tiring, never lost their appeal or their ability to summon the headbanger in you. How could anybody knock the quality and sheer brilliance of *Piece Of Mind*?

Impressively, the opening number, 'Where Eagles Dare', was recorded in just two takes, proving the unity of the 'new' group already. With Maiden, the formula was simple, or at least as simple as us mere mortals could comprehend. Write a phenomenal metal track with varying bass gallops, intricate drum patterns, soaring vocals, sumptuous hook lines and melodies, and hair raising, brain melting guitar – then gather the troops to record it. 'Where Eagles Dare' is sophisticated, cutting edge metal which could easily have required 50 takes to nail correctly, yet it was all so easy to the genre's best. Iron Maiden plugged in, played and laid the track perfectly. The song title came from the 1968 film of the same name and, lyrically, the subject was made up of fighter planes and stealth missions, echoed in a reassuringly British manner by the roaring Dickinson vocals. The guitar breakdowns were no afterthought, being deliberately constructed to evoke a key factor in war, as Steve Harris explained; "It's supposed to sound like a machine gun. It's not very loud in the mix, but we wanted it that way so people who listened to it a couple of times would say 'what's that?" In cute fashion Maiden kicked off their greatest album to date with a Nicko special, a drum fill that introduced the riotous opener. This developed from an idea by Steve who told Nicko he thought the song would benefit from an opening drum roll. Eager to impress, McBrain spent almost an entire day working on an appropriate beginning. The next day he played his newly composed part to Steve but the bassist quickly jumped in saying he wanted it another way. Despite being abysmal on the drums Steve played the kind of thing he was hoping for. Nicko went, 'Oh you mean like this?' 'That's it!' Steve responded, and voila – a classic heavy metal beginning was born.

And then it was time for Bruce to show how quickly he had improved. 'Revelations' is a lengthy, ambitious song similar to 'Children Of The Damned' in its acoustic refrains, which progresses to searing heavy sections. Contrary to the widely held view that the nefarious urchins comprising most metal bands could not string two words together unless they were satanic, Maiden's lyrics are akin to the musings a history professor.

The opening wordplay of 'Revelations' is, in fact, an English hymn by G.K. Chesterton and, though certain other metallers would often quote highbrow literature to pass themselves off as intellectuals, you simply believed Maiden really grasped their subject like eager students. It was not pertinent that Bruce was an ex-public schoolboy, he was simply an on-going sponge for new knowledge.

"I read a lot, I listen to people, and I take the time to think and ponder everything I discover in books," he said, eschewing the common roots of many a metal waif. "The thing is, I feel a tremendous happiness and a fulfilling serenity just by being on stage, because I think this is where I belong, and this is, for me, the best way to locate myself in space and time. I think we all have somewhere where we belong, where we can express ourselves and feel absolute satisfaction. The hardest part is to find where." It was also relevant that Maiden as a band felt most at home on a stage as quite amazingly they did not feel as if their songs were suited to the studio. "Revelations' comes together more live," Steve thought. "That tends to be like that with us. Usually the numbers are better live than on record. That has to do with the feel of the songs. Most of them were written to be played on the stage. They're not really for the recording studio."

Nevertheless the Jethro Tull meets Wishbone Ash track comes over perfectly on vinyl and, at the time, only the regular Maiden gig goers could argue the case for 'Revelations' being better in a live setting. It is true though that the song is given new life when performed on stage, and one only has to listen to Maiden's live album of two years later to see this.

'Flight Of Icarus' is another song the band felt worked better live as they could inject more speed into it and, regrettably, felt they could have played the track faster in the studio. Despite this, the Smith/Dickinson number is another standout cut for the band and something typically melodic for Adrian Smith to turn his hand to. It was also chosen as a single with a quite ludicrous promo video featuring Nicko in blue face paint and monk's robe!

'Die With Your Boots On' is one of the criminally ignored Maiden songs – if only real fans could choose the tracks to be released as singles… In many ways this is an even catchier song than 'Flight Of Icarus' and again featured inspiration from a literary giant, in this case French prophet Nostradamus (*"In thirteen the beast is rising, the French man did surmise"*). The title was formed from a phrase whose origin is unknown but was probably linked to the military. The connotation would appear to be if you're going to go down, go down fighting. Better to die on the field of battle, in a blaze of glory, than in your bed. There is also a theory that the phrase emanated from the old West where if you died sick or old, you died in your bed with your boots off. If you died in a gunfight, you died with your boots on.

The phrase evokes a true 'all or nothing' attitude and because of this, the excellently executed song inspires many who fall to its charms. The track was a first for Iron Maiden in that it was constructed by Steve, Adrian and Bruce, as the bass player explained, "Adrian and Bruce came up with the main riff. Bruce came up with the lyrics. I came up with the chord sequence behind the verse and the cross-section that goes into the main chorus. This is another personal favourite of mine."

There is a strong theme of war throughout *Piece Of Mind*, not quite prominent enough to make it a concept album, but clearly there are several songs with military inspiration. None more so than one of Maiden's greatest ever songs, 'The Trooper'. With its intro, a speedily rendered guitar lick, Steve Harris wanted to recreate the galloping horses in the charge of the light brigade. The basis for the song was The Crimean War which was fought between the British and Russians from 1854 to 1856. This song is one of the most intriguing of Maiden's back catalogue given there isn't actually a worded chorus, just the repeated guitar licks and a few hummable 'Oh woah woahs'. Regardless, the song would be a perennial live favourite due to the frantic guitar work and the carefully enunciated lyrics, which Bruce never failed to deliver perfectly. The song was also chosen as a single with one of Derek Riggs' most enduring Maiden covers, featuring Eddie as a soldier in the war, trailing through the carnage carrying a British flag. Steve Harris loved it so much he got a tattoo of the sleeve on his forearm.

Up next is a rather bizarre song in the Maiden timeline. 'Still Life' is, according to Steve "the story of a guy who is drawn like a magnet to a pool of water. He sees faces in the lake. He has nightmares about it and in the end he jumps in and takes his lady with him." This is the only Dave Murray credit on *Piece Of Mind* and it is a strange topic indeed. Musically it is beyond the normal Maiden sphere with lots of time changes and eerie, almost unnerving melodies. Steve drew inspiration from his recurring nightmares, which perhaps explains the rather unusual subject matter, and the bassist must be given credit for managing to compose a competent song from such night-time confusion.

Unfortunately, or amusingly, depending your point of view, the song is just as notable for its introductory backwards message as the music itself. "We recorded it to scare all those fanatics who are so narrow-minded and so hostile to rock," Bruce jibed. "It basically means 'Don't meddle with things you don't understand'. It was Nicko speaking, but he was completely drunk and had such an accent that, even if you listen to it the normal way, no-one can understand this message!"

For those familiar with English actor and comedian John Bird, however, the drunken rantings were a little easier to comprehend. Bird released *The Collected Broadcasts Of Idi Amin* in 1975, which was a hilarious pastiche of the Ugandan Dictator's sayings, musings and comments read by Bird who captured Amin's perceived characteristics perfectly. This came from a radio show Bird had recorded that was written by satirist Alan Coren.

What Nicko actually says is "What ho sed de t'ing wid de t'ree bonce", meaning "What ho, said the monster with the three heads." The second backwards message says, "Don't meddle wid t'ings you don't understand." As the drummer belches, the song bursts to life!

But it was another song which caused Bruce to have second thoughts about whether he could really sing the words. The vocalist said to *Q*, "I remember Steve said, 'Here's a new lyric: In a time when dinosaurs walked the earth, in a land where swamps and caves were home – all to a merry Irish jig rhythm with these octave leaps in the middle.' I said 'Come on you've *got* to be joking!' I thought, 'bloody hell!' But I did it! More to prove it could be done than anything else."

The song was 'Quest For Fire' (named after a film of the same name), a rather more typical heavy metal affair, which draws upon caveman times for its theme, and seems to be one of the only occasions where Steve Harris was really short of a decent idea.

'Sun And Steel' is another Dickinson/Smith composition, again soaked in melody and with the typical fighting talk Bruce would become familiar with, covering a mythical warrior's sword and sorcery. "It's basically about a Japanese guy who builds himself up to peak fitness and wants to kill himself hara-kiri style," Steve relayed. "I think it would be a good live song but we have never played it on stage as of yet."

Another song that would not quite make the regular set-list was album closer 'To Tame A Land', which Steve felt was the best song he had ever written at the time. It should have been called 'Dune' after the Frank Herbert book of the same name and on which the lyrics are based. However, Herbert was so actively against heavy metal in general and Maiden in particular – for no good reason – that he denied the band the rights to his title and threatened to sue if they used it. "He threatened to have the album banned," Bruce later said. "It's stupid because he'd already sold us the right at a very high price. Anyway, we stayed true to the book. If he only knew how successful the album is, and what publicity this could have been for him."

Unfortunately, as it turned out, Herbert probably got as much publicity for his antics as he might if he had agreed. Although it was probably not top of the list for a staunch Maiden fan to go and buy a copy of the 'Erbert's book!

One area where Maiden always felt it important to be clearly identified was in their cover art and nobody knew this better than the band's management. And so, along with *Piece Of Mind* producer Martin Birch and manager Rod Smallwood, artist Derek Riggs was fast becoming another vital member of the Iron Maiden entourage. His artwork for the album was stunning and once again the man successfully reinvented Eddie, this time as a mental case in a padded cell, creating one of Maiden's strongest sleeve themes. "It's an allusion to an old Aztec custom," Bruce said of the inspiration behind Riggs' piece. "Originally, the idea was to kill Eddie, but we thought that it was too much. So we trepanated him, like the Aztecs used to do to the sacrifice victims that they offered to their god. In fact, the album was going to be called *Food For Thought*, but we decided that *Piece Of Mind* was more subtle." Trepanation, or trephination, is the art of drilling a hole in the head to expose the brain, and allow poisons or other diseases to dissipate.

The Maiden front man was in no doubt as to Eddie's importance to the band's image and, in some ways, their longevity. "Look at a band like Kiss, for example, when they had their make-up, what did you see on stage? Well, you didn't see anything else but four Eddies. They didn't look like musicians anymore, but like clowns. Nobody cared about their musical abilities because they were hidden by the image they were giving of themselves. It's the same with Ozzy Osbourne, although Ozzy's music is worth listening to! Nobody considers Ozzy like a musician anymore, but like a clown, which is a shame. So, in order to have this character, this clown, and keep our identity as musicians at the same time, we created Eddie."

It is interesting to note the different slant Derek Riggs has on the character of Eddie, including the fact that he would have been happy enough not to draw him for every Maiden painting. As the artist says, "We used Eddie on the first few releases and the merchandise was selling so well (vast amounts) that the band and management decided to keep using him. I had actually designed several other characters to take his place but they turned out not to be needed. We worked together for so long because the management offered to pay me a retainer on the condition that I didn't work for anyone else. At that time I began suffering from the illness M.E. (Chronic Fatigue Syndrome) and I was not capable of doing other work anyway so I signed the contract. I had intended to be out of Maiden and doing other things within three years, had my health not collapsed."

As important as anyone in the band, the aforementioned Martin Birch was rapidly becoming the silent sixth member. The veteran producer was still radiating enthusiasm for Maiden come 1983 and it was clear this was a very special relationship and one which would need to continue for Maiden to receive the kind of glossy sheen their material warranted.

Piece Of Mind was released to widespread acclaim on May 16th 1983 and reached number three in the UK charts and number fourteen in America where sales were good enough to see Maiden awarded their first US platinum album. Nevertheless, as certain tactless journalists were at pains to point out, Iron Maiden had not 'broken' America on the same scale as fellow Brits, Def Leppard.

Their adversaries in rock, the Sheffield quintet, had recently released their *Pyromania* album. This had taken the rock fans of America by storm with its heavy rooted but specially adapted commercial harmonies. Tracks such as 'Rock! Rock! (Till You Drop)', 'Photograph' and 'Foolin'' were quite different from the meat and potatoes rock of their formative years. Yet it must be observed that Leppard had, since their inception, been eager to crack the States (their 1980 debut album even featured a song called 'Hello America' to deliberately appeal to Stateside audiences) and be the biggest band in the world. In many ways, their songs were geared towards radio play and with the production help of Robert 'Mutt' Lange they had a secret weapon which enabled them to realise their dream.

Bruce Dickinson responded to one particular comparison with Leppard by eloquently observing, "Our success is not 'compromising' in the way that we have our own sound, and this sound has nothing to do with the 'FM' sound of hard rock that is aired on American radio. We conquered our audience more with our gigs than with radio airplay. But we remain a fundamentally 'European' band and I wouldn't want to change this style. Whatever happens, the European scene is much more important to us than the American one."

Some years later Bruce would also make the distinction, for anyone who was in doubt, between rock and metal. "Metal hasn't got the soft, round, flowing rhythms women tend to like," the singer commented. "It's too fast, not at all smoochy, the quick release after the pent up moment. At the root of it, metal is quintessentially male, the equivalent of the female 'not a dry seat in the house' over Jason Donovan. What happens in the concerts is almost ceremonial. We're up on stage but we're very much the channel for the audience's feelings. It's participatory, good stuff to have a frenzy to."

And therein lay the not so subtle difference between Iron Maiden and Def Leppard. Where Maiden gigs were full to bursting with predominantly aggressive males who wanted nothing more than to pump their fists and throw devil horn signs, Leppard concerts were spectacles with more emphasis on pleasing the females. Not only were the Sheffield boys melodic and in sweet harmony with each other, they were, to all intents and purposes, the type of guys American ladies were drawn to. Many of Leppard's lyrics were throwaway fantasy or harmless fun that the listener didn't have to use too much grey matter to understand. Therefore fans could just rock out to Leppard whilst swooning at their idols. With Maiden there were only two choices, ingest the whole caboodle with history, music and imagery or just go completely crazy. As Steve said of certain fans, "They don't want to punch someone's head in but they do want to shake a fist in the air, scream, let off the physical tension you've got at that age. I mean, when I was younger I used to come in from school, stick on a Montrose record and go *berserk*."

And so, to accompany their best album to date, Iron Maiden would embark on the suitably named World Piece Tour, taking in a multitude of countries and playing to rabid maniacs everywhere.

There is no doubt the *Piece Of Mind* material translated superbly to a live environment. Songs like 'The Trooper', that were already pacey, picked up further speed and the galloping ensued. Melodic tracks, which sounded slightly lighter on wax, were given an extra kick when amplified and performed in one take, 'Flight Of Icarus' and 'Die With Your Boots On' being good examples. Interestingly the band decided not to play the epic 'To Tame A Land' and also shunned the second half of the LP generally, which, in truth, was weaker than the first side.

During the American leg of the tour Maiden appeared on television to deny allegations that Dave Murray was going to leave the band. Quite where this rumour started was anyone's guess but it seemed unimaginable that the guitar lynchpin would want to leave. As he would often attest, there was nothing he could not express musically in the band and he loved playing the material Steve and the others had written. "No-one is thinking about leaving, and the band has never been so united," Bruce said. As far as Murray was concerned the statement could not have been truer, as even today he remains the only other original member along with Steve.

There was also an incident involving Murray, which with hindsight was quite amusing, as Keith Wilfort explains. "In Florida in '83, Dave was walking back from a fishing trip and was arrested by the local police because he bore an uncanny resemblance to a robbery suspect! Tour manager Tony Wigens had to go down to the local police station to bail him out."

Such bizarre happenings aside, the tour was a resounding success and culminated with a sign that the little band formed by Steve Harris only a few years ago had now taken on a mammoth significance. Invited to play at a German festival organised predominantly for television, Maiden topped a bill that included everyone from Judas Priest and Ozzy Osbourne to The Scorpions and the Michael Schenker Group. It was a real coup to stand above such German metal heroes as MSG and The Scorpions in their homeland and Maiden took full advantage of the opportunity. "That was an amazing gig," Steve beamed. "Especially on something like '22 Acacia Avenue', when you can see the audience. It was a magical gig, it really sticks in the mind as one of the best ones we've ever done. Four years ago we were playing the Ruskin, now we're headlining a bill that includes all my old heroes!"

Bruce added, "We'd beaten Def Leppard at football as well. And we were billed above Judas Priest, I've still got the poster on my wall. It was a great gig, but the TV Company cut out 'Iron Maiden' from the screened version because they thought it was too violent. For a country that started the Second World War that's a bit steep. But I like Germans, my sister married one, so I reserve the right to make German jokes." Indeed, for an obviously patriotic band, it might be said the staunch Brits were treading on thin ice, but anyone who took offence from the Maiden attitude was in the minority. In fact, Maiden went down just as well in Germany as any-where else because, ironically, the Germans understood them perfectly. The sense of humour was similar and any racism often came from the English side rather than the Deutsch contingent. Enter their country with respect and they tended to return the civility in kind. Still, it was a shame 'Iron Maiden' had to be cut.

Part of the allure to German fans, and indeed many other European supporters was the complete anti-star vibe Maiden exuded. Good time, great attitude British lads who just happened to play incredible music. Martin Birch was long enough in the tooth and had enough experience to note the difference between Maiden and other bands he had worked with was, "Their attitude towards the outside world. They are not into the 'star-system' and remain very accessible. Success hasn't raised any barriers be-tween them and the others, press, audience, which wasn't the case before. Moreover, they listen to you, and they are not convinced right away that they are right. This is why I think that this is my favourite band to work with, the relationship producer/band is much more constructive."

NICKO MCBRAIN, AS KNOWN BY NEAL KAY

"Nicko does everything with a real big smile, a big heart and a big sense of humour. Everything to him is like 'life is worth living' and he just grins from ear to ear. I remember he came to my house in Maidenhead one day because he wanted to join the local flying club and I had a friend who had a plane up there. Unfortunately the chief flight instructor up there refused to let him fly because he didn't like his American license. The twin rating over there is not recognised in England, you have to do a European twin rating.

But we went back to my house and I said, 'look I've got a buddy who's got a really sleazy pub dive in town, do you want to come in for a liquid lunch?' Nicko says, 'yeah yeah,' and we go down to see my mate. We're standing in this little sweat hole bar at lunchtime and there's no-one in there. And the door opens and these two young heavy metal fans come in, wearing all the denim and badges etc.

And they pull up at the bar on Nicko's side and he kind of half has his back to them. And they're talking *very* loudly and we're listening to their conversation about the new Iron Maiden album and all that. And they don't even realise that they're stood right next to the fucking drummer. By now I'm on my back on the floor absolutely creased up, I'm laughing so much my stomach's hurting me. Nicko was just laughing in his beer.

But I said, 'don't you want to say something?' And he just went, 'no, if they don't fucking recognise me I ain't going to talk to them!' Worse was to happen when we got home, because my girlfriend came in and she didn't know who he was either, but then again she is a Chinese accountant so what do you expect!"

Sources:

Paul Stenning Interviews
Enfer Magazine #8
Best Magazine #185
Metal Attack Magazine #3
Artist Magazine August 1983
John Stix Interview 1983

Chapter 7
Curse Of The Pharoah

"Honestly, I think that this album is superior to the previous one. We took what was best in it, while stressing the aggressive style of The Number Of The Beast *and we released a high-quality record, artistically-speaking, of course!" Bruce Dickinson*

1984 would be a pivotal year in the Iron Maiden timeline. Fresh from their successful *Piece Of Mind* album and subsequent tour the band members reconvened early that year to construct their most ambitious and powerful set of songs to date. Everything about their next move would scream epic and place Maiden in the ranks of the truly legendary rock bands. Steve Harris and Bruce Dickinson were the chief songwriters for the venture known as *Powerslave* and the album would be the quickest the band had yet written. An Egyptian theme, spawned lyrically by Bruce, would add spice to proceedings. No band in the metal annals (unless ludicrously obscure and untraceable) had committed to wax a paean to ancient Egypt. Yet the inspiration had always been there, and it begged the question, why hadn't someone thought of this before? Metal was perfect for covering the revered Egyptians. The imagery of hieroglyphs and dank, dark tombs as well as the powerful pharaohs of the society could not have been better suited to the majesty of metal [1].

And there was simply no lyricist on earth who could combine history and metal with such ruthless precision as Bruce Dickinson and the singer hit a personal high with his contribution to the album. Penning two songs alone and another couple with Adrian Smith, the vocalist had improved immeasurably. With the benefit of experience in the Maiden set-up, Dickinson was now free to display all his eccentricity and genius while the others simply stood back and watched open-mouthed.

But take nothing away from Steve Harris who, as ever, could be relied upon for consistently brilliant compositions. On *Powerslave* he would go beyond his usual remit and truly establish himself as a gloriously epic composer. There are only eight songs on the album, yet fans certainly get their money's worth. The closing track, 'Rime Of The Ancient Mariner' is close to fourteen minutes in length with most others topping the five-minute mark. And as always there are no empty sections to any of the songs, Maiden keep the listener spellbound whether a song is three min-utes or 13 minutes long.

Opening with future live certainty 'Aces High', *Powerslave* bursts into life with a crescendo worthy of the sort of glory usually reserved for the likes of fighter pilots. The Harris number brought Maiden screaming into 1984 with a procession of duelling guitars and soaring Dickinson vo-cals. The chorus is a beautiful harmonic section for which one might have anticipated an Adrian Smith credit, being catchy and a touch commercial. The following track did contain a Smith mark, and his clever craft is all over '2 Minutes To Midnight'. With another gorgeously catchy chorus this song would again be guaranteed live hit.

The lyrics revolve around the theme of war and feature some mem-orable Dickinson lines, such as; *"As the reasons for the carnage cut their meat and lick the gravy, we oil the jaws of the war machine and feed it with our babies."*

Strangely, in amongst the embarrassment of musical riches, Harris throws a curveball. The 'Losfer Words (Big 'Orra)' tune clearly belongs on *Powerslave,* though it might be regarded as something of a filler track. An instrumental in the vein of some of their earlier work, it is a song the album could have done without, stretching thinly beyond four minutes. However, the ending bars are worth waiting for as up next is a Dickinson classic, 'Flash Of The Blade'. Beginning with an awesome riff, here was the song Bruce had longed to write for some time. An ode to swordplay, specifically fencing, the song is somewhat autobiographical, telling tales of the young boy growing up. To fight with honour and pride is the moral of the story – don't mess with Bruce or he'll put his sword through you! Musically, here is the vocalist at his unflinching best, making an argument for being Maiden's finest songwriter. Even 'Back In The Village', which has been cruelly dubbed a 'filler' track by some, is, in fact, true Maiden steel – taking in multiple rock genres in its captivating five minutes, the song should go down as a classic Smith/Dickinson number. Importantly too, it was the sequel to 'The Prisoner'. As Bruce said, "It's the story of some bloke who's trapped in a village. In fact, he's mostly a prisoner of his own fantasy and can't get rid of it, hence his imprisonment in this ghost-village, the place of both his dreams and nightmares."

But really, the mastery of the band was sealed with the epic title track. Dark, eerie and loaded with Egyptian references, this is the crown-ing glory of the opus. A remarkable vocal feat by Bruce is bettered only by the slinky, emotive guitar parts, which are some of the band's best ever. Lyrically here was the crux of the *Powerslave* LP. Bruce illuminated, "The whole theme of the album is contained in the song 'Powerslave'. The other songs deal with completely different things. 'Powerslave' tells of a dying Pharaoh. He's about to die and he finds himself a slave to the power of death, as well as the slave to his own power. When a Pharaoh dies, all the slaves who built his grave and prepared his funeral have to die too. Even if he didn't want it, his power implies, without question, that these people must die, far beyond his own will. Basically, he's a prisoner of his power. In Egypt, the Pharaoh incarnates life, he's a living god and controls the essential substance of the earth. When life departs his body, it must also quit the bodies of those who served him, as the rule dictates. The paradox is that, even if he's a living god and decides on his deathbed to carry on living, well, he can't. His power is enslaved to the power of death."

It is no coincidence the song is similar, musically, to 'Revelations', another Dickinson solo credit from *Piece Of Mind*. Describing the circumstances behind the writing of the 'Powerslave' track (it came to him while having his breakfast!) Bruce explained, "I was thinking about 'Revelations', on the previous album, and I was looking for something missing. And I indeed found a missing link. In 'Revelations', there are all sorts of signs related to Hindu and Egyptian mythology about life and death. But there was something missing – the power of death over life, which is a theme you find very often in Egyptian mythology. So, I basically wrote 'Powerslave' while listening to 'Revelations', a cup of tea in one hand and bacon in the other." It is an ambitious, giant tale of mythology, perfect for a heavy metal album and there is no question Bruce knew his subject.

'The Duellists' is a Steve Harris song but could easily have been Bruce's handiwork – covering fighting with honour and 'splendour' once again. "It's about a pretty traditional duel," Bruce said, "Steve was able to efficiently put forward the futility and uselessness to die for a question of glory and pleasure to fight. Because, in a duel, there's more than just honour, there's this sick gratuity that discredits any place honour could have in such events."

The closing track would be Iron Maiden's most famous lengthy epic. Though Steve Harris had previously written the now traditional long closing track for *Piece Of Mind* and would pen many more in the future, 'Rime Of The Ancient Mariner' is beyond epic. Totalling 13:39 this is a depiction of the famous poem by Samuel Taylor Coleridge, echoing Maiden's obsession with British history. To undertake the representation of such a lengthy piece might have been regarded as almost ridiculous in its pomposity. But Maiden carried it off with mind-blowing aplomb. Words that would crumble in the mouth of a lesser vocalist are dispatched with clarity and accuracy by Dickinson and the music accompanying the lyrics is simply outstanding. The galloping Maiden stamp is ever present and the time changes Harris was so familiar with appear in abundance. But, like many long tracks, and in the shadow of his progressive rock heroes, there had to be a breakdown, a quiet section. This would allow the song room to breathe before being built up again to its crushing crescendo. The mid section is genuinely creepy and certainly conveys the desperation present on the mythical ship. Bruce carefully constructs his vocals to draw the song back to a steady pace and with one long scream Maiden are back in the throes of the song. The guitar parts are phenomenal, Murray and Smith trading riffs, licks and solos as if it were their last ever song together. After the parting line, *"And the tale goes on and on and on..."* *Powerslave* is finished and Iron Maiden had solidified their place in music history.

1984 was a fairly strong year for metal generally, especially as Metallica had built on their debut album's formula and returned with the stronger, more mature *Ride The Lightning*. There were also new albums by Judas Priest (*Defenders Of The Faith*), Manowar (*Hail To England*) and Mercyful Fate (*Don't Break The Oath*), among many others. But Iron Maiden were untouchable for sheer bravado and majesty. Their material was far beyond other bands' output and would remain so for many years to come. Clear, sharp and precise, *Powerslave* was light years ahead of the competition and rightly gave Maiden a further boost in their worldwide ascent.

Part of the album's allure stemmed from the enormous artwork. Derek Riggs brought Eddie to Egyptian life in a stunning visual landscape. Many would claim the terrific depiction of Eddie as a pharaoh, with the pyramids in the background, was similar to certain Earth, Wind And Fire covers. However, in comparison, EW&F sleeves were woefully inept whereas *Powerslave* was a joy to behold, especially on the detailed LP art where you could clearly see every intricate detail Riggs had inserted. As well as several small but amusing jokes written across some of the statues, there were also genuine hieroglyphics. "I copied them from a book about hieroglyphics," Riggs explains. "They are a small part of the prayer to Osiris. It's a very long Egyptian thing that just says that Osiris is the meanest mother in the world and you definitely should not mess with him."

Maiden was well aware its mascot had to diversify in order to retain its appeal. "Look at Kiss, for instance," Bruce observed, "their make-up shocked everyone when they first started, but after a few years, nobody was paying attention to it anymore. It's the same with Eddie, he's still there, but he's different, bigger, more powerful." Indeed he was, and it was strangely symbolic that, as Eddie grew in stature so too did the band he represented. For Iron Maiden were about to go into orbit.

SCREAM FOR ME LONG BEACH

"It was the best tour we ever did and it was the worst. And it nearly finished us off for good." Bruce Dickinson

To support their best album to date, Iron Maiden would tour far longer than they ever had before. The members knew they would have to be healthy and on form for the duration, but that was only a small part of the undertaking. The band would not only be at their busiest, they would also have a massive entourage with them and everything had to run like clockwork. For 13 months the organisation would tour the world travelling through 25 countries, performing some 220 shows and the whole supporting arsenal would boast 700 spotlights, six huge lorries and five tour busses. This was, as the band themselves state, a first for a heavy metal outfit. Maiden's ambition was only surpassed by their competence and consistency.

Whereas budget had often been a problem in the past, by 1984-'85 money was no object. Although the tour was to see them only just break even financially, not to mention destroying the band members' sanity and wrecking them physically, it would all be worth it. With their huge stage show, the name Maiden would remain in the heavy metal spotlight for years to come.

On previous tours, despite the fact that he walked on stage to rapturous applause, Eddie had just been a papier-mâché creation and something of a bit-part player. Come 1984 however, he had become a giant mechanised 30-foot-tall ogre. This was true heavy metal theatre, surpassing the likes of Alice Cooper, who had, for years brought his own horror show to fans.

Bruce would later speak of the wonders of the tour claiming it was their best ever. A sentiment the rest of the band shared. "The whole set, apart from the lights was done musical hall style," the front man would say. "It was all boxes and ropes and two blokes pulling levers. It was so simple, it was like pantomime. You could set it up in small theatres or big arenas and it would always look fantastic."

The backing was, of course, an Egyptian dream, making use of the idyllic *Powerslave* sleeve. As the band would say, it was like walking into the album cover just being on stage in the *Powerslave*-come-to-life universe.

For the first time, Maiden would crack the American market, bringing a show to the States that was 1984's must-see event. The group would sell out Radio City Hall in New York for five nights running, a phenomenal achievement which could have been greater had illness not prevented them making it seven. According to Bruce, *Powerslave* would be *the* Maiden album to own. Even those who had never before bought a record bearing the famous logo, and perhaps would never buy one again, still had *Powerslave* in their collection.

This brought its burdens however. With Rod Smallwood eager to capitalise on the band's success (lest it disappear quickly), he was keen to cram every town on the United States map into the schedule. But having already laid waste to Europe, the group were beginning to wish the punishing calendar would end. Bruce was beginning to feel, for the first time, that he might well quit the band unless things changed. "I began to feel like I was part of the lighting rig, like a piece of machinery," he would later say. While this never meant Dickinson gave anything less than his best on stage (and nor was anyone on the outside of the organisation aware how he felt), it was clearly no good having your singer verging on burnout.

Besides, everyone else was feeling the heat as well. The biggest problem was that they rarely had a day off during the incredibly intense gigging schedule. As Adrian observed, "These days when bands take on 14 month long world tours, they build in gaps for recuperation. But there were no real breaks on that tour. By the end you don't know how to act properly any more, you don't know who you are or what you're supposed to be doing. I remember, I went to see my parents when I got home and I knocked on the wrong door, honestly!"

Still, there were many highlights on the tour, the first of which came on day one and was a very special achievement. Beginning the World Slavery tour in Poland (at the Torwar Sports Hall in Warsaw where there were 14,000 fans inside, and another 5,000 locked out!), Maiden became the first major band to bring a full touring operation behind the Iron Curtain and would go on to visit the likes of Hungary and Yugoslavia as well.

The tour ended on July 5th, 1985 at the Irvine Meadows Ampitheatre in Laguna Hills, California. After the immense undertaking, the five members of Iron Maiden would enjoy a long overdue, and seriously deserved break. The tour for *Powerslave* had brought the band their biggest success to date and taken them further than they had ever collectively travelled, yet there was a price to pay for such geographical leaping. More prone to introspection than the other members and physically more likely to tire due to constantly using his voice, Bruce Dickinson was hit hardest by the excesses of Maiden's most ambitious tour thus far.

With this in mind, there was no great rush to head straight for the studio and record another album, only to have to tour all over again to promote it. The public was hungry for Maiden yet the band could only do so much. The *Powerslave* album was, in many fans' eyes, the pinnacle for Iron Maiden and in order to equal, let alone outdo it, the group would need a serious recuperation period.

As Nicko McBrain explained in a rare interview, "Three quarters of the way through the last tour everybody, myself included, was going 'Oh wouldn't it be nice to go home and have a nice roast beef dinner and a pint of ale? Throw a few arrows and down a couple of barrels of beer.' So yeah, we all got a bit homesick towards the end, but don't forget it was a bit of a slog we took on there; eleven and a half months! They don't come any bigger. And it always happens, almost every hard-working rock musician I know, the kind who really like to work on the road, they'll all tell you there comes a point where you really can't wait to get home, to have finished the job and done it well." Bruce Dickinson concurred; "Something we'd all been dreaming of and whose meaning had been almost forgotten in almost four years, was taking a break. We took a well-deserved six-month break. We needed time to recuperate after the tour. We'll never tour again so intensively!"

The vocalist was certainly right about that. Even the perennial en-thusiast Steve Harris was in agreement that the World Slavery tour was perhaps too intense, even for the Maiden workhorses. Or at least, Harris seemed to agree with Bruce's comments about long tours – but perhaps he was just thinking of what was best for Iron Maiden, since, in keeping his singer happy, he was prolonging the lifespan of the band.

With this in mind, it was a welcome idea of EMI's to release a stop-gap live record before the next studio album was recorded. Maiden had been the first act ever to play to a sold out Long Beach Arena in California for four consecutive nights, the quartet of shows amounting to performing in front of 52,000 people. To commemorate such an achievement the band chose a concert from one of the nights at Long Beach for the live release, which was to be called *Live After Death*. There would also be a video of the same name to capture the visual impact of the mammoth show. The al-bum hit number two in the UK charts and the video flew in to the top spot. For many reasons, *Live After Death* is considered to be one of the finest rock/metal live albums of all time.

Firstly, and most obviously, the band was firing on all cylinders for the World Slavery tour. It was now Bruce Dickinson's third major jaunt with Maiden and collectively the members were in their stride. They had also recently released three of the finest heavy metal works of all time in *The Number Of The Beast*, *Piece Of Mind* and *Powerslave*, providing them with a highly impressive arsenal of tracks to play live. As would become their custom, Maiden made sure to throw in several current songs to promote their new material the best way they knew – by performing it onstage. For inclusion on the album, four tracks from *Powerslave* were used, but two were the longest songs Maiden could have chosen; 'Powerslave' itself, and 'Rime Of The Ancient Mariner' which was recreated perfectly. The two opening tracks on the band's '84 studio release were used to begin the live show, 'Aces High' and '2 Minutes To Midnight,' both of which sounded fantastic. Prior to 'Aces High' kicking into life, the intro tape used a Winston Churchill speech immortalised during the Second World War: *"... We shall go on to the end, we shall fight in France, we shall fight on the seas and oceans, we shall fight with growing confidence and growing strength in the air. We shall defend our Island, whatever the cost may be. We shall fight on the beaches, we shall fight on the landing grounds, we shall fight in the fields and in the streets, we shall fight in the hills; we shall never surrender..."*

As the echo of the word 'surrender' boomed around the jam-packed Arena, the band burst onto the stage and, after the introduction but before the main riff, the lights suddenly sprayed the attendant throng, highlighting the group's appearance. This was true theatrical heavy metal in all its glory. So many bands had tried, and many more would later try, to capture the incendiary nature of an electric live performance, but none could touch the sparks flying off the vinyl of Iron Maiden's live albums. There were, of course, appearances for the, by now, familiar live versions of 'The Trooper', 'Hallowed Be Thy Name', '22 Acacia Avenue' and 'The Number Of The Beast'. Yet the highlight of the double set was the extended version of 'Running Free' where Bruce divided the crowd down the middle, playing left and right against each other to see who could make the most noise. His famous quote then rang even truer. Throughout the record Bruce would cry, "Scream for me Long Beach!" and during 'Running Free' the singer told the crowd he wanted to go back to England and tell his doctor, "Long Beach fucked up my hearing for good!"

Initially the record would be a two LP affair featuring the concert in its entirety, also captured on the video version. A few years later when compact discs were invented, the *Live After Death* album was transferred to the new format, but, unfortunately, only onto one disc, thus cutting off a fair chunk of the show. Thankfully by 1998, after many requests, EMI reissued the entire Maiden back catalogue with enhanced multimedia sections. *Live After Death* was given the full treatment with the complete LP version recreated for the first time on CD, along with a few extras. The inner sleeve was also extended to include much of the information originally on the vinyl version. This included several superb photos of the band in action, at work and at play. Choice pictures included Nicko wearing joke glasses and a 'Fuck You Man' cut off t-shirt, the group viewed as one in a swimming pool, Steve in mid-flight on stage, Nicko again with questionable eye-wear (goggles with false eyes), Adrian looking knackered, Bruce standing by a limousine thumbing a lift, and some highly questionable clothing; Bruce's yellow spandex trousers, Steve's black and white spandex and Dave Murray's quite appalling collection of blue and black hooped and striped vests.

The reissue CD also featured an in-depth list of equipment Maiden used on tour, everything from the makes of guitars and drums, to the monitors and P.A. used – incidentally, the total power of the front P.A. was a staggering 152,000 watts. The original notes from Martin Birch were faithfully reprinted, as well as a note from Tony Wigens. There was a full list of each date on the tour, a comprehensive list of everyone on the road with Maiden and the daily schedule of the crew, which involved working from eight in the morning to two the following morning. Life in a touring metal band wasn't as easy as it seemed, but the rewards were surely worth it. With *Live After Death,* Iron Maiden rewrote the rulebook on how a concert could be translated to tape. Overall they showed just how to put on the best show possible for everyone in attendance, all over the world.

[1] In 1993 an American death metal band known as Nile was formed. Describing their music as "Itylphallical Death Metal", the group is entirely devoted to Egyptology and their albums are all grand conceptual affairs, evoking images and sounds of ancient tombs. Though the band themselves are all of American, white heritage their overwhelming interest in Egyptian themes and history (specifically front man Karl Sanders) means every one of their albums is draped in the ancient mysteries of Egypt. Nile were the first band to truly embrace the history of ancient Egypt for not just one album, but all of them.

Sources:

Enfer Magazine #17, 24
Metal Attack Magazine #13
Hard Rock Magazine #2
Publishing Credits Iron Maiden (Holdings) Ltd 1984

Chapter 8 –
Time Is Always On Our Side

"I saw us when we first started off as a 'Heavy band', a heavy rock band of sorts but it then became known as 'Heavy Metal', then it was just metal. Now you have all sorts; Death Metal, Black Metal and such. I think as long as we don't turn to rust they can call us whatever metal they like."
Steve Harris

DÉJÀ VU

Iron Maiden was, to all intents and purposes, on vacation. Bruce suggested ironically, "Only Steve never does anything! I think he's busy enough with his daughter and his wife..." Most of the band-mates took advantage of their first real break for six years. Adrian travelled to the Canadian Rockies for a spot of fishing, Nicko perfected his flying, Bruce practised fencing while contrary to Dickinson's suggestion of doing absolutely nothing, Steve kept fit playing football.

As far as relaxing went, Steve certainly did that too, but, as he told *Enfer* magazine, "We're almost all married and have children, so we have to consider the needs of our wives and kids, we have to come home from time to time. I'd be extremely pissed off to have a successful 'public life' while my private life suffers from it. I can't even imagine that."

Ironically enough, even 'off-tour' some of the Maiden members wanted to be involved in playing live. As Nicko would say however, it was necessary even if not completely serious. "Just telling myself that I couldn't play at a moment's notice was driving me mad," recalled the sticksman. "I remember when we told Rod that me and Adrian wanted to get out with our mates and do a couple of gigs, he couldn't believe it! He thought it was the last thing we would want to do after spending so much time on the road together. But we said 'No, we wanna get up on stage somewhere, don't matter where it is, and just burn!' So that's what we did." Indeed Nicko was so desperate to play music again that he asked EMI to "keep their ears open for any sessions that might be going around. Anything, I just wanted an excuse to play, really. But nothing really came of that, or if it was about to it wasn't happening quick enough for me, so in the end I rang Harry Mohan at Sanctuary, this was around October and asked him if he would book a rehearsal room where I could go and just have a practice on my kit. Harry asked me what size room I wanted, was it just for myself, or did I want something bigger than that? And that's when I thought, well, what was the point in sitting there bashing away on my own? I might as well rent a bigger room and get a few of the boys down there for a bit of a jam."

Nicko was about to find there was at least one other Maiden-ite who was still aching to play. Once Nicko had secured a room at E-Zee-Hire Studios in North London on an open-ended ticket, the first person he contacted was Adrian Smith. "The thing is, Adrian has a lot of ideas, and bits and pieces floating around that he's written, that aren't really the sort of numbers we'd want to do with Iron Maiden," explained Nicko. "And the thing with me is I just love to play. So I rang Adrian back and asked him if he wanted to come down for a blow."

As a result, the band The Entire Population Of Hackney was soon born, in which Nicko and Adrian played a few secret gigs including one at The Marquee Club in Soho on December 21st, 1985.

"It was intended as a bit of a pre-Xmas party, really," Nicko explained casually. "And everybody came down too. The Maiden boys who do our sound and lights helped out and Davey, Steve and Bruce came down for a blow on stage at the end. And Pete Way from Waysted got up as well, and everybody just had a ball! It was a tremendous night. We did the Marquee as The Entire Population Of Hackney two days after the Gravesend gig and the place sold out in about half an hour. If we'd thought about it, we might have done two nights as the demand for tickets was that great, only we didn't have enough songs to vary the set too much. So, really, things worked out perfectly the way they were."

The makeshift band's set consisted of obvious Maiden tracks, such as '2 Minutes To Midnight' as well as the rarely played 'Losfer Words (Big 'Orra)' along with other rock standards such as Thin Lizzy's 'Rosalie' and ZZ Top's 'Tush'. Nicko still missed daily contact with Maiden though: "Deep down inside I knew that five or six months off wouldn't be easy," the drummer said. "I mean, five months from the family? The family is what Iron Maiden call themselves, and all who work for them are seen as part of the family."

For Bruce Dickinson, variety was the spice of his time off from Maiden. And what better way to escape from the confines of touring life with a band, where every whim is catered for and one lives in a surreal bubble, than by doing something thoroughly British and completely insane by most mortals' standards. "I spent two weeks at an off-duty Catholic Boarding School, sleeping in a box with no hot water on tap until seven am and no heating whatsoever," Bruce explained. "And all for fencing, the sport of kings, doctors and the unemployed, or, as was the case for six months, me. They actually asked me to teach people and even gave me a piece of paper that said so. I was on a quest, of course, you know, the Grail, the Holy Shroud, tournaments, jousting, fencing, the Esso Open, the Shropshire Open... the bar's open! Let's have a drink." For Dave Murray, who had just married long-term girlfriend Tamar, the first thing he wanted to do when the World Slavery tour was over, was escape with his new wife. "The moment it was all over I scooted off to Hawaii where me and Tamar have got a house," said the guitarist. "It's in a really beautiful spot as well, surrounded by mountains and waterfalls and plenty of sun. Complete paradise. But what with the band working so much I've still only spent about two months at the house in Hawaii, in all, in just over two years."

SOMEWHERE IN TIME

Eventually, come January 1986 and after five months of inactivity in camp Maiden it was time for the band to begin recording the follow up to *Powerslave*. However, where their '84 platter had been Bruce Dickinson's strongest album in terms of song writing, the next studio recording was to be devoid of a single Dickinson credit. This was shocking and confusing for many fans, yet it was preferable to the possibility of Iron Maiden without their greatest vocalist.

"I thought of leaving," said Bruce with regards to his mind state in 1985. "Not because what I wanted to write didn't fit in with the group. It was because I thought, 'well if it's gonna carry on like this, if I'm gonna feel bad all the time, this imprisoned, then I don't really want to go on tour. Me and Steve got to the point during World Slavery where we said, 'if they add another week's shows to this tour we're both going home.'"

For Dickinson at least, the hangover from the tour had continued up until when Maiden was ready to compose the next album. He wrote no material – at least that was considered acceptable – for the new studio opus and he felt loathed to undertake a massive tour that would undoubtedly follow the release. Yet Bruce still fronted the songs Steve, Dave and Adrian had penned and he would also tour in support of the album. So it was unclear at the time what exactly was troubling Bruce. What seems most likely is that the vocalist had ideas, but ones that both he and Steve felt were not appropriate for Maiden.

The final endorsement of this belief lay in the acoustic tracks Bruce had written, initially intended for the new album. Fed up with the heavy metal clichés and perhaps also tired of the wall of sound generated by a live metal show, Bruce switched off, quite literally, and prepared a softer collection of music, the kind of thing he would have preferred to perform on a two-year tour. But this was Iron Maiden, and the legacy already built – that of a behemoth destroying all pretenders to the throne of kings of heavy metal – was not to be tampered with. For Steve Harris there was never a doubt about what kind of material Maiden would compose and perform.

"What Bruce had written didn't quite suit what we'd done," said Steve rigidly. "So, we kept his songs for the next album." This comment seems to have gone unnoticed in the Maiden history, but Steve Harris was being diplomatic rather than totally honest. If the songs Bruce had written in 1985-86 were later used by Maiden then it was never mentioned that the material was pre-existing. It seems more likely that the songs were kept aside by Bruce himself and used for his later, solo work. The ultimate proof of this theory is the fact that the 1988 Maiden album, *Seventh Son Of A Seventh Son* featured no acoustic tracks, save for the short intro and outro pieces. The remainder of the material was typical, ultra heavy Iron Maiden, whereas Bruce Dickinson's solo albums contained a number of acoustic tracks, especially 1997's *Accident Of Birth*.

So it was clear that Bruce's compositions were in a different sphere to that which Steve Harris envisioned for *Somewhere In Time*. But of course, the singer had an explanation for his deviation from the familiar; "After the *Powerslave* tour I really didn't give a shit anymore. I thought 'if this is what it's gonna do to my head, sod it! I'll go and be a folk singer.' When it came to writing for a new album, whenever I started to write 'very 'eavy metal' things, I found I was thinking along those lines, you know, I should do one of these, one of those. So I ended up writing a lot of different things instead, for bagpipes, folk things, stuff like Jethro Tull. Bang went my royalties!"

While Bruce was speaking perhaps somewhat tongue in cheek, and not completely discounting the possibility he might have been misquoted, he seemed to be very confused and contradictory at the time. For one thing, he was stretching the boundaries to suggest Jethro Tull was a folk band, given their place in the echelons of progressive rock and their huge catalogue of material consisting of sophisticated arrangements, and indeed precious little bagpipe playing! But even if Bruce were to consider true folk music to be only that which is entirely acoustic and whereby the artist uses a myriad of quirky instruments shunning the typical guitar, bass and drum format of the average rock act, he had to realise folk musicians were in exactly the same situation as a rock band when touring. Regardless of the style of music, a musician on tour has to face the same distractions from regular life. In fact, history is far more likely to assign the average folk singer with artistic foibles, where he or she deviates from living a 'normal' life, than yer average heavy metaller. Any number of artists, from Nick Drake to Billy Connolly, have preferred to strum acoustically and sing melancholy songs rather than play heavy metal but it didn't stop them from experiencing serious inner demons.

Yet perhaps the most confusing aspect of Bruce's thoughts at the time was the insinuation that if his material was not appropriate then he would not be a part of the band and therefore would not have to go through the rigmaroles of touring. Surely Bruce realised, regardless of who penned the Maiden works, he was the singer with a duty to go out and sing the songs. And he would indeed continue in his role as the group's vocalist, for the time being – it wasn't until some years later that he finally gave up being the singer in a heavy metal outfit.

Steve Harris still maintained Maiden was functioning well at all levels saying, "We get on extraordinarily well on the professional level, but I think it's even better on the personal level. Iron Maiden is a very united band overall. It's much better like this. The bands that have internal problems, but who still want to remain consistent on stage must be completely paranoid. We all try not to tread on each other's toes. When there's something wrong, we all discuss it together. And we don't have any drug problems, which is, I think, essential to keep a band together."

For 1986, despite his personal views, Bruce Dickinson seemed happy enough to front the world's biggest heavy metal act. And no-one seemed to feel that the fact that Bruce came to the table with 'folk' songs detracted from his metal prowess. However Steve remained damning in his reaction to the material Bruce had presented. "I just thought he'd lost the plot completely," he says in the official Maiden biography. "Bruce just wasn't himself at the time. He came in with a few ideas which didn't really suit. It wasn't because it was acoustic necessarily, or even that it was very different sort of stuff, it was just…we didn't think it was good enough really. Luckily Adrian came up with some strong stuff on his own and that was that."

Martin Birch, who was entrusted with production, engineering and mixing duties, followed the group to the Bahamas, where, for tax reasons, they were recording. There was no doubt in the band's mind that, as long as Birch was available, he would be at the helm of a new Iron Maiden record. He had even overseen the *Live After Death* album and Steve had this to say of the man's importance in the Maiden camp; "He's got Maiden's sound in him! He's fantastic, and there aren't so many like him. It would be terrible if we had to do without him, if he didn't have time for us. I know perfectly well that he'll always be available for us, but just thinking about it gives me the shivers."

Before its release Steve reckoned, "This album is very different from the others, it's the best one since *The Number Of The Beast*. It's the diversity that I like so much in this album, you'll see, no-one will be disappointed." *Somewhere In Time* is indeed a diverse set of songs, perhaps Maiden's most forward thinking and ambitious to date. They had much to contend with. Heavy metal was about to hit a peak in 1986 with the strongest respective releases from Metallica, Megadeth, Slayer and Ozzy Osbourne. There were also a few up-and-coming bands who were improving with each release, namely Candlemass, Fates Warning and Kreator.

It was not as if Maiden had fallen behind in the pecking order because of the two year gap in studio output, but, in the face of ever stiffer competition, they still had to put forward their case for continuing to be the kings of metal. As time went on, metal became heavier, faster and angrier. With the specific case of Slayer's *Reign In Blood* record, a recognised landmark in thrash metal (perhaps just pipping Metallica's *Master Of Puppets* in terms of influence on extreme metal) [1], the ever broadening genre referred to as heavy metal, was about to reach new heights of speed, power and mayhem. In comparison, Maiden's sound was somewhat tame and in some quarters was viewed as being 'past its sell-by date'. But for the majority, the material on *Somewhere In Time* was as viable and enjoyable as anything from the past. Besides, the thrash metal movement was not something the Maiden members aspired to, and Dave Murray professes a liking of two of the more melodic proponents of thrash. "I like Anthrax and Metallica. I think the really fast ones are too fast to enjoy, they seem to have got hold of the wrong end of the stick." Murray was clearly out of his knowledge range with such a comment, since for many within the thrash communities it was *all about* playing fast! But he did, of course, have a point, and many agreed that Maiden's brand of metal was worthier. Steve Harris ventured his opinion on thrash too; "My main problem is that thrash bands don't write that many good melodies and that's why I can't get off on them. We've always had good melodies running through the songs. These thirty-second songs, that's bloody stupid."

Again, the man had a point but it reflected a generational shift from the traditional rock of the old days into a faster and, some would argue, more proficient style of playing. But thrash and Iron Maiden would never see eye to eye and were hardly likely to cross paths in future.

As Steve Harris had promised, the diversity of the new record was its strength and the band had stuck to their guns despite adding flourishes to their existing sound. The trademark Maiden stamp was still in place: the jangling of 'Arry's bass, Nicko's tight drumming, the melodic twin guitar interplay of Adrian and Dave and, of course, the unmistakable vocals of Bruce Dickinson. On tracks such as 'The Loneliness Of The Long Distance Runner' there are a number of identifiably '80s guitar licks and harmonies, which proved more than welcome at the time. Tracks such as this are dark in appearance, yet on closer inspection reveal highly melodic guitar textures that gave Maiden an edge over their heavier musical counterparts. True, there is nothing approaching speed metal on *Somewhere In Time,* but it is a very strong record and certainly worthy of the heavy metal tag. The inclusion of guitar synthesisers was a particularly up-to-date twist, providing the overall sound of the album with an ultra modern feel. Though the addition of synths is only noticeable on *very* close listening or on headphones, they are undoubtedly there, lending a solid edge to the band's sound, despite the somewhat 'wimpy' overtone of what was basically a converted modern keyboard. The synths, along with its recording location, helped make *Somewhere In Time* Maiden's most expensive album so far. Their most costly recording yet maybe, but it was all for a higher purpose. For the first time Maiden experimented with a new process invented in Germany, known as Direct Metal Mastering, and previously only used on classical music recordings. As Steve said, "The result is quite remarkable, mostly if you're lucky enough to own a laser compact disc reader."

Beginning with 'Caught Somewhere In Time' the album clocks in at just over fifty-one minutes, with eight tracks. Perhaps not surprisingly the theme is time, which as Adrian suggested was most apt. "If you think about what we'd just done and where we'd just been, maybe it wasn't so strange that most of the songs we seemed to come up with had something to do with time – either time wasted or time spent learning something that cost you a lot. It's all there if you read between the lines." And the titles echo the theme: the aforementioned opening track, 'Wasted Years', 'Déjà Vu' and even the suggestive 'Heaven Can Wait'.

The latter has an interesting topic and would become one of the band's best-known songs and a staple of the live set, though it's worth noting that Steve thought the chorus "could sound mainstream". It was difficult for the headstrong Harris to write anything that did not contain several time changes and intricate riffs, not to mention the odd sing-a-long melody, and 'Heaven Can Wait' was no different. Still, along with 'Wasted Years' and 'Déjà Vu' the track was one of the catchiest Maiden ditties in a long time.

"I finished 'Heaven...' in the first week we were in Jersey, and it sort of wrote itself, and very quickly too by my standards," a satisfied Steve Harris disclosed. "It's about someone in a deep sleep whose spirit rises and leaves the body and is looking down on it. They say that when an out of body experience happens there's usually a strong light, which beckons the spirit to follow. But the person in the song looks into the light and says 'no, I don't wanna go yet... I'm not ready!' Basically, it's about the determination for life. You have to survive."

The song is pure Steve Harris, with backing choral shouts at the bridge section of the track that allow for crowd participation during live renditions. And, as the bassist described, the subject matter is something typically Maiden. A theme also runs through certain other tracks, such as 'Wasted Years', 'Sea of Madness', and 'Stranger In A Strange Land'. "The first two are songs with, as usual, a pretty optimistic message," Steve affirmed. "In life, you have to try and have an optimistic attitude in front of all the problems that you have to face – and God knows that it's not always easy! 'Stranger In A Strange Land', although inspired by the title of a Robert Heinlein book, has a strange origin. Adrian remembered a story that was published in the press a few years ago, about this old sailor who was found dead, perfectly preserved in the ice of the North Pole. In fact, he was a member of an expedition that had disappeared after an iceberg had struck their ship. When they found his body, they awarded him a posthumous medal."

'The Loneliness Of The Long Distance Runner', based on the 1962 British film of the same name, was a particularly apt title, since Steve must often have felt as though he was the only one running the Iron Maiden organisation. Despite the fact that the band had sterling management behind them and amazing musicians who were highly talented and capable of writing wonderful songs, the buck still stopped with Steve Harris. And the writing of *Somewhere In Time* was highly indicative of this – without Steve's credits the album would only contain 3.5 songs!

The one song attributable to Dave Murray is the impossibly catchy 'Déjà Vu'. Not only is the main riff a galloping leap through the Maiden back catalogue encapsulated in just a few notes, but the spooky vocal lines enunciated by Bruce also give the track a mystical feel. It is typical of Maiden's shorter songs, clocking in at just under five minutes, while seeming to be only two minutes long. As usual, with a Murray composed track, it turned out to be something special and yet 'Déjà Vu' remains one of the band's more underrated compositions. Its subject matter could not have been clearer and again fitted in with the loose concept of the album. The only surprise is that this subject had not been previously broached by Steve as the lyrics are vintage Harris; "*Ever had a conversation that you realise you've had before, isn't it strange. Have you ever talked to someone, and you feel you know what's coming next, it feels pre-arranged.*"

Everyone knows how it feels to experience the sensation of déjà vu, but perhaps few have written such a lyrical description, able to stand on its own merits as a poem, yet also fitting the essence of the song and the Murray/Harris musical backings.

But the real jewel in the crown on *Somewhere In Time* is the closing track, 'Alexander The Great.' Known to be a historical figure admired by Steve Harris, it was high time the ancient Greek be immortalised in song form! The bass player takes sole credit for the mammoth eight minute thirty-five second song. Echoing some of Harris' progressive rock faves (especially Genesis and their 'Watcher Of The Skies' track) in the opening phrases of the song, it soon opens up to a glorious riff that struts and swings before a lifetime best performance from Bruce Dickinson. If Bruce felt any doubts whatsoever about fronting the material he was given, it certainly wasn't audible. "It is always a worry that you come up with something that sounds similar to something by someone else," thought Steve, perhaps making reference to Genesis, "but if someone goes 'Oh that so and so song sounds like something else' then as long as you did it unintentionally then it's okay. If you did it intentionally then that's not very good but I suppose anything is possible when you are writing new stuff. *Everybody* is affected by what you hear and see, otherwise you're dead!"

The track is composed in chronological and biographical order, name checking specific battles, countries, religion and a cast of characters from King Darius to King Philip Of Macedonia. Even the opening dialogue is a saying by King Philip, Alexander's father, which Harris paraphrases thus; "*My Son ask for thyself another kingdom, for that which I leave is too small for thee*". As with any Maiden epic there is a long breakdown section during the track where the guitars beautifully feed off each other, and Steve Harris' ability to produce another grand classic is displayed. Unsurprisingly the track had been a formidable undertaking for the bassist and he admitted the song took him as long to write as 'Rime Of The Ancient Mariner' despite its being only half the length, illustrating the intricate and majestic quality of 'Alexander The

Great'. "I suppose I must have taken about two or three weeks to write that one. I end up spending hours and hours on one part at a time, making sure they will work before going any further, very slow. And that comes after I've done all my reading up on Alexander's story. I was reading it anyway, and the more I got into it the more I knew I could make something of the story, because it's a fabulous story, the whole thing." Steve's reading of the history was certainly correct, and the song stands as a cult classic of the Maiden catalogue, although it does not always get the credit it deserves with regards to *Best Of* compilations. It might not be a song widely associated with Iron Maiden, but for the committed fan it ranks highly. Most importantly, the song is a fitting accompaniment to the life of the great warrior Alexander and will probably never be bettered. Interestingly, prior to the finishing of the album, Bruce was interviewed and asked whether there was going to be an epic track, as there had been ever since *The Number Of The Beast*, tacked onto the end of the record. "No, there won't be one this time," Bruce replied. "All the songs have more or less the same duration – four to five minutes. But there is a great instrumental written by Steve." Obviously there was no instrumental in the end (perhaps due to a less than excited reaction to 'Losfer Words Big 'Orra') and Bruce was also way off the mark with regard to the length of the songs. Only 'Déjà Vu' was under five minutes, with the average being somewhere around the six and a half minute mark. It seems extra parts were added once the recording had begun so it was no surprise Bruce was inaccurate with his comments on the album. As Steve would claim, it was virtually impossible for them to fit one more minute onto the vinyl. If they had been able to cram in more music, they surely would have done so, though, as always, the band didn't write more than they needed – in fact they generally only recorded songs for b-sides when a choice of single was already decided. Once the maximum length was realised, the songs were squeezed into the remit. And the definitive take from Steve Harris, on how long tracks were, was as follows; "None of us really pay any attention to the length of the songs. We never have done really."

It was a certainty Maiden would use Derek Riggs for the cover art. As Bruce had stated beforehand; "You can count on Derek doing the painting! I don't know yet what shape or form it'll take, but I trust Derek to use his talent in the best of ways." It hardly mattered given the fantastic finished piece Riggs produced, but the basic premise of *Somewhere In Time* – that of a futuristic concept album – was met with disdain by the artist.

"I don't believe in time travel, I think the idea is silly," he told *Enough* magazine in 2001. "The past has already happened and the future doesn't exist. If you believe otherwise then you must also believe that you cannot change anything in your life because it has already happened in the future and your life is nothing more than a pre-ordained play and you are dancing through time like some kind of a stupid fucking puppet with no control over anything. Also it negates the concept of laws and punishment for criminals because they cannot help themselves because it is all pre-ordained, their future is fixed just the same as their past is and they had no choice anyway. If you think about it, the concept of time travel makes the future into the past. The past has happened, but so, according to this idea, has the future, otherwise you couldn't travel into it. So there is no future, only another kind of past you haven't seen yet. Stupid isn't it?"

Luckily, the idea of a concept album had not been totally serious or intended. Though the cover art matched the majority of themes in the songs, and with an updated Eddie to boot, it wasn't as if the package was all about revisiting the past or indeed travelling to the future. Yet expanding on the tacky '80s themes of many movies, Maiden posed with futuristic *Star Wars* type vehicles for the inner sleeve photos, standing alongside the machine used for the 1982 *Blade Runner* movie starring Harrison Ford. "These machines are in Hollywood. And these are no studio pictures. We had to endure a temperature of 50°C for this photo session," said Bruce. Looking at the pictures one suddenly begins to empathise. It's no surprise the skies were completely cloudless.

Somewhere In Time was released in October 1986 and became the first Maiden album to sell more than two million copies in America. It also reached number three in the British charts. Initially at least, everyone felt the band had delivered the goods. As time has passed there are some who refer to the '86 opus as being one of the weaker Maiden releases, perhaps due to the perceived commercialism of some of the songs. There are also a couple of tracks, 'The Loneliness Of The Long Distance Runner' and 'Sea Of Madness' for instance, where the style was criticised for being 'a little stodgy', with some aspects sounding quite unlike the quintessential Iron Maiden. Yet, as previously stated, the true fans of the band see *Somewhere In Time* as a diverse batch of songs, with the only drawback being no Bruce Dickinson material. The album rates as one of the cult features of the Maiden catalogue, and, as the members often acknowledge in interviews, it takes a few listens to really begin to understand and enjoy the music. Twenty years on, *Somewhere In Time* still provides enjoyment and every so often there seems to be something the listener hasn't heard the other 100 times they listened to it. Ultimately, the music speaks for itself.

THE PAINTING

Derek Riggs' cover art for *Somewhere In Time* was his most elaborate Iron Maiden creation to date. "He spent three months designing and painting this illustration" Steve Harris explained, "that depicts a very futuristic Eddie, *Blade Runner*-style, in the middle of a place where you can find plenty of details related to the band's history. It's a real feast for the eyes, I think."

Best viewed in LP sized format, as opposed to the rather inferior, diminutive recreation for CD purposes, the futuristic nature of the sleeve, along with the many hidden extras Riggs became fond of including, makes the cover a favourite with many Maiden fans. For all those who have never seen the vinyl version, as well as for those who are familiar, but want a solid reference, the following is a list of all the writings, scribbles and doodles to be found in the painting.

• "This is a very boring painting" - backwards message just behind Eddie's right leg.
• Ruskin Arms reference.
• The clock reads 23:58 (2 Minutes To Midnight).
• West Ham 7 Arsenal 3 – to be found to the top left of the cartoon versions of the band members. (A fictional football score in favour of Harris' beloved Hammers).
• Aces High bar, complete with a spitfire flying above.
• *Live After Death, Blade Runner* on at the movie theatre.
• The movie theatre is the Philip K. Dick cinema, who is the author of *Do Androids Dream Of Electric Sheep?* on which the movie *Blade Runner* is based.
• Marquee Club.
• Phantom Opera House (a reference to 'Phantom Of The Opera')
• "Bollocks again and again" under Phantom Opera House. This is likely to be a reference to the hidden "Bollocks" message on the *Powerslave* cover.
• Ancient Mariner Seafood Restaurant (a reference to 'Rime Of The Ancient Mariner').
• Herbert Ails on the overpass (probably a reference to Frank Herbert, author of *Dune*, who wouldn't allow Maiden to use it as a song title).
• "Tonight GYPSY'S KISS", under the 23:58 sign – a reference to Steve Harris' first band.

• Hammerjacks – a reference to one of the band's favourite bars in the US, Hammerjacks Night Club in Baltimore, MD. The Night Club closed on Jan 1st 1994, though the concert hall is still open.

• Long Beach Arena.

• Nicko is dressed in old-time flight goggles (a reference to his being a pilot).

• Nicko is also wearing a shirt saying: "Iron What?"

• On the back cover Icarus is falling from the Sun with burning wings in the top right corner, in front of the Bradbury Hotel. (A reference to 'The Flight Of Icarus').

• The "Bradbury Hotels International" sign – quite possibly a reference to the popular futuristic author Ray Bradbury (author of such works as *The Martian Chronicles*, *Ice Nine* etc.)

• If you look closely, you can see the shadow of the reaper on the back cover in front of the pyramids.

• The pyramids refer to the *Powerslave* cover art.

• "Maggies revenge" on the back cover refers to Margaret Thatcher.

• The street Eddie is standing on is Acacia Avenue, a reference, of course, to 'Charlotte the Harlot' and '22 Acacia Avenue', the Charlotte series. (You can see this above the Iron Maiden poster on the extreme right side).

• In one of the windows on Acacia Avenue, you can see a girl (supposedly Charlotte the Harlot herself) sitting in a chair.

• Bruce Dickinson is holding a brain, a reference to the inner sleeve of *Piece Of Mind*.

• Tehe's bar is where the band found the backup singers for the sing-a-long part in 'Heaven Can Wait.'

• Batman standing under Tehe's bar sign.

• The Tardis from *Dr. Who* is above the Rainbow Club sign.

• Asimov Foundation Building in the background.

• Tyrell Corp. right above the causeway (the replicant manufacturer in *Blade Runner*).

• Eye of Horus above Webster sign to left of Eddie's gun.

• One of Eddie's eyes is actually a 'laser'. This probably comes from the '2 Minutes To Midnight' single artwork. (On that sleeve he had a Pirate's eye-patch).

• There is a litter box right under Eddie's left leg attached to the lamppost. This is exactly the same as the litter box attached to the lamppost on the *Iron Maiden* debut album, to the left of Eddie next to the wall.

[1]. A quote used by Iron Maiden on the front of the *Live After Death* cover came from H.P. Lovecraft and reads, "That is not dead, which can eternal lie. Yet with strange aeons, even death may die." It was perhaps no coincidence that a year after the live album, Metallica paraphrased this very quote in their song, 'The Thing That Should Not Be' from *Master Of Puppets*. Their lyric read, "Not dead which eternal lie, Stranger eons death may die."

Sources:

Nelly Saupiquet, Marc of Hard Rock Magazine (France) – Numéro 6, 21, 26
Pierre Thiollay of Enfer Magazine (France) – Numéro 42
Iron Maiden Somewhere On Tour Programme
Mick Wall Programme Interview
www.ironmaiden.com
www.maidenfans.com
Enough Magazine 2001

Chapter 9
Seven Deadly Sins

"I would say 1986-88 was where all the members were getting on the best and all pulling in the same direction. Everything came together and the band were almost a single entity musically, both on stage and in the studio. The stage production was phenomenal. I think their powers were at their height, everyone was pulling in the same direction and the band's popularity was at an all time high, culminating with setting the record crowd at Donington in 1988." Keith Wilfort

Where *Somewhere In Time* had been almost exclusively the brain-child of Steve Harris, along with a significant contribution from Adrian Smith, Iron Maiden's next album would see a greater unity in the song-writing department. *Somewhere...* had been a successful record, propelling the outfit to lofty heights in the United States, yet when the dust had settled and fans had time to analyse its ingredients, many felt it was poorer for the lack of any Bruce Dickinson penned material.

The singer explained his reduced involvement on the 1986 opus in this way; "The more I look at it now, the more it was like a conscious reaction, like your brain throwing a temper-tantrum saying, 'I'm not going to write any more of this stuff! I hate it! Look what it's done to me! Why can't I stick my finger in my ear and go and be a folkie and drink beer like everybody else?' I was very messed up in the brain department at the time. I was talking to Steve about it and even he had a lot of head problems after the *Powerslave* tour, and nobody had really resolved them by the time we came to do *Somewhere In Time*. I think I came to terms with it more after we'd done the album. We had quite a long gap and then went out and did the tour – which still ended up being two months longer than it was supposed to be, of course! But this year I'm feeling in much better shape. I'm much happier being a singer again."

Dickinson knew whilst being the front man he also had the additional responsibility of participating in the song-writing process. When Bruce wasn't up to it, Steve Harris had little trouble taking on the mantle himself and there was always the clever commercial craft available from Adrian Smith. Yet, since Dickinson's arrival in the Maiden camp, many felt the group worked best when he was contributing suggestions for melodies, riffs and lyrics. An underrated guitar player, the vocalist had a multitude of ideas regarding not only Iron Maiden, but also his own work, which would come to fruition from the early nineties onwards.

Bruce enjoyed working with Adrian Smith perhaps best of all and, to the relief of both, they were now able to write together again, penning along with Steve Harris, the two most instantly enjoyable compositions of Maiden's 1988 album; 'Can I Play With Madness' and 'The Evil That Men Do'. The LP was titled *Seventh Son Of A Seventh Son* and recording was certainly far more relaxed than their previous experiences. As Bruce Dickinson testifies, "Instead of looking at it like Lego bricks – this bit goes here and that bit goes there – it was just getting the feeling right that made it work. Whereas before I think we tended to plan everything out a lot, on the new album we sort of loosened up a bit and that made all the difference. There's a lot more experimentation and, although it's obviously Iron Maiden, it's quite distinctly different from anything we've ever done before."

The album had been written at Steve's house, in a converted barn in rural Essex. The band were collectively happy with both the sound of the studio and the environment but it didn't seem to effect morale too much when they were obliged to record the material on a sojourn in Munich for tax reasons.

"You shouldn't feel obliged to write songs, you should feel enthusiastic about it," said Bruce of his rediscovered penchant for composition. "We had the freedom to relax and experiment. We banned Rod Smallwood from rehearsals. Nobody was allowed to listen to anything before the album was mixed. We made precisely the album we wanted, no more, no less. With no interference from anybody."

By Christmas 1987 the work had been completed though the members could not return home, as they would then have forfeited the benefits otherwise available by taking the tax break out of the country in the first place.

Though Bruce Dickinson and Adrian Smith were in part responsible for the direction of the new material, it was Steve Harris who laid down the ground rules, albeit loosely. The album was to be based on a remote concept, initially emerging from some indirect musings. As Harris explains, "It was our seventh studio album and I didn't have a title for it, or any ideas at all. Then I read the story of the *Seventh Son of a Seventh Son*, this mythical figure that was supposed to have all these paranormal gifts like second-sight and what have you. And it was more, at first, that it was just a good title for the seventh album. When I told Bruce about it he said,

'Wow! That's brilliant! Why don't we try and write a whole album about it, something you can really get your teeth into'."

There were two catalysts for the general theme of the album. First and foremost was the story that Steve had read. Orson Scott Card was the author of the work, *Seventh Son* that was part of a fantasy novel series. The concept is based on a child who is indeed the seventh born son, a mythical child possessing clairvoyant powers. In Card's tale, magic and folklore prevail over science.

"The idea for 'The Clairvoyant' and then the idea behind the album came to me when Doris Stokes died", explained Steve Harris, referring to one of the LP's obvious focal points [1]. "It's just an interesting thought, if she could foresee her own death… from that it led to the legend of the seventh son of a seventh son, which is tied in with the power of clairvoyance."

A concept album was difficult to tackle, and it came at a crucial point in the Maiden timeline. Had the material been below par and the subject more open to ridicule, the whole project could have brought the band crashing down. However, despite reservations amongst certain members of the group, Harris gritted his teeth and decided to go full throttle on the concept. It was Adrian Smith who felt more than slightly unnerved at the prospect of being compared to the types of '70s progressive rock acts who had baffled press and fans alike with overblown, pretentious and grandiose musings. As the guitarist sensibly opined, "It was always in the back of my mind that the songs should be able to stand up on their own if you took them away from the rest."

Thanks to Dickinson and Smith's involvement this was a must for any Maiden opus, where songs are themed and appear in a natural order yet can quite easily be enjoyed out of context. The tracks released as singles are all crucial to the idea behind the record and storyline, yet manage to hold up as straight-ahead rock songs when played individually.

Equally, where many outfits would over analyse the concept album proposal and create something overlong for the sake of it, Maiden kept the basis of the LP short and relatively snappy. The record clocks in at under forty-five minutes and was actually their shortest since *The Number Of The Beast*. The premise of *Seventh Son Of A Seventh Son* was more complicated than the finished product and Harris and co. did a fine job of splitting the basic foundation into eight snippets that were not too complex or difficult to comprehend.

If the overall feel of the album is relatively straightforward, then so too were the recording conditions. The members were in the groove to the extent that the first song on the album, 'Moonchild' was recorded in just one take. This opener is a perfect beginning to a thorough and well-assembled throng of songs. The track, written by Dickinson and Smith, is a dark ride through history. Long interested in mythology and magic, Bruce had no trouble in adapting a famous cult work. Ceremonial magician and writer Aleister Crowley's most famous novel was the source for the track's title and Dickinson cleverly takes the basis of 'Liber Samekh', a piece by Crowley (this is sometimes referred to as the 'Preliminary Invocation of the Goetia' or 'The Barbarous Names of Evocation'), transforming it into lyrics.

The original Crowley text contains lines such as 'Thee I invoke, the Bornless One', which Dickinson converts, in 'Moonchild', to "I am he the bornless one" – the first line of the song.

As usual with much of Iron Maiden's work, the inspirations were wide and varied for a record that purported to be of one concept. Though the general idea was adhered to, there were many references from other literary works as well as personal demons throughout the lyrics on the album.

'The Evil That Men Do' certainly integrates within the overall theme perfectly but its origin is Shakespearian. Taken from 'Julius Caesar', the quote comes from Mark Antony's soliloquy where he utters the immortal words; "The evil that men do lives on after them, but the good is oft interred with their bones."

'Can I Play With Madness' equally conjures up demonic pictures but is simply a mischievous tamper with an earlier title. Bruce Dickinson suggested an acoustic track Adrian had been working on, 'On The Wings Of Eagles,' be adapted into something heavier and given a new label. Smith was quick to pass on the credit saying, "I must admit, it did sound better that way."

The first single to be lifted from the album showcases a commercial side to Maiden's armoury and it is all the more impressive – given its multitude of ideas and rewrites – that it somehow combined to create a flowing tune. "The single's a real collaborative effort," said Bruce with some understatement. "The beginning bit, the riff – with apologies to Pete Townsend! – was me on acoustic guitar at home. Then Adrian came along with some chords and I went, 'Hang on a minute, I've got some words here that fit', so we sat around and worked on it. And I said, 'Can I write an instrumental bit in the middle?' – because I normally don't write bits like that since I don't have to play them – and Steve came in with the time-change bit, the Zeppelin-y bit, and we had a tremendous argument with

Nicko saying, 'Oh it won't work it's too radical'. And I thought, 'no it will work, so long as everyone takes the plunge and does it'."

As is often the case, Bruce was right and 'Can I Play With Madness' would provide a contrast to the first two much weightier tracks. The second of these, 'Infinite Dreams', was the subject of long standing problems for the Iron Maiden bassist. "Steve's songs tend to be about dreams, nightmares and obsessions because he has a lot of those," explained Bruce. "He's a terrible sleeper. He writes a lot of songs about out of body experiences, which he has more of than he likes to admit. I think he has a bit of a problem with that, he's quite frightened of it. He never tells anyone about his nightmares, he doesn't like to go into it, but obviously that's why a lot of his songs follow those themes. For me it's interesting to work with someone who has that sort of imagination, it's that that makes it worth staying in the band."

As Harris would concede, "I do have nightmares, but usually only when we're writing an album. Then your mind just gets so overactive with all these ideas flying about inside that it's difficult to sleep. That's what 'Infinite Dreams' is about."

The challenge for this song (a future single) was to keep it easily digestible for the casual listener as much as the intense devotee. One of Maiden's most ambitious numbers, it begins with a virtual soft rock verse, but builds up into an avalanche of riffs, with Dickinson enunciating a string of difficult lyrics perfectly. The track is different for Iron Maiden and though dark in subject matter and feel, is a form of power ballad, which perhaps explains the choice of the song as a single.

The most complex material on the album emanated from Steve Harris, with the bass player taking sole credit for 'Infinite Dreams', 'The Clairvoyant' and the centrepiece of the album, the just under ten-minute outpouring of psychic energy that is the title track. While fairly straightforward in its chorus structure, the inclusion of keyboards certainly adds atmosphere to a band that were frequently low on anything considered superfluous to guitar, bass and drums. Though the keyboard 'synths' were crudely played, (whoever had a spare finger at the time according to Bruce) the final product could not have been more perfectly formed. The numerous layered harmonies and effects are best enjoyed on headphones, such is the grandiosity of the construction, and credit must certainly go to long time producer Martin Birch for placing a myriad of ideas into one flowing semblance of a rock record. Indeed such is the perfect sheen of the material, that unless those involved with recording had been honest in explaining how crude their methods could be, few would have suspected the choral backings in the title track to have emerged from a synthesiser.

The album climaxes with a crushing number entitled 'Only The Good Die Young'. Though there was already a well-known song of the same name by Billy Joel based on the famous saying, Iron Maiden's version is significantly heavier both on guitar and demons. Starting with the line, "The demon in your mind will rape you in your bed at night", the lyrics once again reference the nightmares of Steve Harris, flawlessly immortalised by the pen of Bruce Dickinson.

Where the conceptual theme also excels is in the striking cover art of regular Maiden artist, Derek Riggs. Here he creates an unusual iced landscape, quite literally chilling to observe. Though the front cover is outstanding, it is perhaps the back that best represents Iron Maiden. With a clever array of iced Eddies throughout Maiden's career sculpted for posterity, this is clearly no ordinary piece of art, perfectly representing an astonishing crop of music.

"What we wanted to try and capture was a Salvador Dali feeling", explained Steve of the cover art. "Derek loves all that. We wanted something weird. It reminds me of some of the early Genesis covers, and I am very pleased with it."

Seventh Son Of A Seventh Son was released on 11th April 1988 and was quickly lauded in Britain. Not only was 'Can I Play With Madness' a surprising hit single (reaching number three in the UK charts) but Maiden managed to appease their legions of fans, even those who had been disappointed with *Somewhere In Time* and longed for a 'return to form'.

Few would argue with *Seventh Son Of A Seventh Son* being placed at the higher end of the Maiden archives and for many fans it remains their favourite Maiden LP to this day. Whether it is down to the conceptual nature of the album or simply the great music, many believed this line-up of the group hit its peak in 1988.

It seemed however, that America was slow to react to the record and indeed in some quarters *Seventh Son...* received a 'thumbs down'. Steve Harris was incredulous; "I thought it was the best album we did since *Piece Of Mind*. I loved it because it was more progressive. I thought the keyboards fitted in brilliantly, because that's the influences I grew up with." It was the inclusion of synthesisers that turned the heads of many American fans, the suggestion being that Maiden had gone soft. "I was so pissed off with the Americans", ranted the bassist. "They didn't really seem to accept it. *Somewhere In Time* had done far better. But you can't just go by album sales: they might buy the album and not like it, and maybe some of the Americans that bought *Somewhere In Time* didn't like it and so didn't buy the next album. I don't know. Who knows what the reason was, but it didn't do as well in America and I just couldn't understand it."

Though Harris was clearly upfront with his disappointment, the sales were more of a blip than a serious setback. Where *Somewhere In Time* had sold to two million American buyers, the '88 follow up dropped to 1.2 million units – still enough to see Maiden pick up their sixth Platinum album in a row. Though Steve was unsurprisingly pleased with another million-plus selling record, his annoyance stemmed more from the implication that the American fans just didn't seem to 'get it'. As he summed up; "Everyone said afterwards it was a very European sounding album. To me it's just a Maiden-sounding album. And I thought, 'Well if you don't like it, bollocks. I don't care!' There is no other way of looking at it. I remember thinking, 'Fucking Americans, they just don't fucking understand us.'"

1989 would mostly be remembered as a year off for Iron Maiden whereby they restored their creative juices and relaxed after an intensive tour. As ever though, Steve Harris could not completely switch off from his band duties. He had been viewing all the footage from Maiden's UK shows at the tail end of 1988, and settled upon using their two-night stint at the Birmingham N.E.C. Arena for an upcoming video release. Titled *Maiden England*, the VHS compilation would be a visual record highlighting the band's career to date.

Not since the World Slavery tour had Maiden looked this good. They were able to combine the classics of their repertoire with a selection of tracks from their current album, songs which were already treated as prime Iron Maiden by many fans. The likes of 'Can I Play With Madness,' 'The Clairvoyant' and a sterling rendition of 'Seventh Son Of A Seventh Son' sat easily alongside such live set regulars as 'The Number Of The Beast,' 'Hallowed Be Thy Name' and 'Iron Maiden.' The set really shone with the inclusion of tracks Maiden rarely performed – and likewise, songs that had not appeared on *Live After Death*. There were spaces for 'The Prisoner,' 'Die With Your Boots On' and an appearance of 'Still Life.'

But by 1990 Iron Maiden were ready to follow up the immensely successful *Seventh Son Of A Seventh Son* album and its accompanying tour. It was certainly not going to be easy to top or even equal the quality and the sheer sales of the *Seventh Son...* record and they would also have to contend with a remarkable year for heavy metal and its more aggressive sub-genres.

As a decade turned, so too did the alternative music fan's tastes. Where regular heavy metal had once been the marker for rebellion, it was now overtaken by the artistic funk metal of Faith No More (who released *The Real Thing* in 1990) as well as the thrash metal genre, which counted multi-million selling acts such as Megadeth (*Rust In Peace*) and Slayer (*Seasons In The Abyss*) among its number.

1990 would see new albums from all the aforementioned bands, as well as Testament (*Souls Of Black*), Anthrax (*Persistence Of Time*) and Celtic Frost (*Vanity/Nemesis*). Only Queensryche and Judas Priest were close to the collective age of the Iron Maiden members and both released highlight albums of their career with *Empire* and *Painkiller* respectively. However one older band who could always be relied upon was AC/DC and they cemented their place at the top of the tree with a rousing set titled *The Razors Edge*.

The beginning of the nineties was perhaps the strongest era for British rock bands since the NWOBHM first hit its peak. Not since that well publicised movement's emergence had there been so many groups releasing such high quality albums. From a hard rock and metal perspective the likes of Little Angels, Quireboys, Thunder, Almighty, Atom Seed, Gun, Wolfsbane, Xentrix and the rejuvenated Whitesnake all contributed to a mammoth year for home grown rock talent. Then there were the mainstays of the British rock and metal scene, Led Zeppelin, Def Leppard and of course Maiden. Each of these would hit the heavy music charts with albums from their past as new fans were discovering their supposed 'dinosaur' charms all the time.

1990 was a time for camaraderie between the British bands. In Maiden's case this meant choosing a British band to support them wherever possible and 1990 belonged to Wolfsbane (see the Tour section). The Donington Festival that year was indicative of this, with three British acts propping up the bill. Alongside the hair metal attraction of Poison and the dependable Aerosmith were Thunder, Quireboys and headliners Whitesnake. Thunder was enjoying a baptism of fire within the rock scene, having hit the racks with the awesome LP, *Backstreet Symphony*. For once, Britain could lay claim to a new hard rock group that did not rely on mimicking the L.A. hordes by pretending to be something they weren't. Instead, the vocalist Danny Bowes and guitarist Luke Morley were the front pairing for what, essentially, was a hard rock and blues outfit. Quireboys were slightly luckier in their fortunes, though in comparison were arguably the weaker of the two bands. Nevertheless they enjoyed a festival where they followed Thunder. Fronted by the gruff Geordie Spike, this band would manage to stave off the critics who inevitably followed, building up a loyal fanbase for their heavy honky-tonk blues-rock approach.

And then there was Whitesnake, the Granddaddy of them all. With the capture of guitar whiz extraordinaire, Steve Vai, the band's *Slip Of The Tongue* album carried an authoritative American edge, despite front man David Coverdale hailing from North-East England. With the likes of 'Now You're Gone,' Whitesnake flooded charts the world over and conquered America, not for the first time. But they were still known as a British band and they capped off a tremendous run of success with a riotous Donington performance of which Coverdale said, "It's great to be fucking 'ome," from the stage, as the night time air drifted across a crowd nearing the 100,000 mark.

Though the rock charts were dominated by the old warhorses of the business (with even reissued Jimi Hendrix works climbing the tree) there were still new bands breaking through from all corners of the United States. Therefore alongside veteran hard rockers Bon Jovi and Aerosmith, stood new albums by fledgling acts Skid Row, Dan Reed Network, Salty Dog, Pretty Boy Floyd and Vain.

However, the beginning of the '90s would see a whole new era of success for heavier, faster bands and in some people's eyes this would signal the end for outfits considered to be veterans, or as they were more negatively referred to, 'dinosaurs'. It seems ridiculous for a band, whose members were hardly into their mid-thirties, to be considered ancient, yet this is typical of the kind of typecasting issued by the music press. Like athletes musicians are considered to be at their peak at some point around the mid-twenties mark, taken seriously up to about 28 or 29, and assumed to have nothing more to offer once beyond this unwritten marker for quality.

Only certain selected groups could avoid being written-off in this way – namely those considered to have produced consistently decent albums 20 years into their career. The list, when viewed objectively is arguably short. And it is a matter of opinion as to whether veteran groups like The Rolling Stones or The Who are capable of writing music to equal their classic eras today. Moving into hard rock and metal territory, precious few worthy bands have managed to carry their impetus and stature into their latter years. For some reason, the hunger seems to dissipate, the quality is compromised and song-writing tends to fall markedly short of classic, once a set of individuals reach a certain age.

However, in the case of Iron Maiden, the members had weathered an internal storm and emerged stronger, with a fantastic album to show for the experience. Since Bruce had not contributed to *Somewhere In Time*, there had been careful consideration as to whether he could really do his job in the band any longer. Yet the singer had proved not only that he could front the material with tasteful aplomb, but also that he could return from the brink to co-write four incredible songs on *Seventh Son*....

Bruce was clearly back in the groove and loving every minute of being in Iron Maiden. He was even allowed to write a solo record on the side, thereby giving vent to the creativity that had seen him write material considered unsuitable for Maiden. (See Chapter 16 for an in depth study of Bruce's solo career). It was therefore a refreshed and chirpy 'Brucey' who returned to the heavy metal fold for the business of creating Maiden's eighth studio album. In reality they had nothing to prove. They had single-handedly revived the heavy metal genre time and again with their studio output and had clearly defined the art of the live rock album. Maiden were still at the top of their game and it should not be forgotten that despite their 'advancing years' they buzzed with an unflinching energy many half their age would have struggled to match.

Only for their up-coming record there would be one member who was not firing on all cylinders and it was noticeable.

COUNT THIS!

Seventh Son Of A Seventh Son was the first time Maiden openly used keyboards, and this time they used a bona fide professional player. An American, Michael Kenny, had been with the band for a while, working as Steve's bass technician from 1980.

"I think the thing I like most of all about working with these guys is their sense of humour," says Michael. "I remember one of the early tours I did with Maiden, it might have been the *Killers* tour, I can't remember exactly. We dubbed it the Heads Will Roll tour, because everybody was constantly getting sacked... When you saw people in the morning you didn't say 'hello, good morning', you said, 'what the hell are you still doing here? I sacked you last night!' I ended up getting fired about half a dozen times myself, but each time it happened I would say, 'Do you mean it? Can I really go home?' and Clive Burr would say 'no, you can't leave yet, you're too happy!' Eventually I think Steve officially sentenced me to life plus twenty years that I have to serve with Iron Maiden... I've been here ever since."

[1] Doris Stokes was a famous medium and psychic. Before undergoing an operation to remove a brain tumour she claimed a disembodied voice said to her, 'Your time on earth is over, it is time for your life in the spirit world to begin.' Shortly after the operation she passed away.

Chapter 10
Dare To Fail

"It was this total belief from both sides that really attracted me to Maiden in the first place – I remember feeling it when I used to go and watch the band as a fan. There is a total understanding that there is no compromise. There's never been a deviation from the band's direction and Maiden have always done what they believe in." Janick Gers

Feeling detached from heavy metal, Adrian Smith had, in his own mind at least, come to the end of his tenure with Iron Maiden. He believed that with *Somewhere In Time* Maiden had been moving in the right direction, since the melodic aspect was always the most pleasing factor for the guitarist. Bruce Dickinson's lack of involvement in the writing of *Somewhere...*had left a void in the band's sound that was filled by the more 'commercial' efforts of 'Wasted Years' and 'Heaven Can Wait.' Now, with the front man returning to creative duties on *Seventh Son...*, Smith felt somewhat dismayed by the band's return to the heavier reaches of rock.

In short, he had become disenchanted with life in a heavy metal act. Smith certainly wanted to exercise his creative flare with a solo project, although his attitude did not display the same level of detachment as his vocalist. Where Bruce could run off and mark his own material with the label 'solo', it was more a case of 'all or nothing' for Smith. Not only was he unhappy, the band had also picked up on his lack of enthusiasm and it was mutually decided that the best thing to do was for Adrian to leave the band.

He would release an album titled *Silver & Gold* under the banner A.S.A.P. (Adrian Smith And Project). Listening to the material on the record it is easy to see how Smith had become disillusioned with metal, for A.S.A.P. was clearly in the AOR vein. Unfortunately it seemed the Maiden fans were not ready to embrace such 'soft' rock, and the album died a commercial death, despite having a fair amount of promotion behind it.

For Smith's replacement the band turned to one Janick Gers, who had known the members for a long time anyway, and had previously been roped in to play on Bruce's *Tattooed Millionaire* solo debut. As Gers explained to *Metal Rules*, "I was playing football with Fish and he asked me to come to the gig to watch him and he ran me out and said he was looking for a player and I said okay. So, I got that gig and Bruce was doing that same gig as well and we met again in a few years and basically we hadn't seen each other in a long time. I was recording a Bowie track 'All the Young Dudes'. Tony Hadley from Spandau Ballet was originally supposed to sing the song, but he got sick in the last minute, so Bruce sang it. That's how we got together. The rest is pretty much history..."

The credit has to go to Bruce for bringing in a guitarist who at that point had been considering finishing his music career for good. By 1989 Janick was nearer to the point of selling his gear than playing in a multi-million selling rock band, but Bruce made sure Gers would get his due. When the singer was approached by Rod Smallwood to compose a song for the soundtrack to the movie *Nightmare On Elm Street 5*, he knew exactly who to bring in for the guitar parts. And the song would be pertinent to Iron Maiden the band not just Dickinson. 'Bring Your Daughter To The Slaughter' was a track Bruce admitted came out of nowhere and took him just three minutes to write. The singer told Mick Wall that EMI partners, Zomba, "went absolutely mad. They were like, 'this is fucking great!' The guy called up the office and says, 'I can't believe this, have you got any more stuff like this?' and I went, 'well, yeah, there's a few things kicking about.' Lying through my teeth again, I said, 'look, how about if we do an album?' He said, 'fuck it, yeah all right.' So I called up Jan, and said, 'you definitely can't sell your gear now, you bastard, we're making an album!'"

Bruce and Janick did indeed go on to work with each other on the well-received *Tattooed Millionaire* album, but ironically the song which brought Bruce and Janick together again was the one track Steve wanted for Maiden. He told Bruce it was, "a song that would be great for Maiden." Steve had thought Bruce would be more than pleased at having a song he wrote for a solo album snatched back by his full time outfit. However, according to Bruce, the original version of 'Bring Your Daughter...' (which only appeared on the American version of the *Nightmare On Elm Street 5* soundtrack) was significantly different to the eventual Iron Maiden take. "The arrangement is identical," Bruce commented, "but mine's kind of slinky. Maiden's just really goes for it, but I was happy that Steve liked something that much. In actual fact I wandered back into Maiden to start the album a very happy-go-lucky little leprechaun. So there was no intention of leaving whatsoever at that stage. If anything, the joy of doing my own album had made me sure I was happy where I was."

"My old band White Spirit and Samson were often playing in the same kind of places," Janick would say of his union with the Air Raid Siren. "We both came from the same genres and we had the same kind of backgrounds." Indeed Gers had been a long-standing guitarist who would forever be synonymous with the NWOBHM. From 1975 to 1981 he played for White Spirit, a band from his native North East. Born in Hartlepool on January 27th 1957, Janick Robert Gers grew up with Deep Purple legend Ritchie Blackmore as his predominant guitar influence, so it was no surprise that White Spirit was something of a tribute outfit, with Malcolm Pearson's keyboard playing highly reminiscent of Purple's Jon Lord. The band was quite successful in the UK, getting decent support slots with the likes of Budgie and Girl, and ironically they even supported Iron Maiden, which was where Gers and the other Maiden members had first met.

White Spirit secured a slot at the Reading Festival and soon their self-titled debut album was released. The Deep Purple comparison was natural, given the direction of 'Don't Be Fooled', 'No Reprieve' and 'Midnight Chaser,' but WS did give the material their own stamp and in the grand scheme of things, were a prominent addition to the NWOBHM scene, even holding a prestigious slot on the notorious Neat label. The departure of Janick Gers threw the White Spirit line-up into confusion and they didn't last much longer once he joined up with none other than Ian Gillan. The former Deep Purple vocalist admired the White Spirit style, which was unashamedly rooted in Purple worship, and specifically Janick's hi-octane axe-tickling style. Gers played with Gillan for a year and a half before the singer decided to drop his solo career in favour of rejoining Deep Purple. This was to come sometime later in 1984, before which Gillan fronted Black Sabbath for their *Born Again* album.

By the time of the Purple reunion, Janick Gers was in limbo, where he remained until 1985 when a chance meeting with Jonathan King led to Gogmagog, a band eventually remembered for what they *didn't* achieve rather than what they *did*. In fact, the project was a warning to other bands of their ilk, and the warning read: don't be anything other than yourself or you will come unstuck.

"That was a great thing," Janick would later reminisce of the project, with a somewhat melancholy air. "I got a phone call from Jonathan King who assembled that thing around 1985. He liked my blues style kind of playing and... he wanted me to join the band with Neil Murray, Clive Burr, Paul Di'Anno and Pete Willis. So we got together and we did a session, which we recorded. We put it out and it was quite a good fun thing actually."

It may have been fun on the inside, for a time at least, but Paul Di'Anno for one would never talk about the project again once it all fell down around their ears. In fact he gave the impression of feeling embarrassed about the whole affair and that his involvement had almost harmed his reputation.

The shenanigans started when King (a publicity guru and Radio DJ) saw the NWOBHM as a potential vehicle for making lots of cash. Of course it was cash he saw for himself in the future, but he also turned on the charm and managed to assemble a group who were by now well-experienced musicians. Most importantly they had all been in big bands and for one reason or another, now found themselves seeking new ventures of equal stature. There was Clive Burr and Paul Di'Anno who had of course been ousted from Iron Maiden. Janick Gers had seen his shot at the big time apparently vanquish after Ian Gillan reverted to his former band. Pete Willis had been fired from early NWOBHM proponents Def Leppard for alcohol problems and he too thought his time had passed. Finally there was bass player Neil Murray who had been in Whitesnake and also played with Gary Moore. The collection of musicians could have been likened to footballers past their prime, who, with their career nearing its end, try to relive the glory years at a lesser team than they were remembered for – with, almost universally, dismal results. As in football, the feeling is always one of 'perhaps the boy still has the talent and the desire, maybe he can be successful again', and this may well have been true of the Gogmagog members. There is certainly nothing to say that just because they had lost high profile gigs that they weren't capable of stardom once again.

This was certainly true of Janick, in particular. Where Di'Anno, Burr and Willis had lost their respective jobs because of a lack of application or an unprofessional attitude, Gers was simply out of work due to bad luck, which was also the case for Neil Murray.

King's vision was to assemble a super-group and take full advantage of the NWOBHM moniker, by creating a band that adhered to the template associated with the movement. What was not instantly apparent was that the group of musos were not exactly first choice. King had initially sought The Who's John Entwistle as well as Rainbow and Whitesnake drummer Cozy Powell, all of whom turned him down (perhaps as a result of being a little older and wiser than the eventual recruits). Nevertheless, for his subsequent group, King had already founded the material which the band were to perform, co-writing the tracks with Russ Ballard, a renowned composer who knew exactly what it took to pen a rock hit.

Indeed, and perhaps as a consequence of having Ballard onboard, with his penchant for catchy pop-rock, the songs Gogmagog had to record were mostly bland and overtly pop. There was a cringe-worthy attempt at rebellion in the shape of the track, 'Living In A Fucking Time Warp.' And also the stupidly long titled 'It's Illegal, It's Immoral, It's Unhealthy, But It's Fun,' – words which could quite easily be applied to Jonathan King. In 2001 he was imprisoned after being found guilty of indecently assaulting 14 and 15-year-old boys, allegations that he denied.

However, it was sheer avarice, which halted the Gogmagog project before it ever really got off the ground. King insisted on a million dollar advance when approaching record companies who all, in no uncertain terms, told him where to go. Nevertheless the former Decca Records employee refused to quit, he simply dropped the advance request and was eventually accepted by Music For Nations, on their Food For Thought Imprint. Gogmagog's first 12" was called 'I Will Be There' and the title track was reminiscent of fellow NWOBHM luminaries Blazer Blazer in particular. The song also appeared on one of Russ Ballard's own recordings, his *Into The Fire* solo LP.

Perhaps predictably, the EP was not lapped up by a Gogmagog-hungry public. In fact the project was viewed with disdain by many fans who, in reality, had by now moved on from the NWOBHM. It was difficult not to be cynical about a super-group who were plying a style that had seen its best years some time earlier. Most of the bandwagon hoppers who were calling themselves NWOBHM came in the mid-eighties, desperately trying to cling to a genre that had already come and gone. So Gogmagog never stood a chance. Whether it was their ridiculous name, their misinformed and greedy manager, or simply their sub-standard soft rock, the project was a calamity as Pete Willis acknowledged, "I wasn't really sure what to do after Def Leppard but I had some really strange offers. Jonathan King enrolled me, Paul Di'Anno and Janick Gers to play on these songs. Frankly they were terrible. We all stood around in this studio for a day trying to make the best of it. The whole thing was pretty disastrous."

Luckily the Gogmagog project did not irreparably damage the careers of its members and most went on to better things. Neil Murray had a successful spell in Black Sabbath and also played with early 90s sensations Vow Wow while Pete Willis had spells with Roadhouse and Nightrun who were both moderately successful.

But the ex-member who fared best had to be Janick Gers and it was all thanks to Bruce Dickinson. Certainly Gers had the ability and the enthusiasm, and he was almost a full time member of Fish's band. The ex-Marillion singer's *Vigil In A Wilderness Of Mirrors* album, released in 1990, featured Janick playing guitar on 'View From A Hill', which he also co-wrote (along with 'Family Business'). The record was Fish's first after departing from the Marillion ranks and it was a very underrated collection of progressive, emotional rock.

Discussing Adrian Smith's departure, Steve Harris remarked, "When Adrian left, we met to think about his replacement and it was obvious to all of us who it should be. We've all known Janick for a number of years and we all get on great with the guy. He's a superb guitarist, lives and breathes heavy metal and has always been a fan of Iron Maiden's music." Indeed, the fact that Gers was a Maiden fan is what really contributed to his energetic performance for the band, as if, in some ways, he couldn't quite believe his luck. Understandable after years in the rock wilderness!

And it certainly didn't do any harm that the man from Hartlepool not only liked playing football but was a formidable goalkeeper. Unfortunately he had to knock the diving and finger-tipping on the head to protect his hands. As Steve elaborates, "Janick's a good 'keeper but we can't let him play in case he does his fingers in. He played in goal against a Maiden eleven once and had a blinding game, I nearly didn't give him the job because of that!"

Keith Wilfort describes Janick as a "consummate showman and talented guitarist, Janick like the rest is a good person and a pleasure to know. He was faced with replacing a Maiden stalwart but accepted the test and passed with flying colours. He has many of the characteristics shared by Rod. Loyal to his friends and family, dedicated to the job at hand and not one to suffer fools gladly. He's also a great companion to have on a pub-crawl!"

Gers admitted to being "shocked" when he heard Adrian had left the band. "My girlfriend said I was as white as a sheet when I got off the phone. She thought someone had died or something..."

The first song the new line-up practiced together was 'The Trooper' and Janick was not the only one to feel that the union just felt "right." The others agreed and they were silently all gunning for Gers when they ran through a couple of other numbers including 'Iron Maiden' and 'The Prisoner.' The rest of the band huddled together in the corner and then turned back to Janick telling him he had the job. The guitarist remembers the moment well; "Steve came over and said, 'you're in, and we start recording tomorrow'. I was like, 'what?!'"

THE ALBUM

"We were going to call it A Prayer For The Dying *but then we thought, 'well Eddie wouldn't give anyone a prayer' so we changed it."* Steve Harris

For their new album, *No Prayer For The Dying*, Iron Maiden would take a looser approach to recording and truly go for the 'live' sound that they had always tried to capture. Feeling they had previously failed to fully bring the excitement of their concerts to their studio work, the band decided to record in Steve Harris' mobile studio. This was conveniently situated next door to his Essex abode. When journalists insinuated that there might be certain distractions when working at home, Harris told them that that wasn't the case at all. "My house, the studio and that is almost separate anyway," he explained, "and since we've always rehearsed there we knew that there was a job to be done, and that there was a schedule for doing it. I always find it very easy to switch between my two roles – one as the musician on the road and in a band, and the other as a father and a family man. They are two different worlds and I don't let the two overlap."

Bruce Dickinson was a notable focus for the 1990 Maiden album. Having both exorcised his solo record demons with *Tattooed Millionaire* and returned to song writing with *Seventh Son Of A Seventh Son*, the vocalist was intent on making sure *No Prayer For The Dying* would be cut and thrust Maiden at its best. "This new record's got to be Maiden as good as ever before, savage, ripping your throat out sorta stuff," he commented. "*Somewhere In Time* was a notable low point for me on a personal level. Sometimes you can't see the wood for the trees. Then it was obvious that for years there was a concept album gestating in the band like a big turd waiting to drop out. With *Seventh Son Of A Seventh Son* we got that off our backs. This new album is going to be completely away from that."

In fact, *No Prayer...* would turn out to encapsulate Maiden's back catalogue pretty well. There are battle ready epics ('Mother Russia'), snappy and catchy numbers ('Holy Smoke', 'Bring Your Daughter To The Slaughter'), daring and somewhat eerie tracks ('The Assassin', 'Fates Warning') as well as heartfelt, emotional power ballads such as the title track – a style Maiden were always so adept at composing. This is undoubtedly one of the band's best songs ever, with a superb, emotive vocal line from Bruce.

The drawback with such a varied set of material was that the breadth of ideas offered little continuity for the record. Silly, upbeat songs like 'Hooks In You' and the first single from the album, 'Holy Smoke' are interspersed with the heart tearing seriousness of 'No Prayer For The Dying'. Of course this paradox was Maiden all over, and it invariably happened when the song writers changed from song to song, but still for some the album is a low point in the Maiden timeline. Perhaps this was down to the fact that the group had been assigned the task of following up one of their most successful albums to date, a job they would have found hard to do, whatever they composed.

The raw spirit the band wanted to capture certainly came across, despite now having enough money to make the most polished record possible. It was admirable that the now multi-millionaires literally wanted to go back to basics, their desire being to return to the sound of *Killers*, and one has to conclude that with this they managed it.

No Prayer For The Dying was nevertheless something of a wildcard Maiden recording. Those who love it *really* love it, yet for others it's a hit and miss album with some good songs but a few questionable ones too. Perhaps it is the absence of Adrian Smith material (he only managed one co-credit, on 'Hooks In You'), which upset the balance, though as always, Steve Harris delivered the goods and it is the songs credited to him alone that are the strongest.

A Dickinson/Harris track, 'Tailgunner', opens the album, which proves to be an excellent advert for the album and is the one song universally appreciated amongst the Maiden faithful. "The title came from a porno movie, about anal sex," explained Bruce quite contentiously, "then I thought, 'well I can't write the lyrics about that!' So I wrote it about real tailgunners. I had some words, which began 'Trace your way back fifty years, to the glow of Dresden, blood and tears.' I know we shouldn't mention the war but it's about the attitude of bombing people. It was real death in the skies back then. But there aren't any tailgunners on planes anymore. It's all done by computers, using missiles. At least it used to be man-on-man, but now it's machine-on-machine. Who uses bullets anymore?" Steve told *Metal Forces*; "Bruce said the intro reminded him of planes, and so working along that school of thought he had the lyrics written in an afternoon."

The song gave Bruce license to wax lyrical about his aircraft passion. Indeed, one line would confuse many a fan. *"Nail that fokker kill that son"* is pronounced with such gusto that it sounds more like 'fucker' than 'fokker' – and what is a fokker anyway? Anyone curious enough to find out would have discovered that the name comes from the Dutch Aircraft manufacturer, so named because of its founder, Anthony Fokker. Though the words are approached with no small helping of satire, the song's subject is actually a serious one, despite the potentially racist overtones (*"Cologne and Frankfurt have some more!"*) and with lyrics that could well have inspired those really entering war or combat.

One of the major talking points of the album however would be the first single, 'Holy Smoke,' (which had also initially been touted as a possible title for the LP). Without ignoring the fact that this was one of Maiden's catchiest songs of all time, with a supreme main riff, the subject matter was in fact to be the cause of most interest. The theme centres around television evangelists immortalised as *"Jimmy Reptile and all his friends."* The Jimmy Reptile character had actually been referenced previously in Bruce's novel *The Adventures Of Lord Iffy Boatrace* (see chapter 17): *"I have great pleasure in confirming your appointment as United Kingdom liaison officer for Jimmy Reptile Evangelism Incorporated."*

"I've got a book by Jimmy Swaggart at home, *Music: The New Pornography*, with a big picture of Steve on the front!" Bruce would say. "It was sent to me by a Bible-basher and a letter came with it, very sincere. She sent me a copy of the Holy Bible, which was good because I didn't have one and I needed one to research for some songs."

Swaggart was, along with Tipper Gore and her PMRC organisation, part of the religious right in America who were so appalled by heavy metal they sought to blame the music for crime, Satanism and Lord knows what else. It almost worked too. As part of the crackdown on 'unsuitable' lyrics for minors, Parental Advisory stickers were introduced. Yet, the real prize for the zealots was in gaining serious media exposure. Through this they could broadcast their religious views on prime time television whilst simultaneously denouncing heavy metal music, as well as rap. Maiden had faced this kind of shallow narrow-mindedness before however, and emerged victorious. The likes of Jimmy Swaggart were hardly likely to convert the youth to religion if they were talking to kids who lived and breathed heavy metal.

And as for free thinking adults, well they only had to delve into Swaggart's private life to see he was not all he seemed. A self-made man, he'd begun his career as a street corner evangelist and gradually, with the help of music and a clearly defined husky singing voice, built his evangelical empire. He was at the helm of a large group of religious musical artists and took his cut of all the royalties received by them as well as getting regular donations from those who believed in his mission. By the 1980s Swaggart was grossing $500,000 a day.

His first bugbear was pornography, which, he proclaimed, constituted a form of addiction and that it "represents the worst our great nation has to offer, the scum on an otherwise tranquil pond."

But Swaggart himself was caught leaving a cheap hotel with a prostitute in 1987. This, quite understandably, dented his credibility and his organisation began to disintegrate, despite his 'repenting' and asking for forgiveness on public television where he cried, "I have sinned!" Only he obviously had not learned his lesson as he was caught again with a prostitute in California sometime later. Further adding to his embarrassment was an article in *Penthouse* magazine featuring the prostitute herself, Debra Murphree. She claimed she had had this conversation with Swaggart; "He'd ask me if I'd ever let anyone screw my daughter when she was that young, and I said, 'No, she's only nine years old.' He asked me if she'd started developing or if she had any hair down there, saying, 'I can picture my cock going in and out of a pussy like that.'"

Of course, bands like Iron Maiden were the real problem! Their kind had to be stopped. Rather than let themselves take idiots like Swaggart too seriously, Maiden simply poked fun at the whole pretentious business of evangelism.

A rather low budget video was filmed to accompany the single, with the band frolicking in and around Steve's country house with a few mock preachers involved for good measure. "I must admit that it does capture the mood of the band right now," Steve said, "but it was not filmed to be used as a promo. Everyone knows that I'm interested in videos and that I also always have someone filming whatever we're up to. So, after watching all the stuff we'd collected since Janick joined, this just seemed like a good idea, to put something out that the fans can relate to, and laugh at, rather than a high budget impersonal, story boarded piece that everyone else seems to use.

"I think the *Maiden England* video was very representative of us live," Steve continued. "That is why that video is a faithful fan's eye view of a Maiden show, and then 'Holy Smoke' shows the human side of the band, it offers them something from 'behind the scenes' and it displays no pretensions."

It was great to see a predominantly serious band having such a laugh and a joke.

For the inner sleeve pictures however, the band were all business, pulling solemn faces in a smoke filled graveyard.

Creating songs such as the epic title track was indeed serious stuff, and 'No Prayer For The Dying' has to rate as one of Steve Harris' finest compositions. The epic song could rank alongside the likes of 'Hallowed Be Thy Name' and 'Children Of The Damned' with its gradually mounting crescendo. In the grand scheme of Maiden material this song seems to have been largely overlooked, hardly ever being played live, and never included on subsequent compilations. Perhaps Steve Harris did not receive many compliments about this particular track, whereas he seemed to be bowled over by the response to 'Bring Your Daughter To The Slaughter' that Bruce had composed. Really, comparing the two tracks is like comparing 'The Number Of The Beast' with 'Black Bart Blues' (the B-side to 'Can I Play With Madness').

Nevertheless, 'Bring Your Daughter To The Slaughter' was a song Steve insisted on being recorded for Maiden, halting Bruce's attempts to use the track for his solo album. The lyrics had to be suitably gruesome given this was a song for a horror film soundtrack, but it was still surprising to hear Bruce speak of the meaning behind the words. "Here I tried to sum up what I thought *Nightmare On Elm Street* movies are really about, and it's all about adolescent fear of period pains," he outrageously commented. "That's what I think it is – deep down. When a young girl first gets her period she bleeds and it happens at night, and so she is afraid to go to sleep and it's a very terrifying time for her, sexually as well, and *Nightmare On Elm Street* targets that fear. The real slaughter in the Freddie movies is when she loses her virginity. That is the rather nasty thought behind it all, but that's what makes those kind of movies frightening."

Quite remarkably – though it was admittedly a catchy number – 'Bring Your Daughter...' held the honour of being Iron Maiden's one and only number one single, which was understandably a source of pride for the band, despite their opposition to mainstream music. Radio 1 could not have been more blatant in their disgust at Maiden's place at the top of the UK charts and despite the song remaining there for three weeks, *Top Of The Pops* played only a minute of the video, where a top single usually received the 'honour' of either a full play of the video or a complete, lip-synched 'live' performance by the band on the show. Quite frankly, from Maiden's point of view, the likes of *Top Of The Pops* could screw themselves, they had never previously been responsible for the band's success and that wasn't about to change now. It was loyal fans who took 'Bring Your Daughter...' to number one, lapping up the myriad of different formats which were released all on the same day.

There are lyrical intricacies to be found in other tracks on the album too. Not least of these is the only song Dave Murray co-wrote (with Bruce), 'Public Enema Number One' – a typically stirring Maiden number. "It's actually about... green hypocrites," Bruce explained of the environmental subject matter. "It's about a big guy with his fast car, and he's leaving the city in a cloud of smoke leaving the children crying in fear. He's got a one-way ticket out of here. Fine, see ya. Because he can afford it, he's left everyone else behind and in the cities, there is overcrowding, guns and riots and it seems like everything is gonna snap. The politicians just lie to save their own skins, gamble that they are gonna do the right thing, and they give the press scapegoats all the time... California dreaming as the earth dies screaming! That's what it's about, people talking about the environment and not doing anything." This topic was at the forefront of the news in the early nineties, and other metal bands, specifically thrash acts, had also given their opinions through the medium of song. Perhaps one of the most famous tracks of this green-friendly era was Testament's 'Greenhouse Effect,' (released in 1989 on their *Practice What You Preach* album) which summed up the sentiments of numerous other bands who couldn't put it quite as eloquently as the Bay Area thrash veterans.

Where thrashers were obvious in their beliefs and their lyrics, Iron Maiden had always made their listener think a little bit more. In reading the words to 'Public Enema...' without Bruce's description, the casual observer might struggle to find a specific topic. This was Bruce's true strength as a lyricist, his amazing aptitude for story telling and his abundant imagination meant he could create a mini novel within many of his songs. Often he needed to clarify the meaning of his words simply because his thoughts were a few steps ahead of himself, let alone everybody else!

Another of these songs was 'Run Silent Run Deep' (again, this was mooted as a possible album title) which had a truly ridiculous source of inspiration that it's fair to say no-one could have guessed. The BBC series *Captain Pugwash* was the basis for the characters in Bruce's own netherworld of submarines. He also penned a solo track ('Dive, Dive, Dive') using the same source.

"These are some words I wrote for the *Somewhere In Time* album," said Bruce of 'Run Silent Run Deep'. "That particular song never made it but I kept the words, and when Steve came up with something, I said, 'You know what will fit brilliantly there – these words." It's a song about submarines, actually the first song about submarines. 'Dive, Dive, Dive' came later.

One slightly vulgar song, containing lyrics that would have been at home in Bruce's *Iffy Boatrace* books, is the paean to S&M called 'Hooks In You.' Though the music is upbeat Maiden at their most succinct, the words are childishly cobbled together and come from the most unlikely of sources, as Bruce admits. 'Hooks In You' is a slightly tongue-in-cheek thing. Me and Paddy (Bruce's wife) went to look at a house to buy and it was lived in by three gay guys. We looked around and it had all these beams, and one of the guys was obviously into S&M and leather and stuff, and in one room there were these enormous industrial hooks screwed into the beams. My mind boggled at what they could be used for. I went home and wrote 'Hooks In You' with the line *'All the hooks in the ceiling, for that well hung feeling.'* I couldn't write it about gay guys, but what if you went round to the house of Mr. and Mrs. Average and found all these hooks in the ceiling? What do THEY get up to? At the end of the song the guy thinks his wife has been unfaithful and sets her in concrete in the foundations." Can I play with madness indeed! No-one could accuse Maiden of having ordinary lyrics, though in hindsight perhaps the words to 'Hooks In You' are best forgotten.

Steve's lyrics would be a little more obvious, and the bassist penned two of the album's standout tracks and lyrics in 'Fates Warning' and 'The Assassin.' The former is a typical Harris moment, where he wonders out loud what happens when the body dies. A song essentially about destiny, this is a comforting track to the many others who may have contemplated, 'what's it all about?'

Meanwhile, 'The Assassin' is prime, creepy Maiden both audibly and lyrically. The words are straightforward, viewing life from behind the eyes of a hired killer. Rather than doing the job for money, this is one cold, calculating son of a gun who just enjoys his work (*"excitement running through my veins"*).

Steve also boasts the sole credit for the closing track, the epic 'Mother Russia.' A song literally about the historical plight of the country, this is a positive viewpoint which, according to Bruce, basically asks, "wouldn't it be great if Russia could finally get itself together now and live in peace?" The singer also explains that the song "is about the tragedy of a great land which has an incredible history of being overrun and people being massacred, for centuries."

It is a fitting close to an album that, in the same way as previous recordings such as *Piece Of Mind*, takes time to truly understand. For the most part here is Maiden at its most intricate, with a veritable treasure chest of ideas, enthusiasm and energy. The relaxed conditions in Steve's living quarters meant the band were certainly having fun while recording – one only has to view the 'Holy Smoke' video to see that.

Overall the boys proved they still had much to offer in the changing musical landscape of the nineties, in fact this flurry of quality songs would continue through the mire of heavy metal's changing fortunes.

Q magazine, noted for its aversion to metal of any kind, ran a piece on Maiden once *No Prayer For The Dying* had hit the racks, and observed the following; 'Any takers for the Zeppelin of the '90s? That's the phrase, and perhaps concept, Iron Maiden's publicist is punting about to promote their cause in the new decade. But the band can't really see it getting that big because they won't compromise.'

Dave Murray endorsed the lack of mainstream ethics when he finished the *Q* piece with an enduring quote, "We'll never cross over, we won't make a nice little pop single, so all we can do is appeal to rock fans. But you climb up to the top of one mountain and there's always other mountains to climb."

Talking of climbing mountains, that is exactly the kind of challenge Maiden had to face when attempting to sell albums in America. *No Prayer For The Dying* saw their standing drop in the States, as they only shifted 500,000 copies (which was actually still a supreme achievement, especially as they reached number 17 in the album charts). This was enough to attain Gold status, but their five previous albums had all been Platinum sellers. However, in the UK it was the familiar story, the album sold countless units and climbed to the plateau of number two in the band's homeland charts.

THE TOUR

"Speaking as guitar player, I've always liked to improvise, to make things up on the spot, and it's made the shows very spontaneous. I love the interplay I have with Dave because it's fun. I look out at the audience and I can see people laughing. A lot of people seem to have forgotten that's all part of it. Put that together with the attitude instilled in the band by Steve, that every night is important, and you've got a great combination!" Here was a quote from Janick, the new boy who had just joined the biggest heavy metal band in the world.

This enthusiasm was catching too. Even the stalwart Maiden-ites had been reinvigorated by Gers joining the fold, as Nicko McBrain alluded to in his tour programme notes. "Now that we have new blood in the band it's given all of us an extra boost." the drummer said of Janick. "We're playing as though the band had just formed – we're hungry! I'm having the greatest time watching the other guys. Nobody's in one place for more than a few seconds! Sometimes when we've been doing a long tour in the past there have been periods when we've wanted to be at home in front of the television with a pint of bitter and a roast Sunday dinner, but not now. The fire is there and we keep surprising ourselves with how good we can still be!"

While, to an extent, the entire band was on cruise control, ably performing anything they put their minds to, at the same time they continued to exhibit the level of passion only a new band could understand. To all intents and purposes this may as well have been a new group anyway. With the greatest of respect to Adrian, he was not known for running around the stage and twirling his guitar around his body three times, or playing with a frighteningly acute style. Sure, he made top-notch guitar playing look easy, but Janick was a whirlwind of energy, attacking every song as if he was playing his last ever gig. Much like Steve and Dave, Janick was a quiet, down to earth geezer behind the mask of performing. Yet when he stepped on stage the extrovert in him leapt out at the audience and fired his bandmates up even more. Steve and Dave were always active enough but now they had a kindred spirit in Gers and the awesome fusion was a pleasure for the fans to witness.

Maiden was not about to rest on its laurels by choosing a support band who were vastly inferior either. Nor were they about to take the arrogant step of touring without a support act, as some big metal bands had started to do. It was not in Maiden's make-up to take all the limelight even though they often did. Instead they liked to warm up their crowd in the traditional way – taking out a support act who, like them, played every gig as if it was their last.

In keeping with his usual patriotism, Steve Harris felt it was time to expose the Tamworth quartet, Wolfsbane to the masses. The boys from the Midlands were a revelation and fully justified their place on the bill. Having been formed in the late eighties, the group had built up a righteous head of steam and were commonly regarded as Britain's worst kept rock secret. Several magazines tried to help their cause, notably the *RAW* monthly, and *Kerrang!,* who really tried to push Wolfsbane onto the next level. Despite constant exposure and a succession of truly excellent and awe inspiring records, they failed to hit the big time, which for them, clearly, just wasn't meant to be (for a full rundown on the Wolfsbane experience see chapter 12).

Given the relatively young age of the support act, and their blistering, highly energetic performances, Maiden had much to live up to when they hit the UK stages each night. But as they had always proved when they needed to step up a gear, they did so with assured gusto and prominence. And a stripped down stage show for the early nineties proved a lot to their critics. Many had accused the band of being nothing more than a huge, commercial live spectacle whose only interest lay in expensive light shows and stage props. Well, the 'No Prayer On The Road' tour proved that was nonsense. Old and new fans alike found just as much to occupy their attention even with the absence of icebergs or other fancy additions. As Steve Harris eloquently put it, "all the cynics have suggested we'd be nothing without all the special effects, and you can see what a load of old cobblers that is."

Janick was bubbly and effervescent in his contribution to the Maiden tour and it was no surprise, given the sparkling interplay he was enjoying with Dave Murray. "Maybe it's purely because I have the perspective of being the new boy in the band, but there is one element about Iron Maiden that has really knocked me sideways on this 'No Prayer On The Road' tour, and that's simply the energy level in the band," Janick commented, "In most groups there are one or two members who are never giving 100%, but in Maiden you feel an immense energy blasting out, total energy. The whole thing is reciprocated by the audience too; there's only one word to describe a Maiden audience, and that's fanatical! People at the shows know all the words to the songs before the records are even out!

"I'm still thrilled by the charge that goes through the band when we leave the dressing room and head for the stage," the guitarist continued. "It's like a megaton bomb going off, and the adrenalin rush is amazing. You can hear the crowd over the intro tape when you're still behind the amps and it gives me the shivers. I like it because you should always be a little nervous before a show. The weirdest, yet nicest thing about being in the band is that I feel as if I've been there all along. I remember after the second day playing with the band that Steve said it felt as if I'd been there for ten years, and yet everybody in the band has talked about how fresh the 'No Prayer On The Road' tour feels. There's a sense of fun and danger at the same time. We don't do sound checks so there's a real feeling that anything can happen up on stage and it gives us a real edge."

For Dave Murray the difference was in having someone to bounce off, quite literally in some cases. Where Adrian Smith was more of a rhythm guitarist and front man, Murray had always been just a lead guitarist. For him to be really firing on all cylinders, he needed a captivating partner. With Gers he had someone to keep up with, or as Steve Harris put it, "someone to duel against." This was borne out by the normally stationery Murray suddenly traipsing all over the stage and in some cases, racing Gers from one side to the other. The extrovert in Murray was now enjoying the spotlight and competing for the crowd's attention as much as playing guitar.

Thankfully being on the road for over six months was not going to scare Janick. He claimed he was "revelling" in being involved in such a lengthy road trip, something he had not experienced before. "I'm glad I had three months playing with Bruce's solo band because I think I would have felt phoney walking out on stage with Iron Maiden and playing stadia without doing club and theatre gigs beforehand," Gers noted. "It's like doing a whole career in miniature, but I think it's good for me mentally to have gone down, played at the bottom and worked my way up. There is a greater amount of pressure, I can't deny it, because people expect so much of Iron Maiden that you have to go out and really perform every night on a massive stage. I think that mentally it's harder at the top than at the bottom. Obviously you're not packing your own gear into a van at the end of the night, but...".

As had always been the case, Maiden was still a band who could laugh at themselves despite being consummate professionals. Nicko pointed out that there was always a joke being played on stage whether the audience noticed it or not. Some were more obvious, such as when Bruce moved parts of Nicko's drum kit around, trying to force him to make mistakes. As the drummer elaborates, "But that's what Iron Maiden is all about, isn't it?! Being human. That's part of the reason why we still love being in this band. It's the element of danger! I might have played a song hundreds of times, but there's still the chance that I could mess it up!"

McBrain also acknowledged, "I think the energy level's really high on this tour because the focus of the show is mainly on the band. 'The Seventh Tour Of A Seventh Tour' was like climbing to the top of the mountain as far as a stage show went." This was a view shared by his fellow bandmates, especially Steve. The bass player felt the *Seventh Son...* extravaganza had been a little over the top, with too much emphasis on stage props and the 'ice setting' of the album cover. With *No Prayer...* there was no concept, and thus no fancy stage set-up, just five guys playing rock n' roll. Because of this, the long serving members had their best tour ever in 1990/91.

The media concurred and compliments were wide and varied regarding the new look Maiden. Dave Shack, for example, wrote in *Metal Forces*, "Gers is possibly the greatest thing that has happened to Maiden since Bruce himself injected some new blood way back in 1982."

One thing which had started to permeate Maiden's shows more and more were the activities known as 'moshing' and 'crowd surfing,' where specimens, usually male, attempt to climb on stage and then jump off, or get hoisted onto the top of the crowd, literally surfing across the bodies beneath them.

Moshing is the far more physical act, however, which involves spinning, turning, pushing and sometimes throwing punches. These actions, spawned by the heavier and faster reaches of the metal scene, did not sit well with the relatively reserved Iron Maiden, as Bruce complained to *Q*:

"Moshing is dangerous and it really pisses me off. There were fifteen people down the front absolutely hell bent on beating the crap out of anyone who didn't want to join in. I'm talking about huge skinheads hurling themselves at whoever is in the way, boy or girl. People were getting hurt. My whole thing with rock, especially heavy metal, is that despite the musical aggression, the feeling is always of comradeship, people looking after one another, because you're all into the same bands and it doesn't matter whether you are rich or poor, thick or 'Brain of Britain'. This moshing thing is really egocentric and it screws the show up for everybody."

Perhaps this was a sign of the band mellowing a little, or maybe they were just too mature for some of their fans? Whatever the analysis, the fact was, Bruce had certainly undergone a rapid change of attitude since fathering a child. As *Q* Magazine observed; "Bruce Dickinson sits in a corner of the room, his wife beside him, smiling down at the baby he cradles in his arms with image-shattering gentleness."

"I know it sounds too heavy metal to be true, but I was actually quite surprised when he popped out," the vocalist told the reporter, "the words 'hung like a donkey' spring to mind. I thought, 'Oh my God, what's *that* going to be like in fifteen years' time?' Then the midwife explained that the poor chap had a swollen scrotum. Quite common apparently. Imagine that, most male babies come into the world with sore balls."

In the same magazine it was noted that Steve Harris' only interests, away from Maiden, were his wife, their four children and football.

Q also referred to the fact Steve still played for Melbourne Sports (as he had since his teens) in the Ilford & District League. It was actually Melbourne Sports Reserves Steve often played for, but then since when did a mainstream magazine get their information right?

FIRST TEN YEARS

Though Maiden had been an ongoing concern for Messrs. Harris and Murray since the mid-seventies, they were, to all intents and purposes, ten years old due to their first album being released in 1980. This gave their management something to ponder and an angle to market. Their idea was to reissue all the Maiden singles and dress them up in a smart box. Given compact discs were now being released regularly, *The First Ten Years* set would be available both on vinyl and CD.

The releases came out individually and were in chronological order. This meant 'Running Free' was the first reissue and also that listeners could trace the gradual improvement in the band through their singles – as if proof were needed!

For each single release the eccentric Nicko McBrain gave listeners a personal show, dubbed 'Listen With Nicko Part 1', 'Part 2' etc. This was a lovely package for fans to own and by the time eBay assaulted the internet some ten years or so later, both CD and vinyl versions of *The First Ten Years* were still fetching a hefty price, given they were both produced in very limited numbers.

Sources:

Paul Stenning Interviews
http://www.metal-rules.com/interviews/IronMaiden-Sept2003.html
No Prayer On The Road Tour Programme
Q Magazine January 1991
Metal Forces #56 & #57
http://www.maidenfans.com/imc/?url=album08_npftd/commentary08_np ftd&lang=eng&link=albums
http://moses.creighton.edu/JRS/2000/2000-r18.html
http://www.rotten.com/library/bio/religion/televangelists/jimmy-swaggart/
Malc MacMillan – The NWOBHM Encyclopaedia
All lyrics owned by Iron Maiden Holdings LTD, published by Zomba Music

Chapter 11
The Art Of Chemistry

"It's really satisfying to be able to play shows the way we are doing these days, when you're over thirty! To be honest, I don't think the band have played this good ever!" Steve Harris

1992 would see Iron Maiden return to prominence in the heavy metal scene. With a now stable line-up including 'new boy' Janick Gers, the band had a first chance to pool its collective strength for what would become their ninth studio album. Gers was to co-write four songs on the record and the man from Hartlepool could ultimately lay claim to having written some of the best material on the LP.

But it was not just Gers' enthusiasm and general newness that fired the band up, ironically the stalwarts of the group were also starting to feel closer to each other, as highlighted in Dave Murray's comment at the time. "The five of us have really got to know each other better which I suppose is pretty strange when you think about how long we've been going."

What exactly prompted this newfound openness and closeness is uncertain but it was clear that the Maiden members collectively felt they couldn't be touched during this period. However, as Steve testifies, there were stages even then when things could become heated; "In general, we get on really well. The only thing which does happen, like on every album, is that Nicko and I have a bloody great big row! When I say row, I don't mean a punch up, just a lot of verbal. You can guarantee that he'll throw a wobbler at some point and I'll throw one straight back and after a couple of hours it'll all be sorted out." This view contradicts those aired in interviews partnering the *First Ten Years* release, where it was stated that the 'Mission From 'Arry' track, which featured McBrain and Harris in a full blown argument, was a true one-off.

Being so far ahead of the pack was no arrogant stand by Maiden, it was merely an expression of the confidence they had always exuded, and the attitude, which had brought them to the top of the metal tree. It mattered not that Nirvana had begun to execute a stranglehold on modern music, by breaking into the mainstream with their 'Smells Like Teen Spirit' single. Pearl Jam and Soundgarden were also riding high with their respective albums, and it was indeed this triumvirate of Seattle natives who were to spawn the 'grunge' scene. Though grunge could not be ignored it didn't exactly affect Iron Maiden [1]. It was viewed in much the same way as trends and fashionable music that had come before, only to dissipate, while the British heavy metal institution just kept rolling on, doing the things it had always done.

Except, Maiden always knew they had to keep abreast of even slight musical changes, whether that meant upping the aggression or fine-tuning the sound of their music. In essence this translated into penning some of their most furious work, whilst simultaneously improving the production for their new LP.

Whilst there had been no complaints about the sound of *No Prayer For The Dying* from the fans, inside the Maiden machine there were rumbles of discontent at the way they had presented the record. Bruce Dickinson thought it sounded "flat" and "outdated" so there were inner desires to improve the sound for album number nine. "It was crap," Bruce remarked of *No Prayer*... "whereas this sounds twice as good as *Seventh Son Of A Seventh Son*. We paid real attention to the drum sound too. We hadn't had an update on the drum sound since Nicko joined. This time we said, 'let's make a drum sound that will last until the year 2000'.

"I was really happy with the last album," the front man continued, "when we made it I thought 'brilliant. This has been a good laugh, bags of enthusiasm, loads of energy.' It was only after about six months that I started listening to it and listening to other contemporary albums. Someone gave me a tape of a US band called Dream Theater and I listened to it and thought 'holy Christ!' I got hold of some of their demos for their next album and they were recorded on a twenty-four track and I'm thinking 'Fucking hell!' The world has moved on since you could turn up with a drum kit, stick a few mics up and go."

As long as the core ingredients were present on a Maiden record, however, it didn't seem to really matter how the production was, it always managed to sound great, regardless – at least that's how the fans viewed it. It certainly helped that Martin Birch was experienced enough to consistently present the band in its most flattering light and he was duly hired once again to oversee the beast.

The album was to be titled *Fear Of The Dark*, also the name of the closing track. It really was quite ironic; here were the Maiden team at their closest and strongest for some years, writing an album where several songs tied in with a central theme of 'fear'. "Whether it was a subconscious thing that we all had fears at the time I don't know, it was just the way it was," was Steve's comment, giving little away as usual. For Harris though, there might have been some truth in the idea that the lyrics were sometimes subconscious, given that his were often based on nightmares. Still, despite the ever-presence of the dark, fear-driven lyrics, this was no concept album. As Steve would often have to explain, the only concept album ever produced by Maiden was *Seventh Son Of A Seventh Son* and that was virtually guaranteed to remain a one off. *Fear Of The Dark* was an album with a few strong themes but it equally contained several songs outside of the usual Maiden remit.

Part of the reason for this was the relaxed surroundings Steve's home studio provided. Maiden again had the chance just to be themselves without distractions. "Before when we'd recorded in London or wherever else, you'd get a load of annoying little things happening that just burst the bubble a lot of the time," Dave Murray reckoned. "Things like a cleaner coming in, in the middle of a solo, or a cab driver looking for so-and-so. This time we shut ourselves off and it also meant that instead of leaving the studio and going straight to the bar without passing go, we could go home and relax. It made it a lot more enjoyable and relaxed."

With this sort of home-comforts, quite how Maiden churned out the fury behind *Fear Of The Dark* was anyone's guess but one thing was certain, the band were here to stay in the nineties and if anything, the success of grunge fired Maiden up even more. Bruce Dickinson in particular was bursting with enthusiasm for the songs the group had recorded, and it was his most powerful contribution to the album which made the opening slot and the choice of first single.

'Be Quick Or Be Dead' is one of Maiden's heaviest ever tracks, and certainly one of the fastest yet recorded. With this song, the veteran outfit proved their muscle and their mettle, deliberately releasing as a single their most 'un-radio' number, possibly because they knew radio wouldn't touch them anyway. Bruce described the album as "classic heavy metal for the nineties" and his feeling was accurate given this was prime, pumped up Maiden, bursting with life despite their ageing limbs. "As far as I'm concerned, I don't think I've sung so well since *Piece Of Mind*. I think that my voice has never so perfectly matched the songs than on *Fear Of The Dark*," he added, suggesting that if he could be that satisfied with his performance, the album must be pretty special.

Perhaps it was the lyrics, which made 'Be Quick Or Be Dead' such a riotous opener. It deals with corruption in politics and the media, and as Dickinson illuminated to *Metal Forces*, "It's quite topical I guess. It's about the Robert Maxwell/BCCI kind of scandals. But it's not just about that, it's about the fact that the only way to live your life if you're a kid now is either to be more crooked than them or to be so quick on your feet, so smart you can do what you want. The only way to do what you want in this world is to outsmart the crooks. To out think them is the only way to achieve what you want. Not necessarily to live like they do, but understand what they're doing and how they get away with it. If you're going to survive and not get caught up in the shit."

Robert Maxwell had been in the news since his death in November 1991. The media man who had built his own publishing empire had, prior to his death, been caught stealing staff pension funds to try and save his businesses, which were on the decline. Yet his death was suspicious. Maxwell had accidentally fallen off his boat and drowned, but it was suggested he had possibly either committed suicide or been murdered. It was a situation, doubtless riddled with mistruths and barefaced lies, which was much like the government corruption that was also topical then. Though 'politicians being caught doing naughty things' was nothing new, it seemed at the time to be on the increase. Yet perhaps the only thing that had really changed, come the nineties, was the fact that they were becoming easier to catch.

Bruce would claim most of his lyrics tied in with the theme behind 'Be Quick Or Be Dead' and the inspiration for the words came from an unexpected source. As the singer explained; "My wife said to me, 'if you were a sixteen year old kid growing up now, what a horrible fucking mess. What would you make of it all? The governments around the world are corrupt, and those that aren't are fiddling the books. They won't do anything about the drug cartels and if they do, they usually let them off with a slap on the wrist.' Everything seems to be falling apart."

So, no safe uncomplicated living for the multi-millionaire vocalist. On the contrary he was as angry as he'd ever been despite being professionally successful. And he was at his most despondent on 'Fear Is The Key.' Another Dickinson/Gers composition, this is a social commentary quite unlike anything Maiden had ever released. Not only is the song a bumpy emotional ride musically, the lyrics cover a topic that was depressing, current and unusual for Maiden. Since 1991 when Queen singer Freddie Mercury had passed away due to AIDS, there had been a newfound awareness of the disease and suddenly many realised they had been living on the edge. Where in times past, anyone could sleep around if they wished without need for protection (the only risk being unwanted pregnancy) the late eighties epidemic brought a crushing blow to the sexual arena.

It had become known through that decade how deathly AIDS or HIV was, yet it took Mercury's death to awaken several generations to its very real dangers.

"Sex has become a synonym for fear", Bruce thought. "When we were writing the songs, we heard about Freddie Mercury's death. There's a line in 'Fear Is The Key' that goes: 'nobody cares 'til somebody famous dies'. And that's quite sadly true. In the States, mostly, nobody really cared about AIDS until 'Magic' Johnson, the basketball player, announced publicly that he was HIV-positive. As long as the virus was confined to homosexuals or drug-addicts, nobody gave a shit. It's only when celebrities started to die that the masses began to feel concerned." The Freddie Mercury Tribute concert of 1992 raised AIDS awareness and celebrated the life of one of rock's finest performers with tributes by such diverse acts as Metallica and George Michael.

Still on the subject of sex, the last Dickinson/Gers track on the album rues the loss of sensuality in relationships whilst on tour. 'Wasting Love' is a cleverly written jibe at the groupie mentality. Bruce had been upfront and honest in the past about his enjoyment in pleasures of the flesh whilst on tour. It seemed a reflective stance had now been taken, brought about, no doubt, by being settled with wife and child, which gave the singer a different outlook.

The meaning of the song goes beyond sexual gratification however. The true moral of the story is that sleeping with anyone available on any given night is simply an attempt to compensate for emptiness in your life. For Bruce personally, this had meant taking the easy, gratifying option to mask the void in his existence and the feelings of loneliness. "Life on the road is tough," Bruce admitted "and I know that many musicians find it hard to emotionally 'open-up', because they have those worries and those feelings that they cannot share with anyone, and that they keep buried within themselves. They believe that, in their position, it is impossible to have 'true' relationships with people, so they end up in bed with those of the opposite sex, without thinking any further."

As Bruce delicately put it, he "stopped fucking groupies" when he found someone he truly loved – his girlfriend Paddy, who became his wife in December 1984. It did seem a little strange to suddenly come up with a song on the topic of groupies so far down the line. Nevertheless, it is a welcome diversion in the Maiden catalogue, although, as a 'power ballad' it could arguably have been better suited to Dickinson's solo work. It was certainly indicative of changing times and attitudes, revealing Steve Harris' willingness to progress and take chances on different themes occasionally.

Fear Of The Dark as a whole took a number of risks, though it remains clearly identifiable as Iron Maiden. It is only with hindsight one can truly analyse just how bold a record this was, and the extent to which the album really stands out in the Maiden pantheon. Certainly, of the Bruce Dickinson fronted material, *Fear Of The Dark* was the most diverse set yet compiled by the band, coupling hard and classic rock with true metal and the occasional pop or soft rock flourish. To Maiden novices the album is unlikely to entice further delving into the band's back catalogue, and it remains a record only fully grasped and appreciated by long time Maiden devotees.

These are seriously catchy songs nevertheless, in an upbeat style that Iron Maiden felt more comfortable with since the success of 'Holy Smoke'. Therefore, to offset the negativity of certain lyrics, there simply had to be another ode to Charlotte The Harlot, this time in the form of the fantastic 'From Here To Eternity', also released as a single. Dowsed in sexual innuendos, here is Maiden again at its most juvenile, but at the same time at its kooky best. The words are peppered with *Lord Iffy Boatrace* smut such as the line, *"she'd never sat on a piece so mean"* – the surprising fact being these are the words of Steve Harris and not Bruce!

So, Harris had weighed in with a light-hearted song for once. On the surface, another of his sole compositions 'Weekend Warrior' could be mistaken for being somewhat throwaway. The tune itself is basic beyond belief, and the lyrics are just a tad *too* British, mentioning 'mates' and going back to work on Monday. The sentiments expressed are commendable, a hatred of football hooligans being the underlying theme, but the song itself is a step too far even for the football loving Harris and it seems wildly out of place even on such a varied album.

Elsewhere, however, Steve is on good form, churning out prime Maiden fodder such as 'The Fugitive' (a great fantasy style adventure romp in the vein of 'The Assassin' from *No Prayer*...) and 'Fear Of The Dark' itself. Indeed it was the title track from the 1992 album that received most praise and was also to become a staple of the live set. This is no surprise, since its galloping chorus is perfect for crowd participation. In fact so good are the live versions of this track that a studio version has never been used again on any Maiden compilation to date.

"Steve is really afraid of the dark," Bruce said of the meaning behind the song. "It's the story of a man who walks in a park at night and, as it's getting darker, he sees all sorts of worrying things. He becomes totally paranoid because his imagination is working overtime. It's a great track." Indeed it is, giving the album a more typical Maiden edge and ending the opus with the characteristic 'longest song on the record' – an epic with many twists and turns. True to form the band had taken a relatively innocuous topic and turned it into a riveting story.

'Chains Of Misery' is only one of two songs where Dave Murray pops up for a credit, co-writing with Dickinson. "I haven't written as much stuff as Steve or Bruce because their song writing's pretty powerful," the bashful guitarist conceded. "When I have got some songs though, I want to make sure that they're really going to suit the band." 'Chains Of Misery' is certainly suited to both Bruce's voice and the musicians, being a nifty, melodic hard rock track. The lyrics are more 'in depth' than might have been expected too. "It's about the little devil that sits permanently on our shoulder," Bruce explains. "This little devil who can ruin your life. For instance, you meet a girl, you have a great relationship, and all of the sudden you do something stupid with no apparent reason, and you wonder… 'Why am I doing this?' You don't really know why you act the way you do, but you feel that you have to do it. Maybe it's a feeling of guilt that drives you, maybe you feel that you're not 'good enough' to deserve all this… In any case, you act against your own interest without really knowing why."

The duel guitars are used to full effect here, with the song containing some of the album's most memorable guitar work, begging the question why Dave Murray didn't write more material. The six-stringer explains, "Ever since I joined Maiden in '76 I've just had this huge springboard that Steve's song-writing has given me, to do what I want as far as guitar playing is concerned. There's loads of room to expand and I've never had the feeling that I needed to go out and make a jazz funk album or anything. I love being in this band and playing the way we do allows me total freedom. I've got other stuff that I've written at home, but at the moment when I get time off I'd rather spend it with the family than go fiddling around with it."

Nevertheless, his other credit – for 'Judas Be My Guide' – makes an argument for strongest track on the album. Again, it is highly melodic and a daring variant on the Maiden foundation. "This is a pretty ironic song, actually. I don't know if it will be well received 'cause it's somehow perilous to be ironic in the world of rock music," Bruce quipped. "It's about the dark side in all of us, and I decided to call this dark side 'Judas'. It's this trend that would make anyone sell anything, that would make them care about nothing, that's this little Judas who's inside all of us, and if he becomes powerful enough to rule the world, then… bye-bye!"

'The Apparition' is one of the album's standout songs and certainly another strange turn for the Maiden workhorses. The guitar breakdown following the first verse is truly unexpected, so extravagant it almost misses the direction in which the verses are going. Lyrically it's more direct and characteristic of Steve Harris.

"Roughly, these are Steve's views on the world. He exposes all his feelings, his anguish, his fears, his preoccupations," Bruce commented, throwing light on the song's meaning. In typical Maiden style, the lengthy diatribe fuses several different directions, covering almost random thought patterns and revealing Steve's views on a possible afterlife, destiny and friends.

The bassist must also have been in melancholy mood when he wrote 'Childhood's End,' a rather depressing view of the world children now grow up in. Given many of the Maiden members had young children at the time it was rather disconcerting to hear Bruce say, "There isn't a single place in this world where humans can remain kids. In ten years, we've made almost completely disappear the water, the air, the sun... and now, you have to be out of your mind to be willing to give birth to children when you see the current state of the world. So we wonder where this will all end."

Considering world events during the months preceding the album's conception makes the mostly bleak lyrics in *Fear Of The Dark* perhaps more understandable. Tackling a subject with which Maiden were already familiar in 'Afraid To Shoot Strangers', Steve Harris ponders the Persian Gulf War. "It's about a soldier who starts shooting during the Gulf War," Bruce explained, "and he doesn't want to kill anybody, but he knows that his duty will force him to do it. But if he doesn't shoot, maybe another one will shoot him. So, he hasn't got much choice. It's a cruel dilemma, but there's no other way to get out of it."

The song is a somewhat clumsy variation on the Maiden epic style, featuring a rather irritating drum-beat during the verse. It also seems to be placed poorly in terms of the running order of the album. Clearly Maiden was attempting to repeat its feat on *No Prayer For The Dying*, whereby 'Holy Smoke' was followed by the epic title track.

However with 'Afraid To Shoot Strangers' and *Fear Of The Dark* the same sequencing simply could not and did not work, due to the quick turnover on various styles within each song.

Though anyone purchasing *Fear Of The Dark* would instantly see how diverse the songs were, for better or worse, there were doubtless fans who would buy anything with the Iron Maiden stamp. On the first day of release Maiden's grunge era record sold a million copies world-

wide, proving true metal still had a place in the charts. For further proof
there was the welcome sight of *Fear Of The Dark* assaulting the British
charts, flying in at number two in the band's homeland. Though America
had long been a struggle for Maiden sales-wise, their new opus still managed to carve out a very respectable twelfth placing in the US charts.

THE COVER

*"It's really funny how people pay attention to Eddie. We just thought that
since we'd changed so much on this album musically and we'd brought
the production up into the '90s, people'd do a double take. He looks even
more evil, like he's had a few more hangovers!" Dave Murray*

1992 would mark the end of Iron Maiden's association with artist
Derek Riggs, the man who had been painting Eddie for over a decade.
According to Bruce at the time, Maiden "wanted to stay nasty and we felt
that some of Derek's stuff was getting a bit posy and he was getting pissed
off with drawing Eddie."

Not surprisingly there was some animosity from Riggs regarding
the breakdown of relations with the band.

"There were a couple of unfinished pictures for things like *Fear Of
The Dark*" he told George Matsagouras, "but they got abandoned half way
through for other reasons, not because they were rejected (Maiden never
saw them) but because Maiden changed their minds in mid-flow as it were.
So I had to start again which is why I got pissed off with them on that
project. They kept on changing their minds all the time, then I would get
grief for not knowing what they wanted. Working for Maiden is neither as
straightforward nor as lovely as they would have people believe."

Though Riggs claimed he had half finished the *Fear Of The Dark*
cover, and therefore a third of the cover is all black, the illustrator credited in the album notes disagrees. Melvyn Grant is, according to Maiden,
responsible for the cover and the man himself states, "Derek Riggs had
nothing at all to do with my painting of *Fear of the Dark*. It was certainly
not his idea. It was completely my idea and one of several. All I was given
was the title. It was not inspired by Derek Riggs, or as I've lately heard
claim, Maiden's management. In fact I think very few people realised that
the Eddie creature was actually coming down the tree.

"Maiden called me in to come up with an image for the LP cover.
I produced, I think, about seven or eight different concepts, including the
one used. Maiden then asked me to try adding bat type wings to Eddie's

Early days with Paul Di'Anno

Second line-up with Bruce Dickinson

Top **Oundle Schoolboy Bruce Dickinson 1974**
Bottom **Perpetual Schoolboy Steve Harris (with friend) 1995**

The Earlier Recordings

The Later Recordings

The Collectable 7" Singles

The Collectable 12" Singles

The Collectable Picture Discs

The Collectable Concert Programmes

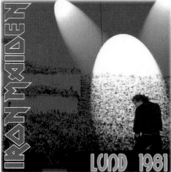

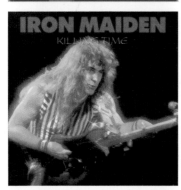

The *Real* Collectables...

...for more information see discography section

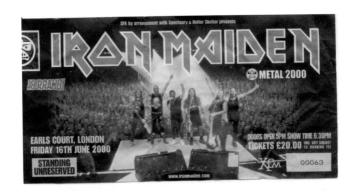

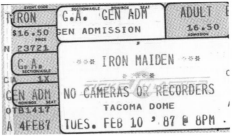

The Collectable Tickets and Passes

The Collectable Memorabilia

The Classic Line-up

Blaze Bayley

Then and Now

shoulders, which I did. But it didn't look as good, so they finally settled on my original concept. I also tried to improve the design of Eddie, but Maiden insisted that I did not stray too far from the previous examples.

The *Fear of the Dark* Eddie does not represent a Dryad as such, although it could be. The concept was based around the thought of something that you defiantly do not want to meet on a moonlit night while walking around in a wood. The image is really two-fold, While Eddie's shoulders, head and arms are the same, and the body is both sitting in the tree and coming down the trunk. The dark branch at the top edge of the moon is a kind of tail and the legs would carry on up the main trunk. Or maybe his lower body is more snake like. So Eddie is not actually sitting in the tree, but hanging down its length. I think it could be something else sitting in the tree. Possibly the future of the viewer."

"We are not changing for the sake of it," explained Bruce of the decision to dispense with Riggs (though according to Riggs he left of his own volition). "Eddie is so obviously Eddie on this cover, but he's so evil. When I looked at it, it sent shivers down my spine. It's not Hammer Horror monsters, it's really nasty. I think Eddie became a bit sophisticated, and with *Fear Of The Dark* we didn't want an Eddie that people could say, 'oh, it's a sci-fi Eddie' or another kind of Eddie. It's a horrible thing and he's back."

At a distance the cover art does indeed look fairly ominous and striking, the union of the archetypal Eddie and Iron Maiden. But closely viewed the art is not incredibly detailed, and actually looks fairly amateur. It is also worth noting Grant spelled Maiden's long time mascot's name 'Eddy'.

THE AFTERMATH

The video made to accompany 'Be Quick Or Be Dead' could not have been more indicative of Maiden's renewed fire. With a captivating performance, Bruce Dickinson merges his lyrics with a suitably angry visual recital (complete with dirty hands – a nice symbolic touch). The images include the stock market and political parties, alongside a rampant battering of the song by the other Maiden members. Shot on a cold Friday morning in the heart of London's docklands the filming was over in seven hours. The final edit of the video happened in Chicago and despite weather problems whereby the city was heavily flooded, a copy of the video was beamed via satellite around the world. The piece was well received and 'Be Quick Or Be Dead' stormed the UK charts, reaching number two, continuing on from the band's previous good showing for the *No Prayer...* material.

In a typically British move, the band filmed their follow up single 'From Here To Eternity' at Pinewood Studios, the hub of the British film industry. The famous company had been responsible for all the *Carry On* films as well as *Oliver Twist* and numerous James Bond movies and here were another great British institution, Iron Maiden, filming in the famous halls.

Promotion for *Fear Of The Dark* hit a peak when the group all flew in different directions before reconvening for a number of UK signing sessions. Bruce visited four countries in nine days, Steve took in twelve European cities in just four days whilst Janick and Dave visited Korea, Japan, New Zealand, Australia and Canada in two weeks.

The real fun was about to begin however, as the band had only been on home soil a few days before getting itchy feet and deciding to warm up for their forthcoming tour by playing a low key secret gig. Billed as The Nodding Donkeys ('Nodding Donkey Blues' had been the b-side to 'Be Quick Or Be Dead') Maiden raced through a set of old and new numbers in front of a sardine-packed 350 punters. The venue, owned by a friend of Steve Harris, was The Oval public house in Norwich.

In part due to the warm reaction to *Fear Of The Dark*, Maiden were invited to appear as headliners for a second time at the Monsters Of Rock festival in Castle Donington. 1992 would see one of the most diverse bills assembled under the Derbyshire skyline with thrash metal masters Slayer, shock rockers W.A.S.P., the rapidly improving Skid Row as well as Brit rock hopes Thunder and The Almighty. Maiden were of course the biggest draw for the organisers and August 22nd proved to be a fantastic homecoming performance for the band. It was therefore strange to consider the fact that the members hadn't been quite sure whether they should actually say yes to the festival at all. This was not because the band had any reservations about playing there – far from it – it was simply an act of nervousness, based on the question – could they really compare to their 1988 spectacle?

"Going back, it's still going to have that thrill," said Dave Murray alluding to their appearance four years previously. "And of course Janick's in the band now so in a way it's like a new band going back. This time it's going to be a whole new show. It's just something that we're looking forward to very much. Donington is the main gig of the whole tour." Indeed, while the yearly festival was a huge part of the heavy metal fan's calendar, it meant just as much to the Maiden members. Donington, like metal itself, was in their blood and it's interesting to note that at the supposed height of grunge, here was a bill filled with good-time rock and metal bands, with the notable exception of the blood-spattered Slayer. In fact Donington '92 would be the last stand for regular heavy metal, where bands like W.A.S.P. and Skid Row could command such audience figures. In 1993 there would be no Donington, and by 1994 the musical landscape was rapidly changing. But for the old school of rock and metal, this was the place to be in late summer.

Janick Gers in particular knew just what it meant both as a fan and performer. "It's gonna be ten years to the day that I actually played Donington with Ian Gillan", he recalled, "so I'm gonna be pretty scared when we go up. It's gonna be very exciting for me personally. And I was there in '88 when Maiden played and I think that was a phenomenal gig, so we've got to try and match that really."

Being more experienced with big crowds and the Maiden spotlight did not automatically immunise the veteran members of the group from a certain nervousness either, with Bruce Dickinson in particular sharing his anxiety with the multitude of interrogators as August 22nd approached. "I must confess I am still pretty nervous about it because I know there is gonna be this pressure, and because we have a hell of an album to live up to regardless of our reputation," the front man confided. "So I'm a bit nervous about it, but I'm looking forward to it in the sense that it's our home territory and I'm determined to go out and enjoy it and just have a great time. To be honest with you it's the most comfortable I've been singing Maiden material for years. A lot of the time I find singing Maiden tracks quite uncomfortable because they're not very singer friendly."

Going back to basics meant relying upon the quality of the music rather than elaborate stage sets or even such convoluted long drawn out songs. *Fear Of The Dark* is unique in that it only features one song above seven minutes, proving Maiden really had stripped down a step further from the *No Prayer...* material. There was a decidedly rock'n'roll edge to much of their new material, understandable with Janick Gers on board. Though this lighter edge did not always work ('Weekend Warrior' being a case in point) it lent Maiden a stronger appeal in a live environment where they could truly move the crowd and push the momentum of their snappy hook-filled tunes.

As headliners and chief rabble-rousers at Donington, Maiden could take their pick of bands to support them. Though Slayer seemed inappropriate it was Steve Harris' way of showing he did not feel threatened by a renowned, very strong live act (many contended it was impossible to follow Slayer) or indeed by a newer, younger band like Skid Row. They were unfortunately restricted to only a six-band line-up, Harris mentioning that had he been able to choose a seventh, the slot would have been offered to Wolfsbane or Gun. Initially the choice included Van Halen and The Cult but neither could commit to the gig.

In any case, many would have travelled to the festival just to see Maiden, and the Brits capped off a successful year with a superb home-coming performance. As ever, the show was recorded and would later be issued as a Double CD and Vinyl set for posterity.

This was released in 1993 (there was also a three LP set, limited to just 5,000 copies) along with two other live albums, *A Real Live One* and *A Real Dead One*, which though of good quality, did suggest Maiden were either running out of ideas, or that something in the camp was not quite right.

In fact, the latter was the case, with Bruce Dickinson feeling unset-tled in his role as front man for Iron Maiden. This would perhaps not have been so surprising in 1990, but given that he had got so fiercely behind the *Fear Of The Dark* material, claiming Maiden to be so relevant that he didn't want to do any other job in the world, it came as something of a shock at this point.

Initially his explanation consisted of "tiredness due to long touring bouts," but fairly soon afterwards the animosity between Bruce and Steve emerged and it seemed there were personal reasons behind the inevitable split. Unsurprisingly Steve did not take it too well, firing off a barrage of sniping comments. Bruce, to his eternal credit, didn't engage in a war of words, he just got on with his solo career. Clearly, the problem for the ever busy Dickinson was not that he had become jaded with the music scene, more that he was convinced the time had come to leave Iron Maiden and venture out on his own.

It is understandable that Steve felt hurt and abandoned by this move. After all, he knew there was no singer on the planet who could compare to Bruce, with the possible exception of Judas Priest's Rob Halford (whose singing ability could not be doubted, though Bruce's stage presence was undeniably superior). Equally, there was annoyance, an almost 'how dare he' kind of attitude. With Maiden still enjoying ongoing popularity, Steve did not understand why anyone would want to leave that guaranteed ap-proval. But Bruce was unique, which is why people loved him, and he was simply determined to do whatever he felt to be necessary.

For Bruce at that time, it was either leave Iron Maiden or get stuck deeper in a rut. The vocalist in fact presaged a huge shift in the rock music scene by departing the Maiden machine just at the point when it would have to fight harder than ever before to keep its status as one of the biggest bands in the world. And Bruce bailing out just as the going was to get tough only helped to underline the bitterness between the band members. But, if anything, the singer was making things even harder for himself in attempting to forge his own career rather than remain within the relative security of a ten-year plus established outfit.

Dickinson's last concert with the band was a strange concert-cum-magic show featuring illusionist Simon Drake. Whether intentional or not, the rather ridiculous 'illusions' took emphasis away from an otherwise historic moment. This was the end of Bruce's tenure with the band after over a decade singing for them and he undoubtedly deserved better than the mock 'David Copperfield Show' send-off. Clearly the rest of the band felt it was worthy not only of broadcasting on television, but also ultimately for release on a video entitled *Raising Hell*.

Rumours of Dickinson's replacement began almost as soon as the door shut on his Maiden career, and the overwhelming favourite was Helloween singer Michael Kiske. Quite why this was remains a mystery, though it's easy to speculate as to the reason. The first time Steve Harris had been made aware of the German vocalist was when Helloween released their classic album *Keeper Of The Seven Keys Part II* in 1988. Always a Harris favourite, he was regularly spotted wearing a t-shirt baring the album cover print. To such an extent in fact, that *Kerrang!* felt it necessary to ask him to stop wearing it in the pages of their magazine!

The second reason behind the mooted acquirement of Kiske was the fact that he was considered on a par with Dickinson both for power and range. Some even suggested their respective pipes were very similar. In reality however, it is difficult to imagine Kiske at the helm for Maiden and, coincidentally, it was not be long before he too made the bold step of leaving Helloween, the group with whom he'd been synonymous for the most successful years of his career. He also took the unprecedented step of disassociating himself with the genre of heavy metal altogether, claiming the fans could no longer understand or appreciate the soft rock direction he wanted to pursue.

And so the search for a new Iron Maiden front man continued – but just who was not only British, but a singer capable of leading the mighty metallers? The choice was indeed surprising, though the seeds had been sown long before.

1992 – A PERSONAL POINT OF VIEW

"I don't think we worry about what's in vogue or what people think of us. If we did, on this album we'd be like a funk rap thrash thing wouldn't we? Nah, it'd be death metal now wouldn't it?" Steve Harris

Whilst grunge is often accused of being the movement which effectively killed heavy metal off, this blame is often attached through laziness and lack of insight rather than being based on any kind of reality. It is all too easy for both journalists and bands alike to put the fact of many metal careers ending around the same time entirely down to the grunge phenomenon. For the bands themselves, they had an immediate scapegoat, relieving them of any blame for putting out poor records, and for journalists it provided a convenient excuse to banish a form of music of which they had never approved.

You will often hear reports of how Nirvana single-handedly destroyed real metal and hard rock but this really isn't true at all. Sure, Nirvana was a global phenomenon, rising to prominence across worldwide airwaves, firstly with 'Smells Like Teen Spirit', followed by the album *Nevermind* containing that track. What music historians have failed to point out however, is that the entire alternative/metal/rock music scene was already shifting on a far bigger scale than Nirvana (or their fans) could control.

It is easy to use grunge to explain how heavy metal and its extreme sub-genres were gradually pushed out of the spotlight at this time. Many music writers certainly hail 1991 and 1992 as the years when it all changed, where suddenly the record buying public got sick and tired of songs about boning groupies or listening to bands who used more hairspray than was healthy for the ozone. And in some ways this is true. However, the notion that people suddenly wanted to immerse themselves in lyrics about sadness, loneliness or misery (as grunge and the Seattle scene in particular were accused of producing) is stretching the truth a bit far.

If you look at the rock charts of 1992 for instance, they reveal a still healthy cluster of hard rock outfits that were all about the good times. Electric Boys stormed the rock world with their *Groovus Maximus* album, and their feel-good paean to ladies, 'Lips N' Hips' single in particular. The Black Crowes returned to the world with a second helping of upbeat blues-rock, *The Southern Harmony And Musical Companion*. Kiss reinvented itself with the hard-hitting *Revenge* opus, Def Leppard continued their development as American radio darlings with the ridiculously soft

Adrenalize (and it's lead single 'Let's Get Rocked'). Guns N' Roses were still in the reckoning with *Use Your Illusion,* a double set from the previous year, and the happy-go-lucky American quintet, Ugly Kid Joe, was enjoying its five minutes of fame with a debut EP, *As Ugly As They Wanna Be* (containing the huge hit single 'Everything About You').

There was also continuing interest in the Queen reissues, released after the death of Freddie Mercury. ZZ Top featured high in the charts with their *Greatest Hits* collection as did AOR stalwarts Foreigner. Gary Moore continued to morph his reputation into a blues performer and even Hawkwind enjoyed ongoing popularity with a new album *Electric Teepee*. So there is no doubt that 1992 was the year in which the music world was *not* turned on its head. There was little sign of the predicted reams of miserable grunge bandwagoners clogging up the charts, in either the UK or the United States, though there were appearances from those who would later be accredited with leading the grunge genre, Nirvana, Pearl Jam (with their 1992 debut *Ten*) and Soundgarden. The members of Soundgarden were actually already veterans of the Seattle scene, long before they released their then best seller, the brilliant *Badmotorfinger* album. Bruce Dickinson had always approved of the band and even back when he was with Maiden he'd stated, "Chris Cornell is a *great* singer. Out of all the Seattle bands, Soundgarden are the one that should succeed."

So in reality it was really only the 'soon to be giants of the Seattle scene' who were making any headway into the charts in 1992. And there were also signs that major label owners should start to pay attention to newer forms of alternative music. Ice T burst onto the rock scene with his flammable crossover unit Body Count, and its self-titled album shook the rock world. For good or bad, this was one of the early mergings of rap and metal music (following on from the Aerosmith and Run DMC collaboration, Anthrax's flirtation with hip hop and the successful blend of many styles released by the Beastie Boys on *Check Your Head*). Where the metal and rock scene was really changing was not so much through grunge, but rather the new, heavier climes of Pantera. This band had successfully remodelled itself from what was originally a glam rock outfit, through to a highly individual extreme metal unit. Their *Vulgar Display Of Power* album was the beginning of a new scene which would influence recordings from '92 through to the present day.

Pantera's modern take on metal, combined with the different and unique edge coming out of a wide range of bands, from Soundgarden to the Red Hot Chili Peppers (with their funk-rock *Blood Sugar Sex Magik* breakthrough album) were in fact primary causes of the change in the musical landscape of the early 90s. Metallica must also take credit for revitalising the rock scene and again, for better or worse, spawning the thousands of clones aching for their million-selling status. With their self-titled fifth studio album Metallica had straightened out the creases of its sound and successfully morphed into a hard rock beast, eschewing their thrash metal roots.

1992 also saw the furthering of the death metal scene, which had been growing in stature since its inception a few years earlier. Thanks to bands like Deicide, Napalm Death and Obituary, underground metal fans had enough to be thankful for.

Also, in the same year there was the *Wayne's World* phenomenon, a film centring around two main characters who are huge fans of bands such as Aerosmith and Van Halen, and including a memorable scene in which grown men are filmed head banging to the guitar break in Queen's 'Bohemian Rhapsody'. This movie was an instant hit, although perhaps ultimately damaging to the image of your stereotypical heavy rocker. For those less familiar with the rock scene it would be easy to assume all rockers to be as dense and idiotic as the characters of Wayne and Garth. And then there were the awful mullet hairstyles! Two films starring dozy duo Bill and Ted (*Bill And Ted's Excellent Adventure* in 1990 and 1992's *Bill And Ted's Bogus Journey*) followed which did little to create a more positive image. It is just a theory, but is it possible these films were made with an ulterior motive in mind? Considering the PMRC's attempts at killing metal in the mid to late eighties and beyond, it is interesting that such movies (along with even more bone-headed rockers in the likes of *Airheads*) now presented rock and metal kids as harmless oafs.

Certainly by the time these films were released on video, the rock scene was changing even further. As we have seen, the impact of grunge was not immediate and nor was it solely responsible for many metal bands losing their record label contracts and splitting up, but despite this there was a gradual shift of tastes. As with the decline of many styles and phases of music what this basically boiled down to had very little to do with the music itself, rather it was the *image* of metal that died. You only need to look at the bands that did actually change the course of rock music over the next few years for this case to be proven. Pantera were without doubt a heavy metal band, yet front man Phil Anselmo ditched his long hair to shave his head and his appearance spawned thousands of look-a-likes worldwide. Other bands such as Biohazard mimicked the antics of gangster rappers and forged a bond between hardcore, metal and rap to begin yet another new scene which also included bands like Sick Of It All and

Madball. Most of the members in these bands had short hair and dressed 'street', i.e. very differently to the likes of Poison, Def Leppard, or indeed Iron Maiden.

And then there was the appearance of Nirvana. Front man Kurt Cobain wore cardigans and had a fetching blonde bob haircut. Never before in the history of rock 'n' roll had a front man worn a cardigan onstage, this was preposterous! Yet, in turn, fans mimicked Cobain's dress sense and soon plaid shirts (a staple of the Seattle scene's wardrobe) were all the rage, while conventional heavy metal garments were increasingly sneered at. Pearl Jam's Eddie Vedder even developed a penchant for brown corduroy trousers and jackets, attire which really couldn't have been further removed from the average hard rock or metal uniform.

Bruce Dickinson was found to be in humorous mood when pondering the grunge scene. "Some of the stuff is good, some is bollocks," he surmised in typical brash mode. "It's actually what the English bands should be doing because all they've done is nicked from Sabbath and recycled English rock. Seattle's just like fucking England for God's sake; it pisses down with rain all the time, it's freezing cold, you might as well be in Birmingham!

And what are they doing in Birmingham? All tying fucking bandanas round their heads and pretending they're in L.A.! Too many English bands are doing that, pretending to be something they're not."

There were many decades of hard rock and metal music. After only a few years after the emergence grunge it was a ludicrous exaggeration for writers to pronounce that metal had been killed by the emergent genre overnight. Rather more simply, grunge took precedence over metal bands. But as mentioned, Pantera made a long lasting career out of playing fast metal and their ascent began in 1992. So it was not that metal was completely ignored, nor that it died a quick death at the hands of grunge. Heavy metal survived, with long time leaders of the style, such as Black Sabbath and yes, Iron Maiden continuing throughout the early '90s and beyond. The next tier of metallers, such as W.A.S.P., Megadeth, Metallica and Manowar would also survive.

If any single band was to blame for the demise of so called 'real' metal, it was Metallica, by deliberately moving away from the trappings of the heavy metal sound and avoiding playing fast throughout most of their fifth album, shunning their speed-metal past. As the nineties progressed Metallica even changed their image, collectively cutting their hair and wearing make up. On the surface these changes should not have brought an entire genre to its knees and it would be a ridiculous exaggeration to suggest this is the case. In any event it was not until 1994 that traditional heavy metal most suffered and by then the fad of grunge had virtually passed. Sure there were still new bands shooting up, but they were just too late to hang onto the coattails of the originators.

Grunge didn't really ever consist of more than a handful of bands, but when broken down many of these groups were closer to metal anyway, consider Alice In Chains for instance.

Metallica were, nevertheless, a band people listened to and looked to for inspiration. When they disassociated themselves from metal it did signify the genre to be in some kind of a rut.

"Metallica are unquestionably bigger than Maiden in the States," Bruce Dickinson remarked in 1992. "What they've done at this point in their career is something that we could have done around 1984. We could have made that decision to change producer, and slow everything down to a nice medium tempo. Keep the riffs, but slow everything down a little bit, take the edge off the guitar a little bit for radio. Just do a few little tweaks here and there and all of a sudden you're on the radio. We could have taken that route in 1984, but nobody wanted to, and I think that was the right decision."

Steve Harris underlined just how relevant Maiden still was even in the nineties when he observed that "there's people who are like twelve coming to see us now. They weren't even born when we started going! That's amazing." However, in hindsight many might say the albums Iron Maiden released during the grunge era were indicative of a metal scene that needed a shot in the arm. In some ways Maiden, like many of its peers, sounded tired and this was best underlined by Dickinson's decision to leave the band. "The sales figures for each Maiden album generally increased over its predecessor but started to level off after *Fear Of The Dark*," says Keith Wilfort, "I don't really know much about 1996 onwards. I would imagine they declined during the Blaze era."

Luckily Maiden survived, and progressed sturdily through the nineties, but at times they only just clung on. Many smaller bands didn't have a chance and consequently lost their recording contracts and their place in the rock charts. There are many reasons why this happened, just don't blame grunge entirely!

Sources:

Paul Stenning Interviews
George Matsagouras Interviews
www.ironmaiden.com
Kerrang May & August 1992
Metal Forces #71
Hard Force Magazine #2
Raw Magazine April 1992

Chapter 12
Going Down In A Blaze Of Glory

"I had recorded an album, crashed a motor cycle, done Top Of The Pops, *made a video, been interviewed on T.V., radio and in magazines, met fans in places I couldn't pronounce, stayed in hotel rooms that were bigger than my flat and eaten more airline food than I ever have in my life." Blaze Bayley*

"When Bruce announced in 1992 that he was leaving we were all very devastated." So said Maiden guitarist Janick of Bruce's departure, which almost ended the band. "He, however, agreed to finish the tour and played his last gig with us on August 28, 1993." Dickinson claimed his leaving was amicable, but according to Steve Harris "His departure wasn't really friendly at all."

But once Bruce had made up his mind there was no changing it. Maiden would have to find a new singer if they were to remain active.

"To be honest, there were a couple of times it came across my mind," Steve admitted of possibly disbanding Maiden, "but it'd only last a few hours before I'd realise that I didn't really mean it. I think it has more to do with your frame of mind and what's going on around you rather than what's actually happening with the band. I just love it too much to ever want to give it up!"

An initial thought for many who had followed the band was, 'could there ever be a reconciliation with Paul Di'Anno?' The simple answer was 'not a chance'. "It would of been a step backwards for both of us," Janick elaborates. "I worked with Paul before in Gogmagog and he's a lovely chap, but we have to move onward and look into the future and not go back and relive the past."

This sentiment was no doubt echoed by all in the band, especially those who'd been in the line up when the problems with Di'Anno occurred. In fairness to Paul, there had been no public claim that he wanted the job and even in his later autobiography *The Beast* he makes no reference to the possibility. Iron Maiden had moved on and would not look to the past, but neither would Di'Anno. Besides, Maiden were not the kind of cabaret band who would reconfigure just for the quick cash-in. For one thing they did not need to and more importantly they were always eager to do what was best for Maiden as a whole, rather than for any individual satisfaction.

Thanks to their remarkable sales, totalling some 40 million accumulative units, the band was clearly not hungry for money. And equally they had to consider there would only be a small section of fans crying for Di'Anno, the kind of fans who would always believe he was the best Maiden vocalist ever. There would always be a pocket of fans who did not support Dickinson for whatever reason, but who might have considered listening to Maiden again once they knew Bruce had left.

The group decided the best thing to do was find a completely new vocalist. They needed someone hungry, young, with bundles of energy, someone who would re-ignite the band and keep them afloat after the crushing blow of Dickinson's departure. Predictably the response to Maiden's search for a new singer was overwhelming. Though the band really didn't need to advertise as such, it seemed anyone who was a half decent singer put themselves forward for the vacancy. The most important criteria aside from a burning desire to further Maiden's reputation, was the nationality. The front man for Maiden had to be British – there was no leeway on that.

"We received boxes and boxes of tapes from everywhere in the world," Janick remembers. "We tried to give everything a good listen and we actually auditioned sixteen vocalists. But one singer came in with all this energy and enthusiasm. He really blew us away with his deep oppressive voice. We felt that he was just right for the Maiden sound."

"We all wanted someone who could fit in yet make the band different in an exciting way to us," Steve said. "If we couldn't find that person we wouldn't have continued to carry on. So we all felt it was important that we made the right decision."

That decision was to take on one Bayley Cook, a Tamworth native born on May 5th, 1963 who later became known as Blaze Bayley. He created an onstage persona while fronting Wolfsbane and had connections with Maiden from that time. The quartet, also featuring bassist Jeff Hateley, drummer Steve 'Danger' Ellett and guitarist Jase Edwards, had been heavily influenced by the modern glam rock scene, and the 'Tamworth terrors' soon created a buzz with a series of corking demo tapes and incendiary live shows.

Gradually the four-piece honed their influences which included everything from the Ramones to Black Sabbath, transforming themselves into a brasher, harder rock outfit. But they had trouble capturing a record deal, despite much promotion and praise in the pages of *Kerrang!* It was widely believed Wolfsbane was the best unsigned band in the whole of Britain. Eventually, Rick Rubin's Def American label secured the group's services. Rubin was well versed in rock music from around the globe and was known for putting his money where his mouth was by signing bands who represented a risk for many other companies. He was also prolific in his workload and even sat at the helm as producer for Wolfsbane's debut album, *Live Fast, Die Fast*. A riotous romp through various genres with a large helping of their own character and verve, the album was an instant success. The band humorously included a few record company rejection letters (and they had plenty to choose from!) for the inner sleeve of the album. *Live Fast, Die Fast* is one huge raised middle finger to the companies who had believed "Wolfsbane are unsuitable for us at this time."

Capturing live favourites such as 'Manhunt' and 'Money To Burn', the ten track LP hit the streets in 1989 spawning many other British rock acts who then decided to get their gear on and give it a shot. If Wolfsbane, after their numerous attempts and failures to be signed, could finally end up on a well-respected worldwide label, then others could follow suit. Predictably, there were many bands who came and pretended, only to find their music falling short of the kind of explosive attack of which Wolfsbane were capable. Edwards' inimitable guitar playing was incredibly fast and dextrous, Ellett and Hateley held the band together like glue despite their temperamental personalities. But fronting the band like some Los Angeles rock star, Blaze captivated all who heard his soulful, powerful vocals. There was no doubt that here was a British band who would never attempt to be anything other than itself, but Wolfsbane also exuded an ability and confidence most American acts could not buy. And it was no wonder listening to the unique battering *Live Fast, Die Fast* provides – Rubin had certainly made a shrewd move in nailing Wolfsbane to his roster.

The album spawned a minor British hit with a paean to hot, steamy love making, 'I Like It Hot'. The song shows the penchant for melody, lulling the listener into a false sense of security since much of the album is actually full on, speed-laced rock. As the back of the album sleeve states, 'Car crazy, speed crazy, girl crazy, the nightmare has just begun!'

The following year Wolfsbane issued an EP, the mature *All Hell's Breaking Loose...* The band's sound had been refined through months of touring and they had also secured the services of renowned producer Brendan O'Brien. The knob twiddler had emerged from the Georgia Satellites in the '80s to establish himself as one of the most important musical figures of the '90s. O'Brien's stamp permeated the likes of 'Steel' and 'Paint The Town Red' with a tougher sound whilst still retaining the likeable Wolfsbane character. Many realised Wolfsbane were one of the brightest hopes of the British rock scene and they displayed their diversity with the track 'Kathy Wilson' that closes the EP. A superb pastiche of old time B-movies with convincing narration from Blaze and with a chorus to die for, the EP is clearly the mark of a band who deserved maximum exposure.

In fairness to the music press of the time, they attempted to move Wolfsbane up the musical ladder. They had little choice in the matter as they could hardly ignore the thousands of 'Bane fans (lovingly dubbed Howling Mad Shitheads) who bombarded the likes of *RAW* and *Kerrang!* with letters bursting with enthusiasm for the best British band in years. In *Kerrang!* a campaign was even launched for the group to grace the Donington stage from 1990 to 1992. At each festival however, Wolfsbane were cruelly overlooked in favour of such no hopers as Quireboys, the inconsistent Thunder and The Almighty. The decision was quite frankly bizarre and readers were incensed and confused.

The Wolfsbane members were also hurt by the absence of a Donington offer. They tried to keep on with the same motivation and belief that had brought them so far, but it was a worry that, with the band at their peak in their homeland and still no offer of a bigger stage, their time might never come.

Still Wolfsbane did keep on and with O'Brien in tow once again, they released a second album in 1991. *Down Fall The Good Guys* is an underhand snipe at the treatment of the band from certain quarters, and even with this remarkable collection of songs, Wolfsbane still found themselves treading in quicksand when trying to push their stardom to the next level. It was not enough to play shows that were never short of incredible, the band bursting with sweat and desire, or to keep improving with every new release. For some reason the powers that be just did not rate Wolfsbane and here began the decline of British rock's greatest hope of the '90s.

Had Wolfsbane played Donington in 1990 or 1991 it is far more likely they could have increased their popularity. Instead they were reduced to the 'also rans' of the era. *Down Fall The Good Guys* is nevertheless an excellent record, and the ultimate marker of the talents Wolfsbane possessed. More emotional and contemplative than its predecessors, the '91 record contains bitter love songs such as the goose-bump raising 'Moonlight' (which showed Blaze's adaptability as a vocalist), quirky, intelligent up-tempo rockers like 'The Loveless' and 'Ezy' and everything else in-between. As always the band had fun during the recording sessions and this came across in the video for the first single, 'Ezy', not to mention the fan club production video, *In Bed With Wolfsbane*.

As if to underline Wolfsbane's immense live presence, the band released *Massive Noise Injection* in 1993. A phenomenal recording from The Marquee in London, the set is prime, feral 'Bane at their best (also featuring several classic one-liners from Blaze) and should go down in history as one of the greatest live records of all time.

Their final studio album, the self-titled 1994 opus sees the band in a fairly black mood and now on a smaller label as well as with a different producer. Here they were more pissed off than ever and the heaviness of the material reflects this. *Wolfsbane* is a good album but unfortunately it proved to be the end for the band.

Unbeknownst to the other members, Blaze had put himself forward for the Iron Maiden post. In their eyes he had betrayed the friends with whom he had spent the best part of a decade travelling and recording together. Unsurprisingly the band were upset at the circumstances and when Maiden offered Blaze the post and he left to take his chance, the 'Bane disbanded.

Though it is easy to empathise with Messrs. Ellett, Hateley and Edwards, one might also understand Blaze's temptation to take up the chance of joining the world's premier heavy metal band. Wolfsbane was struggling as usual and he simply felt compelled to seize the opportunity. "We didn't have a proper record deal and it was getting increasingly harder to write new material as we all had different influences," said Blaze. "I was offered the job in Iron Maiden and the Wolfsbane manager at the time said 'if you've got the chance go for it, as it won't come along again.'"

And so, to many people's surprise Blaze was now the front man of Iron Maiden. It is easy to trace the lineage of the union, Wolfsbane having supported Maiden a few years before and going down a treat with both the Maiden members and their legions of fans.

"With Wolfsbane we had been royally fucked so many times making the compromises we had to make, especially after the first album," Blaze would later say. "The record company or management would always have their way, yet they would blame us if the record didn't do well or if the show wasn't well received. The few times that we did stick it out and manage to get it our way, it was successful. We were broke the whole time as well, which didn't help. But, I'm very proud of the records I did with Wolfsbane."

When asked for his highlight whilst with Wolfsbane Blaze replied, "Looking right back, it was when we had our own transit van," that comment alone showing the step up in stature from Wolfsbane to Maiden. "The year or so before we were signed, we were going round the UK playing original material and playing to sold out places, albeit small places," the singer continued. "Looking back that was probably the highlight before we went on to albums and then supported Ozzy, Iron Maiden, Guns N' Roses and we went on to see the world. I think the early days, there is a lot of crap that goes along with a record deal that isn't really about the music."

Blaze would soon learn the way things worked in a more professional set up. Maiden were in control of everything and never again would he be scrimping and saving. In fact, to commemorate the new Maiden front man, *Kerrang!* placed Blaze on the cover with the quote, "I joined Maiden and bought my first Jaguar!"

Talking of the huge leap in fortunes, Blaze would admit it was "a bit daunting" joining the band, "but once we started writing, things got a lot easier. Thinking about what we were going to do was a lot harder than doing it. We had a lot of ideas. The first couple of sessions were very nerve-racking but once we'd got songs like 'Man On the Edge' underway it was a lot of fun, as I really loved the music. I had great support and encouragement from fans all over the world."

Steve would comment, "This is obviously a very important time for us with a new line-up. It takes time to fully integrate a new singer. Everything went well with Blaze from the word go. We're very proud of the songs. We're delighted with the way things have gone and can't wait for the fans to hear the new band and new songs. We're also dying to get out and tour again – it's the longest we've ever been between gigs."

The X Factor would be a lamentable argument for Blaze's place in the band. Featuring some of the darkest material the band had written, the album came together naturally and "quietly" as Blaze put it. The songs were demoed and laid down mostly in one take, giving the record a truly live feel, with Blaze's enigmatic voice.

There was no doubt this was a difficult album for long-time Maiden fans to embrace, simply because Bruce and Blaze were so different. Clearly it no longer sounded like the Maiden of old, but this was to their advantage. It was almost as if they were a new group, given a fresh lease of life due to unfortunate circumstances. To the credit of the band they made the most of a difficult situation. Blaze passed his unofficial audition in front of Maiden fans with flying colours, belting out their classic songs like he'd been there his whole life.

Most unlike Maiden, they recorded more tracks than needed for the album, so there were several 'extras' floating around, some of which were used for the Japanese release of *The X Factor*.

The title was a clever reference to many aspects of life in the Maiden camp at the time, as Blaze confirms; "In the studio we were listening to these different takes, and each song had this unknown factor to it, plus the album itself had unknown factors, you know, new engineer, and a new singer, and so we decided to call it the X factor, X representing something that is unknown." There was also the fact that this was Iron Maiden's tenth album, and X, of course, represents 'ten' in Roman numerals.

There was, as ever, the guaranteed inclusion of Eddie on the album and single sleeves with Hugh Syme this time around, ensnared to produce a painting. The band wanted to bring Eddie away from the two-dimensional illustrated sleeves. Thus he became a horrific Frankenstein type creature with several mechanical implements pierced through his skin – the mascot was now being electrocuted with 25,000 volts running through him! This was undoubtedly one of the nastiest sleeves Maiden had ever put their name to.

And the album's lyrics are suitably gloomy, thanks to Blaze's fascination with the "darker side of the human spirit" as he coined it. 'The Edge Of Darkness' references the movie *Apocalypse Now* and the book which spawned the film, Joseph Conrad's *Heart Of Darkness*, while William Golding's book *Lord Of The Flies* provides inspiration for 'The Sign Of The Cross', a bold track and a strange move for Iron Maiden.

Their new singer is introduced with a mournful opening track over eleven minutes long. It's certainly recognisable Maiden, especially with its mid-section instrumental work, and it has to be said Blaze's sombre vocals suit the material. He was certainly extending his range, an opportunity which his time in Wolfsbane had rarely offered. His voice was clearly not going to be everyone's cup of tea, but it was obvious from the first note of the new material that Maiden had diversified. They had not taken the easy option of attracting a vocalist who mimicked Bruce Dickinson (as Judas Priest had done when original singer Rob Halford was replaced by Tim 'Ripper' Owens, who sounded almost identical to Halford). Instead Maiden had, as ever, stuck to their guns, hiring a characteristic singer who was comfortable with the dark material that now consisted of several songs about war, although as Janick Gers explains, "There was no plan for us to write on the subject of war. A lot of the material was written separately. I do think, however, a lot of it had to do with what was going on in Bosnia.

When we were home, that's all we would see on TV. It was difficult to avoid it."

The war Janick spoke of pitted Yugoslavia against Bosnians, who sought independence from the country. The resultant fighting produced a casualty list that constituted the worst European death toll since the Second World War.

"We all felt very close to it and it was going through a lot of people's minds," Steve Harris commented, "the situation in Bosnia could of really got out of hand. That's basically how the First World War started. And it could all happen again." It was therefore no surprise that songs such as 'The Aftermath' were depressing in their depiction of the futility of war. At least this sombre edge was tempered with the likes of first single 'Man On The Edge', an up-tempo rock 'n' roller which gave Maiden a chance to appear on *Top Of The Pops* and for British fans to see Blaze in action with the band for the first time. There was no denying his enthusiasm and ability, though some still maintained he was not the singer Maiden needed.

This was emphasised by the reduced size of venues now graced by the band on their subsequent tour. Whereas just a couple of years earlier, with Bruce, they were storming huge stadiums, they were now reduced to theatres of a third that size. "To be honest, it's a little disappointing," Steve conceded. "But on the other hand, we weren't even sure that we would sell out the clubs with all the change in the music scene and the fact that we haven't played here in four years. So we are pleased that we can still play in front of a decent audience."

And that in itself was no mean feat given 1995 was a turning point for heavy metal generally. Here was Maiden with relatively slow and miserable material, whilst in comparison new acts of the metal world such as Machine Head were blasting the world with clever updates of the thrash metal sound. Pantera and Slayer had both released new albums the year before that upped the ante as far as speed and aggression were concerned, whilst the then little known Fear Factory blew a huge hole in the popular metal world with their diverse and highly technological *Demanufacture* album. Maiden, meanwhile, retreated into its collective shell. *The X Factor* was thus a disappointing album for many fans. Even Bruce would have found it difficult to bolster the likes of 'Fortunes Of War'. Had Harris lost his song-writing knack, or was he merely hampered by a bad phase in his style of music and a questionable singer? This is unarguably the weakest album of Maiden's career, and 1995 was certainly not the time to release anything below par – in fact they were lucky not to disappear off the metal radar altogether. It was very likely only their identifiable image and long time success that managed to keep them in regular sales. That and fans who were so unquestionably loyal that a ventriloquist's dummy could have sung for the band and they would still have bought the material.

"Our album's doing well considering everything," Steve neverthe-less reckoned. "So far we've sold over 230 thousand copies in America. It's a Top Ten album all over Europe and Japan and our catalogue sales have exceeded forty million worldwide. We'll continue to play as long as we get that kind of support." It is interesting that Harris referenced the band's back catalogue as it was really the strength of this which kept the group in business and Harris knew it. *The X Factor* was largely a combina-tion of Harris and Gers material but despite this union, it was barely of av-erage quality. Iron Maiden had never before been merely run of the mill.

At least the tour was successful, despite, and perhaps in part because of, the intimacy of the crowds. Bayley managed to front the Di'Anno and Dickinson era material with equal aplomb and it was difficult to argue with the quality of dyed-in-the-wool Maiden classics. This became more pertinent when the band performed new songs such as 'Lord Of The Flies', about which the crowd were often less enthusiastic. It was clear they were simply not good enough.

Talking of his role as Maiden front man, Blaze was visibly stimu-lated. "I don't know how you can describe being on stage and in Maiden at the same time, or how it feels singing 'Fear Of The Dark' or 'The Trooper' for the first time in front of an audience. The nearest I can get is this... Try to imagine the loudest fuck-off stereo ever. It's wired directly into your brain and all the time it's playing there's no bullshit. It's the most perfect narcotic ever. You look up and thousands of people are wired into the same fuck-off stereo and your whole life comes into sharp focus and every mo-ment is like the start of your favourite record, and no-one can tell you to turn it down!" Asked at the time for his opinion on *The X Factor,* Bruce Dickinson was good-natured in pronouncing it a "decent" album, but went on to politely suggest the band should change their musical direction to suit Blaze's vocal style.

It would be three years before Maiden released another album. But before this, in 1996 came their first 'Best Of' compilation. Titled *Best Of The Beast*, the mere presence of some of the tracks was shocking in itself. With appearances of the *X Factor* numbers, 'Sign Of The Cross' and 'Man On The Edge' as well as a new track, the unremarkable 'Virus'. Of course, a compilation will always be a talking point, as much for the material absent as that chosen. But here were countless strange inclusions such as 'Afraid To Shoot Strangers' and 'Seventh Son Of A Seventh Son', with far better songs available that were overlooked; take your pick from 'Alexander The Great', 'Powerslave' and 'Die With Your Boots On' *et al.* At least Maiden justified the purchase by including 34 songs altogether in a double CD set. Though many fans would buy the album for completion purposes, this was clearly a release for those unfamiliar with the band.

It was also doubtless produced to serve as a reminder, dreamt up by the marketing wizards behind the group, to anyone questioning Maiden's relevance in the modern metal scene. The songs from the band's golden era would jog the memory of anyone casting aspersions and the set's release would keep Maiden in the public eye for another two years.

Come 1998 the group were ready to release their second studio album with Blaze Bayley in tow. Though the record would ultimately suffer another dip in sales figures, ironically it was a vast improvement on *The X Factor*. Surely this was testament to the 'new' line-up now having had four years of togetherness and plenty of collective experience to draw on. "Recording 'Virus' gave us a lot more confidence when we started writing for this album," Blaze reckoned. "I had learned so much about the different areas of my voice and I made it stronger. I feel that the recording of this new album was also a lot more spontaneous than the last. We just got the arrangements together and started recording before we even rehearsed the songs."

For once the typical 'new album syndrome' bragging was justified. Maiden really had improved and Blaze in particular was able to stretch his voice and finally cope with the epic Maiden style. This is especially evident in 'The Clansman', a glorious song of battle, over eight minutes long and finally a track which justified his position as Maiden front man. Equally, opener 'Futureal' was prime, catchy Maiden and it was to be one of the best tracks Harris and Bayley wrote together.

Yet there remained weaknesses, chinks in the armour, which would be difficult to patch up. 'The Angel And The Gambler' was a nice enough title, but this sub par record (released as a single) was way short of Maiden's past achievements. Similarly the album contained several filler tracks and considering there were only eight altogether, this did not bode well. The public concurred and *Virtual XI* became Maiden's worst selling album.

At least the imagery was memorable, the band deciding on a football theme with each of the group members integrated into a dream footballing side and wearing a Maiden football shirt (which had recently been added to the Maiden merchandise line). Steve explained the idea; "This is our eleventh studio album and over the last couple years in particular, more and more young kids are getting into soccer, not so much in America, but in the rest of the world people are soccer mad! So, we thought it would be great if we could tie the two together. It's our eleventh album, the World Cup is coming up, and we're totally into soccer. So to tie in with *Virtual XI*, we have the five members of the band and the eleven is made up of six international soccer players." Illustrator Mel Grant describes the process behind the creation of the artwork. "Maiden asked for an idea to do with Virtual Reality. The concept behind *Virtual XI* (which I originally called Virtual Insanity) was of a boy sitting in a very tranquil setting seeing Eddie and chaos through the VR set. So which world is the boy actually in? They then asked me to include the football game. I was told one of the members is keen on football, which is how the title became *Virtual XI*."

However the music was dressed there was no doubt Maiden was struggling to retain its status as the world's greatest heavy metal band. Steve Harris had been thinking for a while that it was time for a change and in the end the group decided it was best if they find a new singer. Blaze had always been the wrong choice in some people's eyes.

"To me Blaze couldn't sing, I hated the bloke," Neal Kay says. "And I heard him do an interview on radio in Lisbon. And he was talking such bullshit, I phoned Steve up and told him actually, I was so annoyed with what I heard. I said 'your fucking singer's mouthing off in Portugal about this, that and the bloody other'. And I said to Steve, 'why did you take him on board?' And Steve said, 'well there was no one else English who could do the job'. And I said 'fuck me there are hundreds of yanks with voices like you wouldn't believe' – that was it. 'I'm not having a bleeding yank in the band!' he said, 'We're a British band'. And that's how it is. Even if the most talented man on God's earth comes outside of England he won't be joining Iron Maiden."

The split was amicable nevertheless and instead of feeling the victim of a conspiracy, Blaze took the news in good spirit. He still maintains his time in the band was magnificent and that both he and the whole of the Maiden entourage enjoyed their time together. It was a strange period for the group and they were lucky to escape a tough time for traditional metal with their dignity intact.

"Basically, they wanted to do something different and that gave me the opportunity to put my own band together," Blaze says of the split. "The result of doing this was *Silicon Messiah*, the album I am most proud of out of all the albums I have done. I remain friends with everyone from Maiden. I don't remember ever getting anything other than great support from Maiden fans all over the world. There will always be room for a Maiden song in our live set."

Blaze's time in Iron Maiden added several strings to his bow. He was now seen as a strong heavy metal vocalist as opposed to a hard rock singer. It had always been his desire to front a powerful metal band and with his self-named outfit he got his wish. Blaze has released several competent albums (an improvement even on his Maiden era material) and toured the world over. Not bad for a poor kid from Tamworth.

The period in which Blaze fronted Maiden was vital for both as it enabled them to see where they could go next. It was clearly going to be difficult for the union to remain for another five years and it seems now with hindsight, the decision to split was best for both parties.

They didn't know it at the time but the Iron Maiden boys were about to be reunited with a very special singer.

THE LOST BOYS – WOLFSBANE REVISITED

The last bastions of hope for true British rock, Wolfsbane possessed all the requisite qualities to become a long lasting, classic band. Unfortunately the typical reality of life in a British rock group meant Wolfsbane faded away all too soon. Here I talk with their trio of original members who recall the 'Bane and Maiden experience.

PAUL STENNING: **What are your thoughts now on the records Wolfsbane released?** *Live Fast, Die Fast?*

JEFF HATELEY (BASS): "Recording was a total nightmare from start to finish. When we got the call from Rick Rubin we had been rejected by every label in Britain, so to sign to what was at the time the coolest record company in America seemed like our ticket to world domination. But once we got into the studio I couldn't work out why he wanted to sign us in the first place as he seemed determined to change virtually everything about our sound. After months of torturous all night recording sessions we ended up with a record with inaudible bass, clumsy arrangements, and to top it all, the great Steve Danger replaced by a drum machine! It got good reviews at the time but I've always hated it."

JASE EDWARDS (GUITAR): "Rick later said he had two plots for the band. Plot one was to put us in a room with one microphone and shout 'GO!' through the door and record what happened next. The other, which is what he did, was to manufacture us with drum machines and stuff. He said he chose the wrong one. I agree. No hard feelings though. I always liked Rick and had some great discussions with him about the philosophy of production and music. Stuff I still find useful."

PS: All Hell's Breaking Loose...?

JH: "This is my favourite Wolfsbane studio recording. It was supposed to be a quick mini album to tie in with our support slot with Iron Maiden, but we saw it as our second album and as our chance to make up for the mistakes of *Live Fast*... It only took a few days to record but I think its got some of our best songs on it and you can hear our enthusiasm and general good vibes. We had to fight the record company for the title and artwork we wanted as they were after something more metal, but we were trying to be a classic band and not part of some scene."

JE: "Recorded in about six days, rough, but much more Wolfsbane. Our first real recording. I like the fact that this album is fun. A piss-take at times. The song 'Totally Nude' for example. I loved Wolfsbane for not being afraid to put ideas together that were ridiculous. We were misunderstood by people who thought we were ridiculous by accident. We just liked to accent the silliness of metal as it was at the time whilst still enjoying it."

STEVE 'DANGER' ELLETT (DRUMS): "My favourite recording experience. I never liked recording, I only wanted to do the touring. Unfortunately this was the thing that fucked up our game plan so to speak. The tracks on this were due to go out on our second album, which was all but written. The record company wanted something to coincide with the Maiden dates, so we had to sacrifice half of the album for this EP. The record company managed to fuck up the release spectacularly – it came out just before the end of the tour."

PS: Down Fall The Good Guys?

JH: "This album kind of follows on from *All Hell's Breaking Loose*...in its sound and attitude. We had a bit more time to make this one and Brendan, who was producing again, had a bigger input. He did a good job but maybe smoothed off too many of the rough edges. We were definitely at our most musically ambitious on this album but in retrospect I think we should have concentrated more on rocking out. Typically, the record company released the worst tracks as singles!"

SDE: "I listened to it a few months ago and it's a lot better than I remember when we did it. There are some really strong songs on it and we still had hope."

PS: Massive Noise Injection?

JH: "I know I'm biased but I think this is a storming live album, up there with the best of them. We'd finally got the true sound of the band down on vinyl and in recording one gig at a famous venue the band and crowd really rose to the occasion. The title refers to how the songs sounded compared to the studio versions. I'm really proud of *Massive Noise Injection* 'cos it captures everything Wolfsbane was about in terms of energy, chaos, humour and the audience being part of the show."
SDE: "I was drinking more than ever and loving it. That album (for my part) was fuelled by cheap red wine and speed. I was unconscious until fifteen minutes before show time. Ah well, I think it captures the spirit of Wolfsbane better than anything else we've done. Oh, apart from the video."

PS: Wolfsbane?

JH: "Although none of us would have admitted it at the time, we all knew that our days as Wolfsbane were numbered. We'd been around too long to still be the next big thing and we were starting to lose our audience to bands like the Wildhearts and Terrorvision. But that said, we'd been playing some of our best gigs and were gagging to get back into the studio.
Unfortunately, with a combination of equipment failure, extreme drunkenness, pre- *Jackass* style stunts that landed producer Simon Efemy in hospital with broken ribs and Blaze disappearing on mysterious all-day motor bike rides we sort of lost the plot. Mind you it was still the most fun I've ever had in a recording studio.
We finished recording a few weeks before Christmas '93 and the plan was to do a short tour then go back to Linford Manor in the New Year and mix the album. Of course, halfway through the tour Blaze left the band so Jase and I had to go back on our own and finish an album for a band that no longer existed. With hindsight it would have been better to go out on a high with *Massive Noise Injection*, but I still think there's a few good

tracks on *Wolfsbane* (it was supposed to be titled 'Lifestyles Of The Broke And Obscure' but Blaze thought it was too negative!) and at least we were trying something different even if it wasn't totally successful."

JE: "Not the album we set out to make. Blaze started auditioning for Maiden after we demoed this album. The demo (now lost) was possibly the best thing we ever did. But Blaze changed his vocal style after the demos and the album ended up as the most lifeless thing we did. It's not a shame. It's just what happened."

PS: Can you tell me a little bit about the whole time when you found out Blaze was leaving, and your thoughts and feelings at the time?

JH: "We'd played a storming gig at Norwich Oval and had a day off before we were due to play in Plymouth. I'd been Christmas shopping in Brum with my girlfriend (who's now my wife) and we got home to about ten messages on the answer phone to call Jase, Steve and the manager, Gary Garner. Basically, Maiden's management had called Garner and told him that Blaze was now a member of Iron Maiden and wouldn't be finishing the tour or album.

I met up with Jase (Steve was living in Liverpool at the time) and we agreed that was the end of the band that we'd both formed nine years previously when he was only 14 and I was 16. Of course we knew that Maiden had been interested in Blaze and we assumed that he would audition for them, I mean who wouldn't? But having been in a band with Blaze for the best part of a decade we knew his strengths and weaknesses and there was no way he could do justice to Bruce Dickinson era songs but he'd probably get away with the Di'Anno stuff.

Blaze had been denying that he was going to join Maiden to us and the music press for ages. It might seem naive now but we had to believe him and concentrate on making the new album. It had always been 'us against the world', so if Blaze said he wasn't joining Maiden then that was it. A lot of water has flowed under the bridge since then, and OK it was only a band and it's not like anybody died or anything, but it was pretty pathetic of Blaze that after everything we'd been through he couldn't tell us to our faces!

I think that after he joined Maiden he was pretty much told what to do, it was like he'd been swallowed up by some kind of machine. So that was the end of the band – he went and bought himself a Jag, while we signed on. Then it got pretty messy as we were chased for all the bands unpaid debts, which dragged on for ages. It's all in the past and although I'm not bothered now, it felt pretty grim at the time."

JE: "We had been close as a band. We had been in situations where we had to watch each other's backs quite literally, places where you could trust no-one but each other. We came through that and we looked out for each other still. We kind of knew Blaze was gonna go to Maiden, but as he never told us he was going, we thought he wouldn't. When he left I remember signing on at Christmas, the 26th, thinking 'Merry Fucking Christmas and thanks a lot'. The band split and it was for the best. We had already said everything we had to say."

SDE: "We found out on a day off whilst we were on tour. Gary our manager called me up and said, 'gig's off tomorrow, your singer's gone to Iron Maiden'. I was well fucked off as I'd just bought a load of pharmaceuticals to keep me happy on tour. I went to my local offy and got a slab of Stella and proceeded to drink and drug myself into a three day stupor, as well as calling everyone in my phone book feeling sorry for myself. I never thought bad of Bayle leaving us for Maiden, fuck we were on our way out. It was just we were such a close family I wish he could have told us. I know why he couldn't as I kept in touch with him. I know it was fucking with him going for the Maiden auditions whilst still being in Wolfsbane."

PS: **What are your best and worst memories of the time in Wolfsbane?**

JH: "I loved the transit tours before we got signed, just gigging all over the country and crashing on peoples' floors, picking up fans on the way. That whole late '80s rock scene. One of my favourite memories is the first time we headlined the old Marquee on Wardour Street. We'd sold it out and the queue was past The Ship. We were in the dressing room waiting to go onstage and after the support band finished each song all you could hear was the sound of the crowd chanting 'WOLFSBANE' like a football crowd and we felt unstoppable.
I've forgotten most of the bad stuff, it's boring. The worst thing for me isn't stuff that happened, its the things we didn't get to do, like go on *Top Of The Pops*, play at Donington, or go to Japan."

JE: "The best was the feeling we could take on the world, and we did for a while. There was no worst…"

SDE: "The best; the fans, the gigs, being in a gang with your mates and doing the biggest doss of a job imaginable. The worst; the end and the industry and the boredom in-between playing and recording. If I could do it all again I would drink harder, take more chemicals and shag until I went blind. I never planned on getting to 35 so bugger me what do I do now?"

Sources:

Paul Stenning Interviews
www.ironmaiden.com
George Matsagouras Interviews

Chapter 13
The Reinvention

"I don't know where it's going with them. While I am not part of them any-more, I still have an attachment to them. I still talk to the band. I always seem to put it this way: 'We may be divorced or separated, but we still share the same bathroom.' I don't want to see them disappear down the tubes or anything like that. It would just be a shame to see all the past work be washed aside if people don't like the new stuff." Bruce Dickinson

"The first thing I said to Bruce was, 'Why do you want to come back?' and the second thing was, 'How long are you staying for?' We didn't want him coming back to just do a one-off tour. We'd rather get someone else. And that's what we probably would have done if Bruce's attitude hadn't been right and we didn't believe that he was coming back for the long-term." So said Steve Harris regarding the surprising return of Bruce Dickinson to the ranks of Iron Maiden. Clearly, though some people assumed a reunion was inevitable, Steve Harris was adamant that a reformation would only take place if Bruce was 100% focused on Maiden. Given the somewhat acrimonious departure of Dickinson eight years pre-viously, it was understandable Harris was sceptical. However, he was also highly enthusiastic about the prospect of the old band reforming.

Rumours had circulated about this as early as 1998 when Adrian Smith had joined Bruce on his *Accident Of Birth* project (see Chapter 17). When things had finally hit a dead end with Blaze, there was only one man fans wanted to front Iron Maiden. Those fans, plus a large helping of the music press, began to ask Harris and co. questions about contemplat-ing a Brucey return. Initially the answer was short and sharp, a veritable 'no'! Why would he? Bruce had left of his own accord and was enjoying a resurgence in popularity with his seriously heavy set, *The Chemical Wed-ding*. From extreme metal magazines to hard rock press, Dickinson was, for the first time in his solo career, being afforded the respect he craved and deserved. Finally he had established himself as a solo performer in his own right – no longer simply regarded as the ex-singer of Iron Maiden. Therefore it was ironic, to say the least, that his most successful record under his own moniker would see him reunite with Maiden.

The wheels were set in motion when Steve asked Rod Smallwood (who was also managing Bruce) whether Dickinson would consider returning. Smallwood spoke to Bruce and returned to the bassist with an affirmative nod. In some ways Bruce was surprised there were even mutterings of acceptance from camp Harris, given the harsh words that had been spat against him. Steve famously told one magazine, "Bruce would make a country and western album if he thought it would sell." Some could see the bass player's point, given Bruce had jumped from hard rock (*Tattooed Millionaire*) to a mixture of serious and tongue-in-cheek rock (*Balls To Picasso*) and traversed grunge sentiments (*Skunkworks*) before returning to fully embrace heavy metal again with both *Accident Of Birth* and *The Chemical Wedding*. There were also those nagging doubts about the singer's temperament. He almost went off the rails, bemoaning his place in the group and writing almost solely acoustic numbers for the band back in 1986. But with Bruce there was no contrived notion of who he should be from one year to another. He wasn't changing to please the public; he varied his material to please himself. The fact that this meant immersing himself in a wide cross-section of solo material was hardly something to criticise him for, or indeed a signal of him being a money obsessed charlatan. On the contrary, one particular quote from Bruce suggested the complete opposite. "Money changes a lot of things, it entices and spontaneously creates a shallow and meaningless entourage. I avoid it," he once said.

What critics failed to appreciate was that Bruce did not make music for money. Come the end of his first Maiden tenure, he could easily have disappeared completely, bought a Caribbean island and enjoyed his royalty money. He could also have pursued fencing, writing, radio broadcasting or flying. More so than most, Bruce was a man of many talents and he didn't shirk from using them. So, was he making music just to sell? Hardly. The days in his first incarnation with Iron Maiden had secured him financially, he was now a millionaire with a steady income just from his past work, as were all the Maiden members. Apart from the fact that their income had always been high, they had now been offered a deal which split $30,000,000 between the group. This agreement was an advance based on future royalties from the back catalogue – assuring there would be regular reissues and repackages. "All of us want to do this," Bruce explained when the decision had been made to rejoin the group with everybody's blessing. "In a lifetime, most people never get to be the best in the world at anything. I've been really lucky, because in my lifetime we were kings of the world in 1984, '85, '86, and I've just been offered a shot at doing it again. You don't pass that up."

In response to the criticism some would fire at Dickinson, it was blatantly obvious that it would have been easier for the singer *not* to try and prove himself musically. Yet Bruce was not one to avoid a test and his longevity was borne from his desire to face a challenge head on – musical or otherwise. Some of the criticism would come from ex-band mates, such as Thunderstick, who were eager to have Bruce in the classic Samson reunion in 1999. "We were talking genuinely and regularly to Bruce on the phone," explains the drummer, "and he was getting a bit disillusioned with his own solo project and we'd written some new material, in fact the material that's around now that hasn't been released. Paul (Samson) sent it to him and he said 'Yeah, I love it, I've got some ideas for it,' and all that kind of thing. And he did a gig at the Astoria. We went up and saw him and we were sitting talking to him and it was actually getting really quite serious. We said 'look, we've got this gig in New Jersey coming up, how about if you do it with us?' And he said 'Yeah, alright, ok.' And about two weeks later it was in the papers that he'd rejoined Iron Maiden, and you just say 'you two-faced fucking bastard.'" Though the desertion clearly rankled with Thunderstick, no-one could blame Bruce for preferring a reunion with Maiden to one with Samson. With the greatest respect to the latter, they were only ever interesting for many folks due to Bruce's involvement. Of course, not to take away from Paul Samson himself, or indeed Thunderstick, there were elements of a great band, even without the Air Raid Siren fronting the material. But if it came down to a choice – which it did – who, other than the Samson members themselves could really accuse Dickinson of choosing the wrong option?

Bruce was not the only one involved in the comeback however. It was Steve Harris' idea also to bring Adrian Smith back to the table, and create an unprecedented three-guitar assault. There was no question of dumping Janick to return to the classic line-up, Gers was now a staple six-stringer for the band. Steve's only thought was to add to the guitar carnage. "I don't think I would have come back in the band if they said, 'if you come back Janick's going to go'," explained Adrian with characteristic good grace. "Unless he left of his own free will. That wouldn't have been cool. I think it's really cool that I've come back and there's going to be three of us doing the guitar stuff. It's like we are going forward, we're not going back. It's like a challenge. It's a bit of an uncertain thing really. But I think that's good because it's a bit on the edge and it hasn't been done before. I think it's going to be great, personally."

Indeed, Adrian's perspective was as unique as Bruce Dickinson's, and the two had the luxury of watching Maiden continue in a different vein from their time with the group. Thus, they brought renewed vigour to camp Maiden, something that even Steve Harris would concede had been lacking for a while. With Bruce's trademark energy and Adrian's laid back but highly competent guitar playing, Iron Maiden was about to be reinvented. And the funny thing was, despite the bickering reported in the press, between Bruce and Steve predominantly, there was no detectable atmosphere or bad blood among any of the band members. Everyone had progressed from being wary of each other to fully embracing everything each member had to offer. In short, they had grown up a lot. Certain questions were thrown at Steve and Bruce in almost every interview after the reunion; obvious posers such as 'does it feel strange to be back together again after all this time?' 'Can you all get along?' 'Does having three guitarists present a problem?' But all these issues were in the imagination of the press, Maiden had matured, their egos had dissipated. No one member thought he was more integral than another and in fact, this was the best the band had ever got along. Bruce had his personal history with Janick and Adrian, and Steve and Dave had always been the best of mates. Nicko got on with everybody and so there was a coming together of the two 'sides', a merger that saw Maiden able to challenge other acts. Bruce claimed that most of the current bands in the metal scene were diabolical and Maiden was here to show the young guns, and plenty of old ones too, how metal performance really should be done. Bruce was boasting about the album that would eventually surface in 2000, *Brave New World*. But first the Maiden members knew they needed something to bond them together, and the easiest way of testing their union was to tour immediately. They had the perfect excuses as well – their PC game and 'Best Of' compilation, *Ed Hunter*, had just hit the racks. [1]

So the band did a short tour (their shortest ever), where their set comprised somewhat unexpected additions such as 'Tail Gunner', a track that had fallen out of the show a long time ago. Yet there was an obvious explanation for cuts that made the collection, and therefore the live set. An online poll was organised, whereby fans voted for their favourite Maiden songs in order of preference, and over just a couple of days, hundreds of thousands logged their opinions. The resultant collection provided a good overview of every Maiden era, from the Di'Anno classics such as 'Wrathchild' and 'Phantom Of The Opera' to standard Bruce-fronted tracks such as 'Number Of The Beast', 'Hallowed Be Thy Name' and 'Powerslave'. There was also a place for comparatively recent numbers with Bruce, such as 'Be Quick Or Be Dead' and 'Fear Of The Dark'. It must also have been pleasing to Steve (not to mention to Blaze himself) that the Bayley era had not been ignored. Fans had plumped for 'Futureal', 'Man On The Edge' and 'The Clansman' to showcase Blaze's Maiden period, proving that whatever the criticism of his tenure with Britain's metal Gods, the fans didn't necessarily concur.

THE 'COMEBACK' ALBUM

As soon as the tour for *Ed Hunter* was completed, Maiden put down their collective ideas and headed off to record what would become their twelfth studio album. Everyone knew there was no room for complacency, and that this had to be cut and thrust Maiden at its very best, lest people became sceptical about the band's motives. But Maiden had never been complacent in their long career and that was not about to change. Every member had to pull his weight and this was underlined by the fact that Janick Gers, Dave Murray, Adrian Smith, plus the dream team of Dickinson/Harris, all contributed to the songwriting. Unusually there was just one 'sole credit' for Steve Harris, the emotional 'Blood Brothers'. Finally, Maiden had created an album where everyone had fused their remarkable energies and talents together to produce their most diverse set yet. Perhaps the strength of the material was less surprising since the band had made a change to their routine. As Steve explained; "This album we approached differently and we actually rehearsed for quite a while before going in and doing it. We'd rehearsed the songs as if we were going to play live."

The result was an emphatic return for the new look Iron Maiden, from the opening single 'The Wicker Man' with its rousing chorus, to the ending phrases of the harmonious 'The Thin Line Between Love And Hate'. 'The Wicker Man' is a feel-good, melodic track that fools the listener into a positive frame of mind, despite being inspired by the classic horror film of the same name. The Christopher Lee and Edward Woodward movie is the story of a policeman (Woodward) coming to a small town with distinctly unusual locals, to investigate the disappearance of a young girl. The town is situated on an island so there is nowhere for Woodward to escape when things become nasty. Eventually the girl leads him to the top of a hill where he is sacrificed by the Pagan residents. He is set on fire within a wicker enclosure, and it was this which inspired the cover shot for the single, where Eddie is dressed in wicker. Mel Grant had been penciled in to do the cover art but couldn't, as he explains; "I was approached by Maiden for 'The Wicker Man,' but I was too busy with other work at the time and they needed it very quickly. I have a 'Wicker Man' painting on my site but it was not for Maiden, it was for a book cover."

193

The other single to be released from the album was 'Out Of The Silent Planet' which, upon inspection, is a superb, catchy number, with the trademark duelling guitars and Bruce's captivating howl. Though Dickinson had written the lyrics, it was unlikely lines such as *"you are guilty, the punishment is death for all who live,"* were going to endear Maiden to radio stations, especially in the band's home country. But that was never really a problem because Maiden didn't expect to be radio or chart friendly, though the *Brave New World* album would scale the top ten in the UK, reaching number seven.

The best songs on the album are, interestingly, some of the longest and the least likely for commercial success. 'Ghost Of The Navigator' (6:50), 'Blood Brothers' (7:14) and 'Dream Of Mirrors' (9:21) drag the listener in with Maiden's trademark hustle. The reassurance of a familiar sound through quality new material ensured *Brave New World* would be universally well received.

'Blood Brothers' is Steve Harris at his most emotional and almost vulnerable, with a set of rather pessimistic lyrics, beautifully sung by Bruce. *"Just for a second a glimpse of my father I see, and in a movement he beckons to me. And in a moment the memories are all that remain, and all the wounds are reopening again,"* were words one would not usually expect from the Maiden bassist. Yet on reflection, his past lyrics had often focused on nightmares and the esoteric, as well as frequently questioning the meaning of existence. So it came as no surprise that after the death of his father, Steve would pen such melancholy phrases. As the Maiden leader confirmed, the song touches on many issues at the same time, be it the 'other side' or the very real and current atrocities in the world. Ultimately though, the song is a reflection on the question: Why do good – or on the other hand, bad – things happen to certain people? A 'some guys have all the luck' mentality. The song sees Maiden at their orchestral best, with a huge, bombastic quality that their earlier material hinted at but never quite delivered. Sure, previously they had penned epic material, but this was something extra and included a higher quotient of keyboard sounds. As Steve admits; "I have always wanted to include orchestral type sounds on our stuff and we have used that sort of sound on keyboards before. This time however it was slightly different, as Kevin (Shirley, producer) knew this guy in New York who does that kind of thing and layers it up. We sent him a tape. I put down on the tape the kind of things I wanted and I was amazed that he came back and did exactly what I wanted. That in itself was very unusual!"

'Dream Of Mirrors' is another epic number, holding the honour of longest song, and, unusually for Maiden, comes in the middle rather than at the end of the record. Once more it sees Steve examining disrupted sleeping patterns:

"I get up put on the light, dreading the oncoming night
Scared to fall asleep and dream the dream again
Nothing that I contemplate, nothing that I can compare
To letting loose the demons deep inside my head"

The music itself is typically Maiden, building up to a huge crescendo where once again Bruce proves his incredible ability to enunciate a series of fast-flowing words.

Maiden are in full, harmonious swing when it comes to material such as 'The Fallen Angel', which Steve admitted was a careful homage to Thin Lizzy, though he was at pains to confirm this was not a deliberately commercial move. In reality everyone knew Maiden did not intend to broach the charts or submit to any demands for a 'hit', that just wouldn't happen. Though a few deadheads had to fire off rumours regarding the new material before it was anywhere near a record store.

Bruce laughed, "I've heard lots of theories about what we should be doing on this album, ranging from 'Get with the program, get electronic,' to 'Oh, it should sound like my solo records. Iron Maiden should do a record that sounds like *The Chemical Wedding*. That would be great.' That's one version, and the other one is, 'Oh, they should remake *Number Of The Beast*'. What we've actually done is none of the above, to my great relief."

He was right. What Iron Maiden had achieved was something even greater than their 1982 landmark, or indeed any variation that had emerged since then. *Brave New World* was simply a fantastic modern metal record and Bruce was clearly enthused, boasting, "This is the album. This is the Iron Maiden album that you've needed for twelve years, and it's also the Iron Maiden album that you don't quite expect.

This sounds like classic, vintage Maiden, but it has a twist in the tail, which is a whole kind of almost prog rock element to it that's come in on several of the songs. This album is completely out of any time zone and current popular music culture. I mean, we know it exists right now, but actually it could exist in 1975 as well, and it might very well exist in 2005 when you come back to listen to it. It exists completely out of time.

It's not dependent upon fashion, MTV, radio, or anything. It's just its own entity."

More than any other member of Maiden, Steve Harris was the archetypal workhorse, with a dogged determination to make the music he liked. Despite having millions of fans around the world there was no doubt his theory had paid off so far, the music he liked was equally something the fans gobbled up in their droves. It just seemed Harris and his cohorts had great taste, and considering how long Maiden had now been an institution it was way too late to change the thought processes behind creating albums. Most bands did not get beyond their second album let alone a twelfth, so Harris had been proved right. And he was adamant the band would never deliberately try to compose a *Number Of The Beast Part 2*, or survey fans to gauge the general consensus. To ask fans for opinions on existing songs was one thing, it was a totally different ball game to ask them to suggest new material. Not a chance. "You just cannot make an album worrying about what other people like. You have to like it yourself first. If they like what we have created, all well and good. Thinking about it logically, what else are you gonna do?" Steve emphasised. Regarding emulating previous work with a contrived follow-up, the bassist grimaced, "What's the point of having part two of anything anyway? A great song is a great song. A sequel won't make it any better."

Credit has to go to everyone involved for the success of such a reunion – from the Maiden members themselves, to the management, to producer Kevin Shirley, who had squeezed an extra bead of sweat from every pummelling riff, kick-drum and vocal yelp. Maiden sounded as if they were 20 years old again, and as Bruce suggests, the album has a timeless feel to it. With the exception of the upfront production values the record could indeed have existed decades before, but the secret ingredient was that it also sounded current. Honour for that must also be awarded to Shirley, whose influence perhaps reflected the fact that he had worked with hip, young rockers Silverchair while living in Australia. (The Australian trio who had come to the fore with their *Frogstomp* album.) The producer certainly had kudos. He had also overseen work by Led Zeppelin, Aerosmith, Slayer and The Black Crowes.

"I had really liked the stuff he has done before", Steve confirms, "and then when we had a meeting with him it was just the vibe and the way he does things and the way he talks about stuff, it was great. Obviously you all have to get on with the guy and we got on well with him when we met him so that was great as well. He has worked on albums for loads of different bands and more importantly different types of bands, mainly still within the broad spectrum of rock, and we just thought he would be the right bloke for the job. I think we have made the right choice as working with him has been really great".

"Kevin took the approach of using the strengths of the band, and one of the strengths of the band is playing live," Bruce adds. "We'd never recorded an album live. It's insane, when you think about it. The one thing the band does the best, we've never actually used as an asset. So we went in the studio having prepared all the new material as if we were about to go do a gig, having come off this really successful world tour last year, and having written the material in the three months before that tour."

Best of all for Bruce, despite the fact that the songs were done in four or five takes, he returned to the studio after a few weeks to polish off his vocals and finish the album. However, to his pleasant surprise, he was told he had already recorded them perfectly and the LP was complete!

Most importantly for the band, who were entering their 25th year as a unit, they could have fun with Shirley in the studio. He wasn't some hyped-up geek twiddling with knobs and expecting a deadpan, dour performance. For Steve Harris, the producer had to be as much fun as his band mates, seeing as it was the bassist who would spend most of his time with Shirley. As Harris preferred a stage and a crowd to the confines of a studio, more than ever now, their twelfth album had to have been a delight to record, and according to Steve it certainly was. "He is a pleasure to work with. When you are recording that is what it should be about, fun! You should be enjoying recording. To be able to say 'I enjoyed it' is important and to work with the right people is important."

It was also the producer's idea to record at a rather unusual studio in Paris. A converted building which had once been a cinema, the Guillaume Tell Studios, which set the scene perfectly. As Bruce describes, "There were little nooks and crannies where we could stick the bass guitar and stuff. Effectively there were three or four separate areas which could all be encased in glass, we could all have eye contact, but the sound would have separation."

ED HUNTER

The PC game was certainly a first for a band in the heavy metal genre, although actually it was surprising no-one else had previously thought of the idea. The graphics look good, the game player has the soundtrack of the fan-chosen 'best of the band', and there is definitely something reassuringly 'Maiden' about it all. Perhaps this is because the game was created with a theme in mind, whereby the participants travel through all eras of the Iron Maiden timeline. As the official promotion spiel records, 'In this death race with Eddie you start in the dimly lit streets of London's East End (*Iron Maiden & Killers*). You must then release Eddie from the Asylum (*Piece Of Mind*) and pursue him through Hell (*The Number Of The Beast*), a graveyard (*Live After Death*), Egypt and the Pyramids (*Powerslave*), the Future (*Somewhere In Time*), and finally to a post-apocalyptic landscape (*Virtual XI*). In the final moments of the game you must help Eddie save the planet by defeating the Four Horsemen of the Apocalypse... that is, if you have the skills to get that far'

Sources:

http://uk.music.yahoo.com/read/interview/12043032
http://www.mtv.com/bands/archive/i/iron00/index2.jhtml
http://www.ironmaiden.com/article.php?section=1&subsection=3&artic le_type=
http://www.geocities.com/sunsetstrip/club/5619/interviews/as1097.html
http://www.cavemanproductions.com/REVS/ozzybrooce.html
http://www.bookofhours.net/samson/
George Matsagouras Interviews

Chapter 14
Flights Of Fire

"The prolific spurt has passed. I have spurted my prolificness! I have squirted my whatever from the whatever, the acatalectic record of mankind and have decided to repose myself until after the new Iron Maiden record." Bruce Dickinson

Everything about *Brave New World* signalled a new beginning for Iron Maiden, from the reunion with Bruce Dickinson to the lavish, futuristic artwork supplied by Derek Riggs and Steve Stone. Of course Eddie is present for the cover, but this time he doesn't engulf the spotlight, but is to be seen merely watching over a future city landscape that looks suspiciously like London. The band still look the part, despite Bruce having cut his flowing locks a long time before, and the group shots are obvious depictions of the one and only Iron Maiden.

"I don't see him developing at all, he will probably go backwards because we're all going forward," Steve said of Eddie. "I thought he would get more haggard but he seems to be getting better all the time. The good thing with Eddie is that he is timeless. He will hopefully mature with age. Who knows what he will get up to next. Surely that's half the fun."

Part of the fun was Eddie's appearance in the video for the first single to be lifted from the album, 'The Wicker Man'. As Bruce explained, "Eddie's involved in the video. In actual fact, for the video, the director had a friend of his, basically this guy's like a giant, he's actually taller than a phone box, has the *Guinness Book Of Records* biggest feet in the world, and he's, you know, huge. And we had a guy called 'screaming mad George' that does prosthetics for movies and really hideous creations out of latex. He did a life cast from this guy's body and did a whole prosthetic Eddie make-up.

"So we've got a latex Eddie monster human being and he drags some poor hapless driver out of his car and lots of semi-naked women dance around a may-pole and sacrifice the guy, and the Wicker Man, which is about a 30-foot straw effigy that we burned to the ground."

Though Steve Harris, and indeed Dickinson, conceded Eddie was a huge part of the whole Maiden aura, and a very special mascot for fans, they did not place too much emphasis on the fact that *Brave New World* would be the last time Derek Riggs would work with the band. This was no surprise given the bad blood behind the scenes and it was Riggs' decision to depart. "They were so rude and unpleasant about everything," the artist told George Matsagouras, "always trying to sound clever and taking credit for the ideas on the covers, that I don't really care if they do well or not any more. According to them, they had all the great ideas and I was just the stupid monkey who painted it for them. The truth is that for about 75% of the time they didn't even know what was going to be on the cover of their album or single. They couldn't possibly have known because I was making it up as I went along. So really even I didn't know until it was on the cover. Basically they were just jealous and insecure because the covers were getting more attention than the music."

However, Melvyn Grant had a vastly different opinion, as he also explained to Matsagouras, "I've never actually met the band, all my dealings have been through their manager Rod Smallwood and he's a good guy. Working with them is A-okay."

Whatever the truth behind the Riggs fallout, it was now a problem for the band, superficially at least. The original designer and long-time painter of Eddie the 'ead was no longer a part of the organisation, ending an association of some 20 years. Riggs would later tell Matsagouras, "Their latest covers are trash. I laugh at them regularly," referring to the likes of *Edward The Great* and *The BBC Archives*, where Eddie still features, but certainly not as we knew him. The artist also made an interesting revelation about the artwork for 'The Wicker Man' single. "There were never any pictures which they didn't use in some form or another. All of my designs were used somewhere (even though they make it sound like they were doing me a favour). If I painted it for Maiden, they used it and it is published in their catalogue somewhere, except maybe for the covers for 'The Wicker Man'. But this is the exception because 'The Wicker Man' was the original name for the album, not just for the single. So the pictures were done with the album merchandise in mind, not just as a single cover. The designs were accepted by the management, the real reason why they got rejected was that I had previously pissed Bruce off (about the *Scream For Me Brazil* cover) and he wanted to get his own back."

Riggs' parting words resonated within camp Maiden, his attitude to the possibility of any future working partnership with Maiden being basically one of 'no going back'. As he summed up; "I have had enough of working with adults who behave like selfish children so I left Maiden to do something else. I thought it might be nice to work with grown-ups instead." Of course, Eddie was never bigger than the band, nor would he ever be, but it seemed a shame the union of Riggs and Maiden would no longer exist. There is no doubting, whatever your view on the spat between them, that the original Maiden covers from the debut album to *Brave New World*, were the best sleeve shots to represent the band. Replacement artists could never capture the Riggs technique and Eddie always seemed to look half deformed in future cover art (and not in a good way).

At least Maiden had Riggs' services for the *Brave New World* cover, though it was a somewhat 'shortened' version of Eddie that presided over the classy metropolis.

The album entered the Billboard charts in the mid-30s, which seemed a touch low for a band of Maiden's stature, especially considering the reunion with Bruce. Yet the singer cleverly sidestepped the issue of lesser sales figures when he informed one reporter, "I think when I went into doing it, at my most optimistic I thought it might go gold. It didn't, but it certainly didn't do the contrary. It sold somewhere about 250,000-300,0000, in the States. That actually is remarkable compared to the derisory figures that any of our contemporaries are selling. We were outselling them by ten- or 20-to-one. When looking at what other comparable new bands and existing metal type bands are doing in the States they are still good figures. So actually I was thinking, wow 300,000 is really fucking good. In the rest of the world and in Europe it was extraordinary. We were pretty much back up to mid-80s type figures."

So, in the age-old battle Maiden had endured with America, it seemed there was no love lost. It seemed they were never going to score a number one hit whatever they did in the future. The name and logo were far too 'old-school heavy metal' for the majority of the American music buying public, and one mustn't forget, radio had never really wanted to touch the band. It was only in Maiden's home country that new music television channels such as *Scuzz* and *Kerrang!* provided them with some sort of platform. Of course, there was never any doubt that cast-iron Maiden fans would buy the album wherever they resided. As Bruce suggested, to sell hundreds of thousands of records in an internet age where downloading was *de rigeur*, well that was some achievement. Equally – though Bruce was tactful enough to avoid the subject – the figures for *Brave New World* eclipsed the Blaze-era material by some margin.

Where one might assume Harris and co. were completely against new technology like downloading music, any such accusations were pleasantly refuted by the Maiden bassist.

"I reckon it's like when CDs first came out," he explained. "The record companies were very worried about the quality of CDs and mini discs and stuff like that. They were worried that people would copy them and not buy them but it has already been proved totally wrong. It's now the same thing with DVD or VHS when they first came out. I think with MP3s it might actually make more people go and see live bands. You can hear the live show on a CD but you cannot see the spectacular excitement that a really good live show like ours brings to the crowd. You have to experience that live and in person. I don't have any problem with new technology and I would be hypocritical if I did."

This statement might go some way to explaining the sheer quantity of live recordings Maiden would subsequently issue, and let's not forget they had, throughout their history, released plenty of live albums and videos. Additionally the comment reflected a typically straightforward Harris viewpoint on a topic others had a problem with. Metallica, for instance lost their dignity when drummer Lars Ulrich and front man James Hetfield spoke out against the new downloading craze, specifically Napster. This service, originally a pirate peer-to-peer file sharing service (where users literally shared music files from their own PCs – basically a modern form of tape trading) put founder Shawn Fanning in trouble when it was found to be responsible for leaking a downloadable demo version of Metallica's 'I Disappear' track, before it was ready for release. The band were furious with Ulrich in particular, for taking on the responsibility of publicly speaking out against the company and other smaller types of p2p services, and then going on to sue Napster. Ulrich was victorious and as a result, the original incarnation of Napster was destroyed, though later the company would re-emerge as a service where listeners could pay for tracks individually or for a whole album.

This did not eradicate the p2p network, other smaller sites still manage to exist undetected for the moment, but it is probably only a matter of time before another band of Metallica's status discovers these and begins court proceedings. Given the huge split between those who favour downloading and those opposed, it was refreshing to hear the attitude put forward by Steve Harris, one, in fact, that many felt should be echoed by other artists. Harris was undoubtedly canny enough to realise, however, that packaging was just as important in some ways to many Maiden fans as the music and therefore it was unlikely a group such as Maiden would really lose out to downloading. Fans would surely still buy the full album if they liked it enough.

Accordingly, it's no surprise to note that the band would soon put even more emphasis on packaging and value for money. Come the turn of the century, the average music buyer expected more for their buck, and thus, many bands resorted to spending lavish amounts on fancy digipak or fold out packaging. In Maiden's case albums like *Rock In Rio* (released in 2002) featured an initial run with 3D sleeves, and also contained enhanced DVD sections.

In fact, the Maiden back catalogue was habitually reissued with new sections to tempt fans into buying them again, or even for the first time. There is no arguing with the quality of the products the group would always release, nothing was particularly throwaway. But Maiden had always released interesting formats, especially for singles, with etched vinyl, picture discs, Christmas cards, etc. Virtually any way of giving something extra to the fans was displayed in the care Steve Harris, Rod Smallwood and co. put into each and every release. Though the band was still part of the huge multi-national record label EMI, they somehow managed to keep their respectability and credibility intact. Statements from their members helped, such as the following from Bruce; "There's a lot of interesting music wandering around. As I said, the whole thing has kind of downsized. And I think that may actually be very good for music. Because, if that means that big commercial corporations take less interest in music, 'cause there's less obvious money to be made out of it, then I think it will be good for music." Regardless of opinion, at least Iron Maiden had sole control over their empire, despite being on EMI. Partly this was due to the fact that the label had to keep the band happy as Maiden pretty much kept them afloat, with their repeated reissues and ongoing sales.

FLY WITH YOUR BOOTS ON

September 11, 2001 will forever be remembered as the date when the financial twin towers in New York were hit by terrorist attacks, with almost 3,000 people being killed. The year had started with the controversial appointment of George W. Bush Jr. as the President of the United States, following a long democratic run with Bill Clinton who had presided, mostly successfully, over the world's most powerful nation for eight years. The country was now in the hands of a Republican. In the United Kingdom, a second term for Labour leader Tony Blair was underway, with millions around the globe unaware of the chaos the union of Bush and Blair would eventually bring to the world.

Following the attacks, life as a band had to go on for Iron Maiden, though it certainly brought about changes in their individual opinions, not least for Bruce and Nicko, given their penchant for flying aircraft. Bruce was actually in New York at the time and recalls; "I was on the roof of the hotel sunbathing. People were wandering on the roof and peering downtown. You couldn't actually see anything. I asked 'what's everybody looking at?' and they said 'there's an airplane crashed into the World Trade Center' and I'm thinking a little Cessna or something. So I went back and lied down again. I thought there's obviously been a few people killed and I don't want to rubberneck and that's that. Next thing I hear is two F-15's going down the Hudson River low and I'm thinking 'that's not right, something's weird, what's going on'?" Bruce spoke with the next man to arrive on the terrace, asking him what type of plane had crashed into the World Trade Center, and as soon as he found out it was an airliner, he immediately stopped his sun bathing. "I watched it on TV like everyone else," he described. "I managed to get phone calls out to London saying that I was ok. 'cause they were watching it on TV as well and they went 'Where's Bruce?' 'Oh, he's in New York.' And everybody thought that everybody was in it for a while. That day and all of the following day I just walked around the city. I managed to get out Saturday morning on the first or second flight to the UK."

Whether Bruce actually flew himself is unknown but one thing was for sure, he had confidence in the security procedures on board airliners, as he revealed regarding the likelihood of a terrorist attack on a regular aircraft. "I am far more worried about, for example, the captain keeling over in the cockpit of a heart attack," he said calmly. "That's much more likely than a terrorist threat and at least people are trained for the captain keeling over in the cockpit. Pilot incapacitation is far more likely to happen than a terrorist threat. In fact last year, 2001, was the safest year for air transport in its history, even taking into account the four jetliners that were deliberately crashed. That's actually a remarkable statistic. If you take out the deliberate crashes and you then take out the old Soviet Union and some dodgy places in Asia and you take out those accidents, then you get an accident record which is virtually nil. You are so much more likely to die crossing the street or in a car crash." Still, for anyone who had not previously considered the fragility of life, and for someone such as Bruce, who tended to cram every available second with entertainment and enjoyment, it was a cold reminder that life would not always run smoothly, whoever you were or however much money you had. Luckily, Bruce's training and mindset were such that this would never result in fear of flying – on the contrary he actually ended up flying commercially soon after 2001. But there was of course sympathy and empathy for everyone who lost their lives, every family affected and every other catastrophe the attacks had created. And inevitably, however optimistic and resilient one was, the world was no longer as safe, or as pleasant an environment as it had previously been.

BRUCEY BONUS

Bruce Dickinson's penchant for aircraft has long been known. More recently he has celebrated this even further. Not only does he now fly Maiden to their gigs more often than not, he also flies for independent charter company Astraeus. Despite his fame, Bruce is just another pilot working for an airline and that is just the way he likes it. Whenever he can cram in extra work, he flies for Astraeus, from Europe to the Middle East and beyond.

Additionally, he filmed a series for the Discovery channel, called *Flying Heavy Metal*. This was an in-depth look at all forms of aviation information.

Bruce explains, "We shot over 75 hours of footage for the series. Only a fraction of that was used, and I spent hours in conversation with some of the greatest designers in aviation history. I think some of the political interference with aviation designers was one of the most tragic aspects I discovered."

There were some hairy moments during filming for the programme, with Bruce happy to get his hands dirty. This nearly became very dangerous at one stage, as the front man remembers. "When we took off in the KC 135 tanker, full of jet fuel, the whole fuselage filled with smoke and I thought we had an APU fire! It turned out that the aircraft HAD actually caught fire the day before over Africa, and the smoke was residual crud and unburnt kerosene sloshing around in the plumbing."

Sources:

www.flyastraeus.com
http://www.discoverychannel.co.uk/flight/flying_heavy_metal/european_ aviation/index.s
http://www.geocities.com/sunsetstrip/club/5619/interviews/as1097.html
http://www.cavemanproductions.com/REVS/ozzybrooce.html

Chapter 15
All For One

"Maiden has always been a family and, even after all these years, we still consider Clive to be part of that family, and as such we feel we should help him in any way possible. We are sure the fans will agree and add their support to this." Rod Smallwood

The tour for *Brave New World* saw Maiden reach all the fans that could remember the glory days with Bruce Dickinson, plus many more besides. As ever, the band was not about to rest on its laurels. Part of the continued enthusiasm for touring through all the years of life on the road was down to the chance it gave to play new material as well as the old classics. Thanks to this attitude and a highly successful jaunt around the world, a live album was to be released for posterity. But this wasn't all. 2002 was to see an absolute feast of Iron Maiden products, marketed for both the casual fan and the serious collector. Firstly the band released a double CD and double DVD of their show from Rio De Janeiro, Brazil on January 19th 2001 which had an attendance of 250,000. A recording that captures the band in full flight, *Rock In Rio* was the ultimate proof Maiden still flourished as dogged road warriors who could play the old and new material with equal aplomb. The *Brave New World* songs had been part of the Maiden set at every date on the tour, where they would play no less than six tracks from the album. And they sounded exactly how the band had imagined, including perfect sing-a-long moments such as the choruses in 'The Wicker Man' and 'Brave New World'. The group were seeing the fruits of their toil with Kevin Shirley (who, incidentally, co-produced the *Rock In Rio* album with Steve) and by playing the studio material 'live' they already had a strong sense of how the material would suit a concert arena. As ever, Maiden managed to reach fans from front to back despite the massive attendance, and this much is audible on the CDs themselves.

Of the band's decision to incorporate so much new material, Steve comments; "I think it is challenging and sometimes I even think it's quite brave of us to play the amount of new stuff that we do. Whenever we go out on tour with a new album we always play at least six new songs. A lot of people don't do that. They are scared of reactions so they only play one new song. They are worried about people bitching about new material but I think it just shows a lack of confidence in their new product. I have always wondered at that myself, I think it is a bit strange. If they think they have written a good new album, go out and play it to the fans, that's the only way you will find out if it really is any good."

Bruce made light of the band's age by introducing 'Wrathchild' with a good-natured jibe; "Here's something from our Jurassic period!" What the fans didn't know at the time was that, given Bruce had not been in the band for a period of eight years, he had, understandably, forgotten some of the words! So the bouncy front man had to take all the lyrics with him to rehearsals, as he confirms; "I thought 'how does 'Number Of The Beast' go?' Now, is it 'torches blazed' first or is it the other way around?' I don't know, let me have a look'. I don't have an auto queue and shit like that. I just have a quick mental refresher."

The DVD was painstakingly assembled by Steve Harris, with the extras taking advantage of the versatile digital disc format with an in-depth look at how the band relaxed while on tour. Steve went to a football match in Brazil, while Adrian went fishing and Bruce went flying.

All together *Rock In Rio* is a fantastic celebration of all Iron Maiden had accomplished since its reformation with Bruce and Adrian, and there's a fair argument for naming it the ultimate Maiden live recording up to this time, perhaps just pipped by *Live After Death*.

"There were a quarter of a million there!" Dave Murray gushed of the Rio show. "We went on stage at about one o'clock in the morning because their shows are very late there and we came off at about three or three-thirty or something and that audience had been there all day. It's tremendous that they'd stuck by until right at the very end and you could just feel it, there was electricity coming off these fans. I think that picture sums it up, that was a tremendous show we had a wonderful time out there and to be able to document it and put it on DVD and stuff like that it's been fantastic."

Though Bruce had already presided over a live recording from Brazil, it was Maiden's first and it showcased the fact that they'd managed to reach places never before breached with the *Brave New World* tour, including Estonia and Ukraine.

Six years on from the first Iron Maiden compilation, *Best Of The Beast*, came another greatest hits set titled *Edward The Great*. It was rather a strange collection which concentrated heavily on the more recent Maiden output. There was no place for hallmark live numbers like 'Powerslave' or 'Hallowed Be Thy Name', instead it was a collection biased towards the material from the late 80s onwards. Overall of course, this was not a compilation for die-hard fans, but simply a quick release by EMI to keep the Iron Maiden name in the public eye.

To this end an advert was produced for UK television. With a typically over the top and 'trying too hard to be metal' voiceover, the ad was somewhat tacky and not entirely honest in claiming that it charted the entire career of the band. There were no tracks from the first two albums! No place for the song that had remained in the set for over 20 years, the signature tune, 'Iron Maiden' itself.

The release of *Edward The Great* prompted rumours of a rather more special offering from the Maiden empire. For once, the reports were accurate and the devoted legions had something seriously juicy to spend their money on – a heavy-duty box set titled *Eddie's Archive*, released on November 4th, 2002. The official spiel referred to the box as a "limited edition casket containing a crystal Eddie Head shot glass and an individually numbered Pete Frame family tree on parchment scroll, detailing the complete Iron Maiden history and rolled in a specially designed Eddie ring!"

But the real jewels in the crown were the compilation CDs, which this time made the purchase wholly worthwhile.

Firstly, there was the official bootleg from the band's 1982 'Beast On The Road' tour. Recorded at the Hammersmith Odeon, the double CD was specially mixed and co-produced by Steve Harris and Doug Hall. This was more like it, a fantastic sounding account of perhaps the most classic era of the group, captured for posterity and featuring songs which had dropped out of the live set years before, such as 'Drifter' and 'Transylvania'. Better still, the inlay was lovingly recreated to the exact design of the original 'Beast On The Road' tour programme. All the tour dates around the world were listed along with band notes written at the time.

Perhaps the best reason of all to buy the box set, though, came in the shape of the *Best Of The B Sides* collection. Literally every track the band had ever included on a b-side was to be found here, and it made for a fascinating romp through the alternative Iron Maiden, where their exploratory side shone through. All the cover versions were there, from UFO's 'Doctor Doctor' to Stray's 'All In Your Mind,' as well as the more comedic moments such as the ludicrous but thoroughly entertaining 'Black Bart Blues' and the tongue-in-cheek paean to Rod Smallwood, 'Sheriff Of Huddersfield'. The manager himself even penned a detailed set of notes to accompany each track and an explanation of their origins.

The box set also succeeded with the superb compilation that was *The BBC Archives*. Featuring the full sets from Donington 1988 plus Reading

1982 and 1980, this was a revealing look at the life of Iron Maiden over the years, climaxing with the deepest time traveller of all, the *Friday Rock Show Session* from 1979, which until then had been virtually impossible to get hold of, mainly because the master tape was still in the vaults.

Though 2002 had been a busy and successful year for Maiden despite the absence of a new studio album, they were about to receive some truly dreadful news. Ex-drummer Clive Burr had been diagnosed with multiple sclerosis.

The band originally heard of this when filming *The Classic Album* documentary on *The Number Of The Beast*, released on VHS and DVD in 2001. MS is a disease of unknown cause, which attacks the nervous system. No two cases are the same and as such it can be difficult to treat. Burr was suffering from intermittent numbness and his balance was affected. The band issued a statement saying, "Some days are better than others. At present there is no known cure for MS, although he is helping test new drugs in the hope that his body's response may contribute to a cure."

"We were gutted to hear of Clive's condition," said Steve Harris. "It must be a very scary prospect for him to face. It seemed natural that we should try and help Clive by trying to improve his future quality of life. We are setting up a special trust, The Clive Burr MS Trust Fund, and are keen to help him as much as we possibly can."

This was the kind of treatment one had come to expect from the band. Even if a member had left years before, as in Burr's case, they were still considered part of the family.

Maiden decided they would put on two special shows at the intimate Brixton Academy in London, with all profits going to the Clive Burr Trust Fund. Tickets were charged at £25 each and sold out quicker than it took Dave Murray to play a solo. This was an even greater gesture given that 2002 was supposed to be largely a recuperation period for the band. The shows were the only gigs Maiden played in the whole of 2002 and this surely contributed to the fact that attendees included fans from all corners of the world coming to show their support. Everyone involved gave their services for free, from management to the promoters. Merchandise was also on sale at the venue and again, all profits went to the fund. To enhance income even further the band also released a single that featured a live version of 'Run To The Hills' that was taken from the then upcoming *Rock In Rio* album. Both Zomba Music Publishers and EMI donated their profits from the single to the trust. Altogether by mid 2002 the fund contained a staggering £250,000. But the band weren't done there. They took to auctioning various memorabilia on eBay.

Thanks to the money raised Clive Burr's life was made much more comfortable. The first thing the cash went towards was a special mobility vehicle. He also had his bathroom moved downstairs so he had easier access to it and an exercise therapy machine was provided, along with home comforts, which included a special bed, a personal computer with internet access and even a DVD player. In addition, he was given general help to pay medical and living expenses as he had been unable to keep up the mortgage payments on his house and was close to becoming homeless. The Trust made a loan of £60,000 to Clive, so he could live in peace at his home.

The eBay auctions alone raised almost £8,000 and, as ever, Maiden looked after their fans. The lucky winner of a signed Fender Stratocaster (signed by the whole band as well as Burr) was Rob Davis from Woking in Surrey, and he had a nice surprise when he went into the Maiden offices to collect his new guitar.

"We thought it would be great if Janick gave it to him," said Rod Smallwood. "Janick extended the invitation for Rob to have a look around backstage the next time the band played in London, which was an added bonus."

OTHER BENEFICIARIES TO THE TRUST: -

It wasn't just Clive Burr who the Maiden organisation was looking after. Part of the trust was kept aside to help other Multiple Sclerosis sufferers – those in contact with the band or friends of friends…

As further explained on the official site, "The trust was able to assist Ralph (an MS sufferer who was at school with Steve and who was a great support to the band in the early East End days) buy a vehicle specially adapted to carry his wheelchair. The Clive Burr MS Trust fund also helped the wife of one of the members of an Iron Maiden tribute band who suffers from the disease. This contribution has gone towards modifications to their home to help with her mobility problems."

Should you wish to make a donation to the Clive Burr trust, just send an e-mail to: donations@ironmaiden.com.

Sources:

http://www.ironmaiden.com/clive.htm

Chapter 16
Mark Of The Beast

"I'd be foolish to turn around and say Iron Maiden are still going to be happening in 2010. I don't know. Maybe we will. It depends how foolish we feel." Bruce Dickinson, 1986

By 2003 Iron Maiden had successfully reinvented their collective persona, bringing the band back to the status they had enjoyed in the fruitful 80s. The high quality releases that had followed Bruce Dickinson's return to the fold had ensured Maiden would retain their respect long into the 21st century. But they still had more to do, and thankfully more to offer. The follow up to 2000's *Brave New World* had been at the planning stage for a significant part of 2003 and come September the band had a new record to promote. Titled *Dance Of Death*, it was to see Maiden at their most epic and glorious.

And yet, as always the members remained grounded and completely unaffected by their status.

Here was a group of musicians who were just damn good at their jobs and *Dance Of Death* would display all of the group's career highs within the confines of its 68 minutes. Once again Kevin Shirley was at the production helm, assisted by Steve Harris and the result was a warm, rounded album. The record begins with the upbeat but strangely average sounding 'Wildest Dreams' which would become the first single, and go straight into the UK charts at number six. "I think that's fantastic," Janick told *Terrorizer* magazine, "Because of the nu-metal thing that happened, instead of listening to Blue and that stuff now the kids are listening to music which has a lot of rhythm, and rock 'n' roll elements to it and so we fit in with that. There's a lot of young kids who are prepared to listen and I think a lot of them probably saw us at Donington, got off on it and thought 'hang on a minute, this is good'. Perhaps that's why the single's gone in there and I'm really pleased."

As a whole, *Dance Of Death* covers many bases. There are lengthy, historic-themed dark numbers, catchy and commercial tracks plus a few surprises. One such revelation is the fact that, for the first time in his Maiden tenure Nicko McBrain contributes a songwriting credit. Along with Dickinson and Adrian Smith the drummer had a hand in the sterling 'New Frontier'. This is the first album (with McBrain at least) where all the members throw their compositional hats into the ring. The result is a spectacularly diverse set, as ever, flawlessly captured and presented. And all this with a new line-up, only on their second album together. *Dance Of Death* hints there could be much more to follow.

It is probably unrelated, but it is surprising to note Nicko had recently converted to Christianity. "It changed my life completely," the drummer beamed. "You just have to be a good Christian to understand how much that means. You learn to love with your body and your spirit. I don't want to swear anymore and I don't like hearing people swearing. I can communicate perfectly without the use of those words. I'd say that I see the world in a different way, through the eyes of Jesus and I feel like a little child, like I've been reborn."

This turn of events was understandably somewhat surprising for the many people contemplating how the man who had often been heard muttering 'Fuck my old boots!' could now commit to a profanity-free life. Equally there was the small matter of many of Maiden's guaranteed live numbers covering the 'dark' side, and in some cases Satan himself! It would be extremely difficult for anybody to argue the case for Maiden's lyrics being pro-Christianity but Nicko did just that, despite the nature of many Maiden classics. With 'Number Of The Beast' for instance, he suggested this was merely proof that both God and Satan, and thus good and evil, existed and was more of a debate on the subject than praising any evil entity. Whatever Nicko's new beliefs however, there was no dispute about the man's drumming talents and he kept the sound tight as reliably as ever for the duration of the album.

"This is a more rounded album than *Brave New World,*" Bruce said to me regarding *Dance...* "Some of the songs have a bit more depth. *Brave...*was good, solid, bolted together Maiden which I thought we did pretty well, but this one has oddities for Maiden, which flesh it out a bit more and give the album more of a personality."

"I think every album we've done is different," Janick adds. "If you go back to *Somewhere In Time* and then play *X Factor* they're completely different, if you listen to *Killers* and *Virtual XI*, again they are totally different albums but once you put them on you know it's Iron Maiden. There's an idiosyncratic sound running through it that is Iron Maiden but every album's different and this is no exception. We don't write an album to try and fit in with the bands that are around now because we're older than them, we're on a different planet. We write what we feel and hopefully people like it but we've never gone in and tried to make a commercial album that will sell to the masses."

Among the highlights has to be the second single 'Rainmaker' featuring an emotive vocal from Bruce and several memorable guitar sections. Then there is the history laced coupling of 'Montsegur' and 'Paschendale', which sees Maiden hark back to its early 80s pomp.

"Given the nature of Iron Maiden in terms of the sounds we make and the things we do, songs about medieval battles and mass slaughter and things like that are a bit of a given really," said Bruce of the two tracks, "there's so many great stories throughout history that you can make parallels with the modern day, that it just makes for very colourful subject matter. If you're going to plunder something you might as well choose something that's real and actually happened rather than make up some crass sword-and-dorkery epic."

These songs in particular are blessed with strong vocal parts from Dickinson. Regardless of subject matter Bruce would always turn up, sing his part majestically and nail the song down. But adding the cut and bluster of a bloody battle to the lyrical equation would doubtless underpin certain tracks with greater gravitas. And here Maiden is collectively able to calm its 'long song' tendencies, controlling the quality and in some cases writing shorter songs simply making them all the more pertinent. There are no overlong mumblings, just stonewall Iron Maiden at its most economic and efficient.

Janick exemplifies the ability of the entire band to provide long-lasting value in this statement; "There are some really strong, thematic, epic songs like 'Paschendale' and 'Dance of Death' where you really have to listen, and you're going to get more from it the more you listen." This is certainly true. 'Wildest Dreams' for instance, is a track devoid of a particularly strong chorus but it grows on the listener with time. Lengthy storytelling epics such as the title track need to be soaked up gradually. But there is no denying, even at first listen, here is a band back to their very best. Again the group play the songs live and the bombastic nature of many of the tracks makes this even more impressive. It also helps the band to see that virtually every song on the album could be placed into a live context, each working equally well.

The three-guitar triumvirate is also more noticeable this time around. Janick agreed, though he also thought the three-guitar sound was notable on *Brave New World* if you listened closely. "What we didn't want to do really was overkill, where there's millions of guitars flying everywhere. It's nice to do that for one song and use that way of approaching it with one or two songs, but really we want the sound of Iron Maiden to be enhanced by the three guitars, and really if you listen to *Brave New World* you can hear the three guitars doing totally different things, me playing the melody, Dave hitting a chord, Adrian will be kind of stomping this weird rhythmic thing behind that and once you look for it you can hear it. On this album it's no different. We really try to pad the song out and make it thicker and more aggressive without that kind of grungy sound. I mean, use one guitar tuned down but keep our sound with the other two, so you have the really powerful Maiden sound, plus a bit underneath with the lower guitar. But if we all tune down we'd have that grungy sound that I'm not really that keen on. I find it a bit colourless and then it's just that dirgy heavy metal, and I think we've got more to offer than that."

Interestingly, there is only one song composed by another member – 'No More Lies' – in this case written by Steve. But despite the fact there are more collaborations than ever on *Dance Of Death*, Bruce made a fascinating revelation in *Terrorizer*; "We never actually all end up in the same room together. Generally I go round Janick's or Adrian's house and then Steve joins us and Steve will be writing with Janick and he'll say 'I've got this song do you want to come in and see if you can do something with the words or the tune' or whatever. Inevitably when someone writes a song they'll run it past me and ask if it's the right place for my voice to be happening and I'll come in and have a stab at the melody and that's how it works."

Steve enlightened fans with the story behind his baby, 'No More Lies' which was to be the third and final single (released as a limited EP) from the album. "It relates to something that's in peoples minds at certain points of their life and the idea of what could be afterwards, whether you believe in life after death it conjures up a lot of different things. It's something some people are scared of, some people are not particularly scared of, or they *say* they're not. It's just something I think is on people's minds and maybe mine more than others! It's like 'Fear Of the Dark', which a lot of people wouldn't admit to but totally relate to, which is maybe why it's such a big song. People are scared or intrigued of the unknown and that's quite a potent thing."

Lyrically on this album, the band is full of good ideas, as always. 'Face In The Sand' is about propaganda and how we all think we're so clever that things we build that we imagine to be timeless just all fade away," Bruce explains. "The whole Iraq war was rearing its head at the time we were writing the album, and I remember thinking about how sand moves and shifts, and whatever you build, like the sphinx or pyramids or whatever, they all eventually crumble away. Whatever empires people try to build, whether it's British, American or Iraqi empires, they will all eventually crumble away into something else. I just thought about a reverse face imprinted in the sand being about the most permanence you can ever get."

And then there is the swooning, acoustic ending theme, 'Journeyman'.

"It started out as just a chorus," Bruce illuminates, "which we thought was a big anthem type thing and we thought 'what do we do with this?' 'cos if we try and turn it into 'Born In The USA' or something it's going to sound crass. So we got trippy and dreamy on the verse and I just got images of somebody making decisions with his heart regardless of where it was going to lead and the journey you're on through the whole of your life. You get the chance to make choices and decisions and you can choose to sit in your cubby-hole and rot slowly or you can choose to do something glorious – it's your choice and that's what the song is about."

Dance Of Death is a crowning glory for the 'new' Maiden line-up but equally it heralds a change in touring patterns. It was at first rumoured the tour following the album would be the band's last full trek. The truth was somewhat more understandable, though no less disappointing.

"By the time we got home from touring and making a new album last time, it was two-and-a-half years later. And we're not at an age now where we can be away from our families for that long," Janick explains, "I know that sounds very family orientated and what not but we're not kids anymore – physically we can't do two-and-a-half-year tours. You say that and then you hear of other bands that go out for like three weeks then have to cancel the tour because of nervous exhaustion! So we're still capable of the big tours, but we don't want to work that hard anymore – I mean, this tour's been going on since May. We've got three weeks off now and then we rehearse for the next part which goes on 'til Christmas and then we go out 'til March. So this has been a pretty long tour anyhow. But after that, when this tour's finished, we're going to look at the way we tour and possibly scale it down a little bit."

"The pattern of touring in the future will be that we just do less," Steve adds, "we're not splitting up or anything, but it means that we'll probably play three or four months of the year rather than nine months which we've done for twenty-odd years. We're not getting any younger, being realistic about it. I don't think we're a bunch of old farts just yet! It just means that we're in fine fettle every night, we always give it 100%. Sometimes there's only 80% to give and you still give 100% of 80% yet it's still not the same as having 100 of 100% if you see what I mean! If we carry on the way we've done in the past I think it will all grind to a halt and no-one wants that, we all want to carry on as long as we can."

Keith Wilfort would finally see his tenure as Mr Iron Maiden Fan Club come to an end, but in his view; "The band were back to a level they hadn't been at since 1988. The album and tour were both excellent." It was at least, therefore, a good time for him to bow out. "I was having problems with my marriage, my wife and kids were in the USA and I was in the UK, which was undermining my job performance," Wilfort says of the eventual parting. "My job was also changing, my role becoming diminished and it ceased to be enjoyable. The band and Rod and I had a meeting and we agreed that I needed to be with my family and have a fresh challenge and so they paid me a very generous leaving settlement and I moved to the USA. I would have liked to carry on with the fan club, but after a couple of unfortunate (and costly) incidents with US-based fan clubs in the 80s Rod and Steve wanted to keep control of the Fan Club in the UK."

Asked of his most outstanding memories of working with the band Wilfort says, "The camaraderie, the feeling that we were all part of something special, one big family who looked out for each other. Being privileged to be where thousands of other people would give anything to be. Singing on stage with the band. Being in a position to meet people I could never have met otherwise, travelling overseas and making so many friends among the fans."

As ever, the fans' first link to the album would be the cover art, and that of *Dance Of Death* is something of a departure from the typical Maiden illustrations. The setting is a masquerade ball with Eddie as host. Mel Grant, who was responsible for the artwork, certainly has to take some credit for furthering Eddie's role and creating a rather unique cover for the band. Later he would also design the sleeve for the live album *Death On The Road* (which shows Maiden at their glorious best in concert, playing much of the *Dance Of Death* material). "My previous two commissions came to me directly from Maiden via my agent." Grant says. "But *Death*… came from a design studio via my agent and I was given a very loose coloured sketch of what they wanted, which was Eddie dressed in 'death's robe' galloping toward the viewer on a horse-drawn hearse, to the background of a red stormy sky.

"This seemed to me a little tame for Maiden fans (knowing what a wild bunch you all are), a bit of a red storm? Leave it out. Even Armageddon is tame. So, death on the roads? Okay lets make it real. Why don't I turn those red clouds into wet intestines? Like all the little creatures that get splattered on the roads. Let's have Eddie with guts in the sky. Eddie with guts all around. Let's have him galloping (or more likely slithering) through someone's guts. Let's give him the scythe too and hang a few scalps and bits from it. Have him scrape the edges as he goes. Maybe have a string of his own guts hanging out. One thing leads to another, and I really got into it. Shows you what sort of mind I've got. Maiden approved and there we are. Keep an eye on your colon on dark nights when the sky is red, especially if you hear the faint jangle of a harness behind you. Eddie is real and out there... and he loves sharp edges."

BEAUTY AND THE BEAST

"The audience supports me morally. To tell you a story, during our last UK tour, in Sheffield to be precise, I got a terrible cold and I had to stay in bed for three days. The day before I fell ill, I already had huge problems to sing. The gig was to last two hours, but after three songs, I had to tell the audience that I couldn't do any more. And they were all very understanding. This kind of support gives you a warm feeling." Bruce Dickinson

Though the majority of the *Dance Of Death* tour was successful for Maiden, one particular gig blighted the otherwise enjoyable shows.

From July 15th to August 20th 2005, Maiden had been performing as co-headliners with Black Sabbath on the US Ozzfest bill. This is a regular event, held since 1996 and the brainchild of Ozzy and Sharon Osbourne. On the last night of their residency on the festival bill, Maiden were treated shockingly.

As one manager of a famous band, who declined to be named, told www.blabbermouth.net, "They were pelted with eggs, bottle caps, beer cups, spat on, had people from the Ozzfest camp talking over the PA during their set, had 'Eddie' delayed from his onstage entrance, had members of the Black Label Society entourage rush the stage with American flags, and had the PA intentionally turned off over six times, all by the Osbourne Camp."

The reason appeared to be down to Bruce Dickinson. A few weeks before he had taken part in an interview for *Kerrang!* magazine in which he made fun of the fact that Ozzy used a teleprompter onstage. Also, at a gig in Detroit, Bruce had sarcastically mentioned a certain reality TV show (referring to the programme *The Osbournes* that the family starred in for MTV).

For the Ozzfest debacle, several bands joined the Osbourne clan in attempting to sabotage Iron Maiden's set. Despite their interruptions and cries for "Ozzy, Ozzy!" Maiden continued in their usual professional manner. As the band came to the end of 'The Trooper' Dickinson called the detractors 'a sorry excuse for an Ozzy Osbourne fan,' and asked how, 'three dozen eggs could get snuck into the front row of Ozzfest by people with Ozzfest laminates?' He then stated the next song would not appear on 'Your local cocksucking corporate radio station, wouldn't be seen on MTV anymore, and sure as hell wouldn't be played on a fucking reality TV show'. The crowd roared in approval. Even though the Osbourne hangers-on were doing their best to bring Maiden down, the crowd realised what was happening and many thousands stuck with the persistent Brits.

Bruce spotted one particular abuser and shouted, "It's gonna take more than eggs to stop Iron Maiden, and if it wasn't for a lawsuit, I'd rip your fucking head off right now, you piece of shit!" Despite Maiden's staunch refusal to be thwarted they were still subjected to several PA cuts, but in response Bruce just underlined the fact that Maiden would be playing their entire set even if it took all night.

When they finally managed to finish playing all their material, as the band were saying their goodbyes to their legions of fans the PA was hijacked by shouts of 'Ozzy, Ozzy!' This was down to 'Big Dave', a hanger on of the band Black Label Society. This openly redneck rock-act features Zakk Wylde on guitar, who doubles as Ozzy's lead guitarist. Big Dave must have felt rather stupid when the crowd responded to his chants with 'MAIDEN, MAIDEN!'

Once Iron Maiden vacated the stage, Sharon Osbourne walked out to pass on some halfhearted praise for their performance. She said the band was "wonderful" with a "fantastic" crew but that "Bruce Dickinson is a prick." The crowd were unimpressed and she was booed and pelted with beer cups. This was no surprise given that tickets for the gig were $150 and many had come specifically for Iron Maiden.

Bruce's close friend Roy Z throws another ghastly light on the whole situation. "What Sharon Osbourne did was utterly classless, not to mention stupid," he told me. "This whole thing could've easily escalated into a full-scale riot had Maiden walked off stage in disgust instead of buckling down and pulling through and giving the fans the show they had paid good money for. The Maiden guys are cool people and if Sharon had a problem with Bruce she should've sorted it out in private. I was actually out there with some friends for that show, but ended up splitting early because I wasn't feeling too well and the tickets and passes Bruce had left for me weren't there and I couldn't get hold of him. When I heard what happened the next day it all made sense – Sharon probably fucked with Maiden's guest list and gave our orchestra tickets to some of her egg throwing minions so they'd be close enough to pelt the band."

Still, nothing would stop Iron Maiden, and the Osbournes' actions only served to cast shadows on their own character. Many felt sympathy for Maiden, even those who were not strictly fans of the group. The level of immaturity shown by vastly experienced campaigners such as Ozzy and Sharon Osbourne was nothing short of pathetic. Maiden passed with flying colours, and it's safe to say that in future they are unlikely to play the festival again.

Bruce immortalised Maiden's take on the stupidity when he held aloft the Union Jack flag and screamed, "This is a British flag, these colours don't run!" Messing with the staunchest bunch of Brits in the music world is not very sensible. And at other times in the past the flag of their homeland had been raised in defiance! "He is a patriot, and intensely loyal and believes totally in his country, the Union Jack is everything to Steve," Kay says of the guitarist. "I can remember when the first Gulf War broke out I was stuck in Hyde Park in Park Lane. I know from speaking to them subsequently, that Maiden were about to take the stage in Canada somewhere and Bruce walked out onstage in front of thousands with this bloody great Union Jack and just told them that 'we're up, we're off and we're flying'."

In the course of writing this book I can happily say the majority of people who spoke to me about all things Maiden were genuinely complimentary about the band and the way the whole Maiden empire goes about their business. These people had nothing to gain by kissing the band's arse so it wasn't a case of doing so just to be kind. Some are still friends with the band (in fact many have remained on their particular friend's radar for many years, since the early days where they first met, whether that was before Iron Maiden or later on).

As Neal Kay says, "You can't say a bad word about them because they are genuinely nice people. They're not like Motley Crue and all the other big-mouthed yanks who think their fucking pricks are bigger than their egos, which are big enough. Maiden are not like that and never have been. They like partying in their own way. But when you're backstage with the band it is kind of like an old working men's club with the old cheese cloth cap on, but in a rich way."

Kay adds, "The band is very much like a unit going into war because unless everybody's that determined, with great leadership and the absolute perseverance to the end of the earth, you ain't going to win. And the whole team is like that, even Rod Smallwood. You can't argue with Rod, he's just a total blunt Yorkshireman."

"I mean we go in there and it's kind of like a football team or something," Dave Murray says of the band's camaraderie. "You all plan together, you want to make it work or whatever and you want to work on the details and I think that's what's important."

Of course many people have pointed out, quite rightly, that without Steve Harris' immense self-belief, desire and passion, Iron Maiden would not be the institution they are today.

Of Harris, Neal Kay says, "I've come to know the man, not fantastically well, we are reasonable acquaintances. And we were for a period of time, quite close really. Initially Steve is a very quiet person, he is nothing like the wild man of rock 'n' roll, in fact, he is exactly the antithesis of that. He's captured the world for his country. He's put Iron Maiden's name firmly on the international map of music for two decades plus. And he's waved the Union Jack on many stages. They are all patriotic actually to a huge degree. You'd have to go back to 1940 to match their patriotism and they've carried that through all their lives.

"I played tennis with him once," Kay continues, "and Steve wouldn't even stop for a drink for about four hours! There are some people in this world who fit that saying, 'cometh the hour cometh the man'. When things have been at their darkest before, this country has always been saved by the greats. You can go where you like, Drake, Churchill, Nelson but when this country has needed its heroes they've always been there. Steve is one of them for me, definitely. He was put here for Iron Maiden and that's been his sole thing all his life. The Wright brothers only did one thing in their lives, they gave the aeroplane to the world. Steve Harris gave Iron Maiden to the world, and nothing and no-one was going to stop him and that was obvious from the moment I met the guy. Total dedication and absolute will and it's with a professionally balanced sportsman's mind, or a military mind. With Steve you are dealing with someone who will never *ever* give in unless he agrees with something.

He is the quiet, confident captain of the Memphis Belle. Paul Di'Anno used to call him Old Mother Harris because he was always nagging them to go to bed and not mess around on tour. He is a real latter day hero because he is unsung. He never blows his own trumpet about one bleeding thing and the whole world knows that Harris is Maiden."

Harris is still an enigma to his legions of fans, but Neal Kay is one of the few who has become quite close to the bass player over the years. He reveals little known jewels about ol' Bomber. "He likes his pints of ale; he likes his British sausages which he used to go all over the world to get! And he is a family man as well, he's not a rebel-rouser. I remember one time on tour, in Norfolk in 1980. We had a night off and the whole crew and band went into town to raise some hell. But me and Steve stayed behind in the hotel and we played ping-pong all night. To the others in the crew he's slightly boring but his word is God. He knows exactly how to get his boys home.

I remember talking to Steve a few years ago about a tour that was going to Beirut, I said to him, 'Are you mad? People who go to Beirut get their bollocks shot off!' He said 'Yes they have removed some of our albums from the record stores there'. I said 'You are a fucking nutcase, I have never heard in my life of a heavy metal band going to the Middle East – go to Israel'. He said, 'Oh we've been there!' They really have gone to places that no one has ever shown the balls to go to. They are very brave. They have gone into places where guns are a fact of life. And it's not for the publicity – that's not the reason they've done it."

There is also no denying that many realise Dave Murray has been a huge part of Maiden's success, and looking in the metal dictionary next to unsung hero you might also find a picture of this chap with the cheeky face and beaming grin. "He is the other side of Steve and there's no Maiden without 'Arry or Murray, not a chance," says Kay. "I met Dave the same time as Steve and he's quiet, almost shy. But he is the consummate professional as well, though he does like a laugh. He is so down to earth, such an Eastender. These guys are salt of the earth, they are guys who win wars. And they're not toffee-nosed officers, they're lads who have come up through the ranks. And I'll tell you something; all the money in the world has not changed these people in the slightest."

The question remains however, how long can Maiden keep going? At some point they will have to slow down, but Kay thinks there will only be one way for the band to end. "I believe if Davey says to Steve 'it's enough' then it will be enough – but I think only those two will know, as old friends. But this band has spent a quarter of a century as Iron Maiden and made millions of people around the world happy and they deserve their millions. The whole thing about this band is, you know when they take the stage you are in the presence of the great ones. When you've been Maiden-ed you know you've been bloody Iron Maiden-ed. There's no question it was meant to be and I know I had to do my part spiritually, I couldn't back out. Lemmy said to me one time, 'well, why them and not me?' 'Well Lemmy, it's simple,' I told him, 'you can't play, write or sing, and they can'."

A CATERER'S VIEW

It's a side of the metal touring monster few actually get to witness. Caterer Lauren Roberts travelled with the band on their *Dance Of Death* tour and can shed some light on the backstage rituals of the Maiden boys.

PAUL STENNING: **Did you actually meet any of the band or crew at any stage, if so whom and what were they like?**

LAUREN ROBERTS: "I met all the band. Steve and his many kids, who were the most polite children of a rock star I've ever met, Nicko, who always came in and had a chat with me, and Bruce who came into catering now and again to talk about gourmet beer. The others we saw now and again, they all introduced themselves at the beginning but they popped in to say 'hi' every once in a while. We travelled with the crew (we were also crew!) and the management team came to every gig we did. So we saw an awful lot of the crew since we were on the buses with them and in the hotels too."

PS: **How big was the catering crew and how does this compare to other tours you have done?**

LR: "There were four of us altogether and this was pretty much the biggest tour I did while working as a caterer. There was normally one chef, one job leader, one front of house person and one dressing-room person. On smaller tours if you did FOH you also did the dressing rooms too. The Iron Maiden tour was the biggest mainstream tour I did. However my first job was on German *Pop Idol* and there were five of us."

PS: **Do you like the band and did you ever watch them?**

LR: "I liked them as people and they all were very nice but I'm not one for their music."

PS: **Did the band eat before or after the show?**

LR: "Sometimes before and sometimes after. They would have platters of cold meats, two roast chickens and lots of choccies and stuff like that to nibble on."

PS: **What did each band member prefer to eat and drink?**

LR: "Bruce loves his gourmet beers like Hobgoblin and Speckled Hen and German wheat beer. Nicko loved guacamole but no chilli 'cause he hates chilli! He also has a big passion for good red wines. He gave me one as a special birthday present... it was lovely! The others I don't really remember being very picky about anything... that's always what stays in my head after a tour...what the performers really liked or hated and how fussy they were about stuff. Some bands have riders (request lists) as long as your arms and are VERY specific about the brands and all that."

PS: **Was there much alcohol consumed by the band?**

LR: "I think they pretty much had the usual as far as booze goes on tours... couple of cases of beer... Corona was popular, and proper beer, a couple of bottles of red and white wines, and that's it I think. I don't really remember 'cause I did front of house and wasn't doing dressing rooms for them on that tour."

Chapter 17
Flying Solo

A Dedication to Bruce Dickinson

"What more can you say about Bruce that hasn't already been written? Renaissance man on steroids! He has often been accused of being egocentric and pursuing his own agenda but his contributions to Maiden speak for themselves. Bruce can rub people up the wrong way and isn't one of the most diplomatic of people but I personally always found him to be a decent guy. You get what you see." Keith Wilfort

If it is unusual to have such an extended section for one particular band member within a full band biography, then that is because the person in question is a truly extraordinary being who deserves his own space. Bruce Dickinson's solo material is inextricably linked with his career in Iron Maiden. Some of the albums were recorded and released while he was still in the group, while others came at times when Maiden seemed to be on a different wavelength. Therefore a full examination of Maiden's career requires a gaze through Dickinson's eyes from the period of 1990 to the present day. Today Bruce combines a sometime-solo career with his full time Maiden position, signifying the solidarity which now exists between Bruce and Steve Harris. Following Maiden's resurgence when Bruce rejoined the band and the success of his solo work with Air Raid Siren, Harris was loath to allow the singer to extend his wings musically lest it interfere with Iron Maiden. But ironically, in attempting to control Bruce's desire to experiment in other musical areas unsuitable for Maiden, Harris actually pushed Bruce away, to the point where the vocalist left the band completely. And it is through his individual work that we get to see the true personality of Bruce Dickinson rather than just the singer for Iron Maiden, with some glorious music coming from the front man's opportunities to express himself.

If ever there was a rock singer suited to a solo career, then it's Paul Bruce Dickinson. Somewhat out of the blue, he found himself leading a band who would conquer the world within an incredibly short space of time, catapulting him to stardom as the very identifiable face of that group. While it's undoubtedly Steve Harris who is the main man of Iron Maiden, it is Bruce Dickinson who personally commands most fans. Of course. it is not unusual for a singer to be the most popular member of a band, in fact it's the norm but that singer needs a certain charisma in order to pull it off, and Bruce has been the face of Iron Maiden for over 20 years.

Yet, with his wide interests and larger than life character, it was inevitable he might seek something other than Maiden to fulfil his ambitions, and true to form he began his solo career just after Maiden's *Seventh Son Of A Seventh Son*, with the well-received *Tattooed Millionaire*. Their album was a taster for the type of material Bruce could hardly include in the Maiden artillery. Songs such as the title track, 'Lickin' The Gun' and 'Zulu Lulu' were schooled in hard rock and gave Bruce license to be less serious, throwing in somewhat sexist, innuendo-packed lyrics and material which was the aural equivalent of Bruce's two novels, *The Adventures Of Lord Iffy Boatrace* and *The Missionary Position*. In fairness there was also more serious work on the 1990 album, songs such as 'Born In '58' for instance – an autobiographical view of his life to date.

Many Maiden fans were eager to hear what kind of songs Bruce could compose away from a band rooted in the heavy metal genre, which had always been too restrictive for Dickinson, as he alluded to during the writing of *Somewhere In Time*. And in truth, the desire to break away from his confines in camp Maiden began at this time. Once his writing for the band's '86 opus had been rejected, there was clearly a rumbling in the Brucey brain as he wondered exactly where he could find an outlet to experiment. Though he'd done a sterling job fronting the *Somewhere In Time* material, and beyond that the remarkable *Seventh Son Of A Seventh Son*, to which he managed to contribute material, rumours started to circulate around the time leading up to Maiden's ninth studio album, *No Prayer For The Dying*, that Bruce was unhappy in his role of mere front man for Harris' band, and that he was secretly penning solo material. Indeed, in the very same year as *No Prayer…* Bruce was to release *Tattooed Millionaire*.

Part of the motivation for this work had arisen out of his firmly held viewpoint on certain British bands – alright then *all* of them – attempting to sound American just to sell. As he stated, "One of the things I found majorly unattractive, and had a bee in my bonnet about, is that for a country that basically single-handedly created the entire music form that is heavy metal, England has this thing about trying to dress up like male bimbos from LA"

This was the inspiration for the lyrics behind the title track where the singer makes fun of the fairly obvious attempts of many English bands to try and cross over. *"I don't want your big city shining. I don't want your silver lining. I don't wanna be a tattooed millionaire."* The lyrics are equally accusing of the *real* tattooed millionaires, the America rock stars themselves, *"He's got a wife, she ain't no brain child. Ex-mud queen of Miami... LA dude. LA Attitude. Laid back, selfish and getting fat. Body guards, Porn Stars, Gold credit cards. Using each other. Running for cover."*

"If you look in the back of *Melody Maker*," Bruce told Jon Hotten, "All the bands are influenced by American bands, and half these bands are shit! There's no feel, there's no soul, there's no nothing. There's a brain scan of zero going through these people. If the whole world started sounding like The Carpenters, they'd get dressed up like The Carpenters and play that instead. They don't owe allegiance or loyalty or anything like that. There's no point to what they do."

However, later in his career Bruce came to hold the view that, of all his solo material, *Tattooed Millionaire* was the odd one out. He would refer to it as "strange," and "unusual." Of course, on the surface this was hardly a bizarre recording in the vein of experimentalism, nor was it artistic arrogance, it was simply a hard rock album. But you could certainly see what Bruce meant by 'odd one out' when compared with his subsequent material. Perhaps this was partly due to the fact the vocalist, along with Janick Gers, only had a very limited time in which to compose a full album of material and their comments explain a lot. Once the record company had heard 'Bring Your Daughter To The Slaughter' they instantly sought an album chock full of such hooks, and Bruce was hardly going to tell the truth and say he hadn't written anything else yet! Janick was more worried than Bruce in fact and felt compelled to enquire, "What are we going to do?" Typically, Bruce was not phased as shown in his reply. "'Oh well, we'll write sort of a freak sort of tune and a Rolling Stones kind of a tune and an AC/DC kind of a tune and we will just have a laugh because these guys just have loads of money and they will pay for us to make a record, so just shut up and have a laugh!' – So we did! So, two weeks one summer we had a great laugh and made a terrifically fun sounding record and unfortunately everybody took it seriously. Everybody was like, 'Aha!'"

Some already considered Bruce a genius, be it in music, or one of the many other areas in which he dabbled. As well as a first outing as a solo performer Bruce also dipped into a touch of novel writing, surprising even himself with how well his slightly eccentric work was received. *The Adventures Of Lord Iffy Boatrace* had a title to which the average Iron Maiden fan would doubtless crease their features in disdain or mockery, but for Bruce there was a serious side to it, even if the whole thing was partly done 'tongue in cheek'. "I was just curious as to what would happen if I started writing a book," he said. "The only reason I continued is because it proved very popular with people, like the road crew who would come into my room and I'd sit there and read them the next chapter. They'd all go, 'Well, what happens tomorrow?' I go, 'Well, I haven't written it yet, come back tomorrow.'

In the acknowledgements for the book Bruce explains how it had been written in various hotel rooms during 1987 on Maiden's European tour. "To all those hotel proprietors who kindly supplied reams of hotel stationery to the peculiar long-haired man at four in the morning, thank you," Bruce cracked. Of course the front man could not resist bringing something Maidenesque into the equation, and the Lord Iffy Boatrace logo was cunningly shaped *à la* the Iron Maiden crest.

"I always fancied the idea of writing a book, and I was bored on the road, so I sat down and started at page one!" Bruce told *Kerrang!* "I had an idea for this character called Lord Iffy Boatrace, who is an upper class chinless wonder. I wrote it the same way I write a song. Write the first note, and don't know what the second one is going to be. About halfway through you suddenly realise what it is you're writing about."

Many who actually read the finished novel might well have wondered what Bruce was on about as well. Although the diction is amusing and the evocative air of an upper class twit is fully encapsulated in the character, the plot verges on the unstable. Nevertheless publishers Sidgwick & Jackson were highly impressed as Bruce continued, "The guy didn't even read it, just looked at it and said: 'How many records did you sell? Wow! I think we should publish this. Hang on let me go away and read it, see if it's rubbish – but we'll publish it anyway." According to Bruce the publisher did not think it was rubbish at all. "He read the book and said, 'look it's really good, you could potentially have a career as a writer.' I was like, 'what!' My editor, the guy who does Douglas Adams and Tom Sharpe said, 'look it doesn't really need editing.' I went, 'you're kidding me!' But that was that really"

The tome was billed as 'probably the most shocking and revolting book you'll ever read,' hardly surprising given the main character's rather taboo habits of wearing high heels and fishnet stockings whilst simultaneously being a dastardly rogue. The archetypal toff is perfectly portrayed and though he doesn't actually say it, there's undoubtedly a little bit of Bruce in there too. All that public school crap had come in useful after all. But the book is overtly vulgar in places, and in some ways it seems not to suit Bruce at all. Nevertheless mainstream English literature has been notoriously vulgar throughout history, so he had plenty of crudeness to live up to. From William Shakespeare's *Twelfth Night* to much of the work of Geoffrey Chaucer there is a "genuine vulgarity running through mainstream literature," as British comic actor Kenneth Williams once observed.

The English newspapers could not get over the fact a numbskull heavy metal singer could even string two words together let alone thousands, and they took a rather condescending and sardonic view of the work. Bruce was typically forgiving telling *Kerrang!* "I don't mind that. You can rubbish their perceptions. We are a metal band. I don't see any problem in being marketed as what you are." The point was fair, but still there must have been an aching grumble in the loins of one of metal's greatest ever front men. Here he was, a champion fencer, a gifted lyricist, now a novelist (and a public school boy to boot), yet because he wore leather, had long hair and just happened to sing about Satan, Indians and Patrick McGoohan, he had to be the subject of derision.

Still, it mattered not; the book was lapped up by mostly (if not entirely) Maiden fans eager to see what Bruce had to offer. The likelihood they were rather surprised is probably high. But Bruce, despite clearly being intelligent beyond his meagre status as heavy metal singer, was unashamed of his role in life, and more importantly, his ability to enjoy his significance in Iron Maiden and heavy metal *per se*. As he opined, "If you get incredibly cerebral about it, you'll end up in all sorts of trouble. It doesn't make any sense. There is no reason why it should. You just enjoy it. That's exactly the trap that a lot of cerebral types fall into. They think themselves out of enjoying something."

Also in 1990 Bruce contributed to a compilation titled, *The Earth-quake Album/Rock Aid Armenia* which was a collection released to aid the Armenian victims of a 1990 earthquake which had devastated the country. All proceeds from the sale of the album went to the Armenian people. Bruce sang the second verse and chorus of the Deep Purple classic 'Smoke On The Water.' Other famous rockers who gave their services free of charge included Ritchie Blackmore, Ian Gillan, Tony Iommi, Dave Gilmour, Roger Taylor, Brian May, Bryan Adams and Keith Emerson.

In 1992 Bruce followed up his first piece on Lord Iffy Boatrace with a successor titled *The Missionary Position*, of which Bruce commented, "This is a bit more directed. In the first one he was a misogynist I guess, but in this one the misogyny is more directed. It's set in Los Angeles and Lord Iffy becomes a TV exorcist with the intention of ripping off the Reverend Hiddy Reptile, who is in no way based upon the Reverend Jimmy Swaggart. There's all kinds of stuff. I think I made a conscious decision that there'd be an awful lot of crapping going on in this book; I think in the last book it was vomiting and in this one it's crapping. There is some vomiting too. That's it really."

Many (Steve Harris included) assumed *Tattooed Millionaire* was a mere one-off, that Bruce was just getting some creative urge out of his system and would return to work, refreshed and focused solely on Iron Maiden. According to Bruce, the Maiden bass player thought *Tattooed Millionaire* would outsell *No Prayer For The Dying*, especially in America. Though Bruce was accommodating towards what he still considered to be his primary musical focus, (even to the extent of scheduling his solo tour around the Maiden dates) Bruce's 'excursion' had created an inkling of doubt in camp Maiden. To be fair, Bruce also claimed *Tattooed Millionaire* provided a means to express his own creativity and individuality, which would indeed be a one off. However the opposite happened once Bruce realised there was a fan base for the kind of material he wanted to write and that he had a very good chance of a successful solo career. Come the time of his swansong with Maiden, 1992's *Fear Of The Dark*, the writing was on the wall and the multi-talented boy from Worksop had decided to leave the group in order to forge a solo career.

Interestingly, in the same *Kerrang!* interview where Bruce discussed his novel, he also told Jon Hotten, "My personal feeling is that when it feels right for us to bow out, we will. I think we'll do it fairly graciously. There are going to be no acrimonious bust-ups in the band. We've been together too long." What a difference a few years can make. Not only was Dickinson flying solo, he was intending to release material that would most probably have shocked his legions of fans. Unbeknownst to many, even at the time, Dickinson had an electronic album written and ready to go.

"Part of me felt like I was trying too hard to be clever," says Bruce of his dalliance with pastures new. "Did I really feel like having electronic anvils, smashing lumps of metal, hissing noises? Nah." Therefore Bruce reverted to type, almost. Though he maintains his 1994 album was "written from instinct", Bruce managed to surprise a few people with his *Balls To Picasso* opus, and gained many new fans along the way. "Metal is irretrievably tied up with American music right now. The Marilyn Mansons of the world have been sniffing around the edges of metal. Soundgarden were a metal band but wouldn't own up to it because it was too uncool. No one's come out and made an unashamedly heavy metal record and said: 'This is not industrial, it's not hardcore, it's heavy metal'." Here Bruce suggests he is still a heavy metal singer, and his ongoing solo work bears this out to an extent, but with *Balls To Picasso*, the singer is clearly embracing his hard rock roots.

This was to be the first album where future long-time guitarist and friend Roy Z appeared on the scene. "Bruce and I met completely by accident," he explains. "Bruce was working at Goodnight LA, producer Keith Olsen's studio at the time, and we happened to be mixing the first Tribe Of Gypsies (Z's main band) record with Keith's engineer Shay Baby at the same place. One evening I stopped by the studio and saw this shadowy figure rocking out to our tunes in the control room. At first I was like, 'what the fuck?' and then I recognised the person – it was Bruce! Shay had played him some of the mixes and he totally loved what he heard. When he left to go back to England he took our stuff with him and presented it to Sanctuary Management who flew out to see the band live and became our managers. Bruce asked me to come over to the UK to write with him for his album. Eventually he ended up scrapping everything he'd done in LA and we wrote and recorded a whole new record, *Balls To Picasso*."

This album is certainly heavier than *Tattooed Millionaire*. Songs such as 'Cyclops' and 'Hell No' pushes Dickinson's affinity with dark, defiant material even further. Yet the real jewel in the crown is the epic power ballad, 'Tears Of The Dragon' which closes the album. Understandably it was used as a single and signalled a mature Dickinson truly branching out with his songwriting. Perhaps the real beauty of the song is its autobiographical nature. The lyrics are undoubtedly personal and possibly refer to his breaking out of the Maiden stronghold: *"For too long now there were secrets in my mind. For too long now, there were things I should have said... In the darkness, I was stumbling for the door"*. Yet within the same song is the underlining of the new Bruce, the one who had learned and moved on, as the chorus states, *"I throw myself into the sea, release the wave, let it wash over me, to face the fear I once believed"*

It seems clear from these lyrics that a fear of the unknown, or a hanging on to the 'devil you know' syndrome were long gone for Bruce who, with *Balls To Picasso*, had validated his worth as a songwriter and performer. 'Change Of Heart' also references Bruce's fears but states the need for moving on, *"You, you're walking away, you couldn't stay. You need a change of heart."*

"Obviously that album will always hold a special place in my heart because it was my first album ever," Roy Z recalls. "Not only was it exciting to be working with a legend like Bruce – we did the thing in London, England. A bunch of cats straight out of the LA barrio making a record half way around the world – pretty mind-blowing stuff! We had a lot of fun in London."

It's a shame that the album was most publicised at the time of release for the fact it captured Bruce rapping! 'Shoot All The Clowns' is a somewhat throwaway song that did indeed have a brief rap section, which enraged or amused many who heard it, and even those who had just heard 'of' it. Yet those who viewed a deep set of lyrics and accomplished songs with such superficial disdain missed out on some prime Bruce material, such as the ambitious and highly melodic 'Sacred Cowboys' with its riotous, memorable chorus.

"'Sacred Cowboys' was written by Roy and myself in the studio," Bruce explains. "It started sounding like, 'Run To The Hills,' so Roy and I went down to the pub and got readjusted and came back and finished it in 20 minutes." It is significant that *Balls To Picasso* was the first Dickinson solo album to feature the talents of Z (real name Roy Ramirez) as this formative alliance changed Bruce's outlook on creating heavy music and established a partnership which would continue for many years. Roy Z had played in a number of small bands before forming the Tribe Of Gypsies in 1991 for whom he was to be chief songwriter and guitarist.

"I was exposed to all sorts of music as a kid," Z remembers. "I grew up in an ethnically mixed neighbourhood – lots of Mexicans and blacks, people from Central America, and whites, too. So you had the Latin stuff, blues, soul, and my white friends turned me on to Led Zeppelin and Black Sabbath. When I was 13 I bought a guitar for 50 bucks and I just tried to learn as much as I could from listening to cats like Van Halen, Schenker, Rhoads, Uli Roth and Jimmy Page and started playing in bands doing backyard parties and eventually clubs. I've always had an appreciation for different styles and a lot of different things are in my blood. That's why I have no problem going from Latin to heavy metal to whatever and feeling comfortable doing it all."

As for the development of the single letter surname Z explains, "When I started playing around LA as a teen having an ethnic last name wasn't considered cool, not to mention that there was the Nightstalker, a serial killer named Richard Ramirez, who had terrorised the city back in the 80s. So I flipped my name around and it became Zerimar. I used to go on auditions for all sorts of things, including Dio and Alice Cooper, and one day they listed my name as Z and a friend of mine who was with me at the audition started calling me that and it stuck. It's kind of funny because now Ramirez is a cool name to have. You have star athletes and rock stars with this name, oh well."

Elsewhere on *Balls To Picasso* Bruce writes of politics in '1000 Points Of Light': *"You can't take a mother and give her back her son, tell me what kind of freedom is bought with a gun."* The lyrics make a fairly obvious stand against dictatorships and show the futility of war. The title itself was actually taken from a George Bush speech focusing on welfare and poverty ("I have spoken of a thousand points of light," the US President boasted, "of all the community organisations that are spread like stars throughout the Nation, doing good").

While overall *Balls To Picasso* was a good, solid rock record, it came out at the wrong time. In 1994 all sorts of new bands with unusual or more popular sounds emerged. 1994 saw Korn create a new genre with nu-metal and also the likes of Machine Head update the template of thrash metal. Meanwhile Soundgarden were still riding the waves of success and their *Superunknown* album rounded off a spate of popular 'grunge' recordings, which also included multi-million-selling sets by both Pearl Jam (*Vitalogy*) and Alice In Chains (whose EP *Jar Of Flies* didn't quite sell millions, but still sold amazingly well for a mini album). Bruce meanwhile was seen as something of a dinosaur in terms of credibility, and his rapping exploits certainly did nothing to help his *sale*ability. Therefore it was perhaps inevitable he changed tack for his next album.

"*Balls To Picasso* is probably a bit underrated, there are some great tunes on that album," reckons Z. "I'm not too thrilled with Shay Baby's production anymore and I was going to remix the whole thing at one point before the re-issues came out but it never happened. Looking back I'm not surprised *Balls...* wasn't wholly embraced because it was definitely a departure from what people knew Bruce as and expected from him. It's an eclectic record – almost like an African Black Sabbath in places – very dark and brooding. The percussion element that we, the Tribe, brought into the mix, certainly is not standard heavy metal. I'm sure that threw some people for a loop. I wasn't disappointed the album didn't go huge – I was way too excited to be part of it all, period. As for Bruce – I don't think he expected platinum success either. He just really needed a break from the typical Maiden metal world and wanted to stretch and experiment musically. *Balls...* was more about having total artistic freedom and expressing it than selling as many records as possible."

Before Dickinson's next studio opus came the *Alive In Studio A/Live At The Marquee* double set, for which Bruce made his customary appearances in many record stores throughout the United Kingdom, undertaking several signing sessions. The first part of the set had basically consisted of the Dickinson band (members) running through Bruce's best solo tracks thus far, while the obviously titled ...*Marquee* set was simply an extra – a true live recording featuring many of the same tracks. Although it seemed fairly incongruous to release a live record so soon after going into a full time solo career, there was no arguing with the quality of the music on offer. Unlike many other band's live releases, the packaging was faithful to the value for money creed Bruce had always endorsed.

"I probably overreacted a little bit after *Balls To Picasso*, but I couldn't have done another metal record. I was burned out. I needed some space." So said the Air Raid Siren after his 1994 LP failed to receive the recognition he felt it deserved. And so he was to try something radical to appease himself more than anyone else, but Bruce also genuinely felt his next project might be the one to push his solo career forwards. After much debate in the pages of *Kerrang!* magazine as to what Bruce's new project would be called, the singer finally announced he was to blood a new band – Skunkworks. The name came from the Lockheed Martin project that built the U-2 (the aircraft which penetrated the Iron Curtain), the SR-71 Blackbird, and the F-117A Stealth Fighter. Lockeed Martin itself was so called due to Al Capp's *Li'l Abner* comic strip which featured the 'Skonk Works', where Appalachian hillbillies ground up skunks, old shoes, and other foul-smelling ingredients to brew fearsome drinks and other products. Although a strange choice of name, it was one followers of Bruce's passions would entirely understand, given the vocalist's long held interest in aircraft.

The collection of band members for the project would be as interesting as the moniker they would play under. Roy Z would not be involved however, as he explains, "Basically, my band, Tribe Of Gypsies, who had backed Bruce on *Balls To Picasso* got signed to Mercury/PolyGram, and there wasn't going to be any more time to continue working with Bruce, so he had to get new players."

In wondering who to bring into his new venture, Bruce recalled that in 1988 he had watched a guitarist, Alex Dickson, play in a pub near where he lived and had been "completely blown away." Once Dickson had been ousted from his band – the Scottish rockers Gun – in 1995, Bruce found Alex and recruited him for Skunkworks. He said it "was like finding a soul mate." This was borne out by the fact that all the songs on the *Skunkworks* album were composed solely by the two of them (with the exception of 'Innerspace', where bassist Chris Dale also contributed his talents). Dale and Alessandro Elena (drums), completed the quartet. These two had been playing in American band, Machine, not altogether happily until one day

Dale just happened to spot an interview in *Kerrang!* In which Bruce discussed the imminent release of *Balls To Picasso*.

"In the interview he said he needed a live band," Dale related to me, "He already had Alex Dickson and just needed a bassist and drummer. I knew a couple of the guys from Skin at the time who were also managed by Sanctuary, so I got the phone number from them and called up. They said to send a tape, photo and biog in." This was not just another gig for the rhythm section however. The two had been "big Iron Maiden fans," as Chris testifies. "The first album I ever bought was *The Number Of The Beast*. If someone had told me then that I would one day play with the singer from that album I'd never have believed them. There are so many good points to getting a job like that. Yes, I liked the idea of a high profile gig; yes the idea of playing for Bruce was very cool. A trip around the world with free beer playing heavy metal appealed a lot too!"

Dale had cut his teeth in cult British band Atom Seed, who released just one album (*Get In Line*) and an EP (*Dead Happy*), but will be forever remembered by their dedicated fans. They hit the UK at a time when the funk metal phenomenon could have plucked them from obscurity and propelled them to loftier heights where it has to be said, they deserved to be. Unfortunately, they could not transcend the fringes of the Brit metal scene, which for a long time had struggled to find even one group who could break out of the shadows and take on America's finest.

But finding a job with Bruce Dickinson had revived Dale's fortunes and there was to be no shortage of material. Altogether the band produced 22 tracks in just over seven weeks. Thirteen appeared on the *Skunkworks* album, with a few being released as b-sides. Bruce's new project was not simply a vehicle for self-promotion and the singer confirmed himself to be "the lead singer of *Skunkworks*, not the former singer of Iron Maiden." At the time Bruce was clearly unhappy with his reputation preceding his every move, and explained part of his reason for leaving Maiden was because he had become a parody of himself. Ironically, he reverted to his earlier days with Samson for his vocal approach on the *Skunkworks* album, claiming he had lost the desire to perform "operatic" vocals. He felt more comfortable in the company of early Paul Rodgers (of Free) and the soulful style of Soundgarden screecher Chris Cornell, who would later release a rather un-Soundgarden like solo album titled *Euphoria Morning*.

Despite combining a variety of styles, *Skunkworks* was destined to be short-lived. Though there would be more signing sessions across the UK, Bruce later blamed lack of promotion for the demise of the band, which was at least amicable. "*Skunkworks* politely fell apart, due to musical differences," explains Chris Dale. "We all had a beer and said this can't go on, so we shook hands and said 'let's be friends.'" The musical differences were chiefly rooted in Bruce's rediscovery of his metal pedigree, and he had already decided that *Skunkworks* was not the right vehicle for his next move. "After we finished touring the *Skunkworks* record we got together to discuss material for a new record, which Bruce already wanted to call *Accident Of Birth*," Chris Dale remembers. "He wanted a more traditional metal album after the disappointing sales of *Skunkworks*. Us three meanwhile wanted to do a more alternative record. There had been some musical differences along these lines before, but this one was final. Bruce said he was going to do an album with Roy Z and advised us to make our own record, which we did with the first Sack Trick album, *Mystery Rabbits*."

For once in the music industry, the commonly claimed 'disagreements of a musical nature' did not lead to tantrums or bad blood, and it is with a pleasant degree of nostalgia Chris Dale recalls his time with the Bruce Dickinson Four, and especially the music which emerged from their period together. "*Skunkworks* is a very underrated record," the bassist claims with no degree of exaggeration. "I think people will discover it one of these days but I'm not going to push it down people's throats."

Chris Dale and his cohorts still have good memories of the whole era, as he emphasises, "It was all a good time, really. We had good fun, made some good music and got to see the world at the same time. We all got on very well together as friends as well as musically. Alex Elena and Alex Dickson are both great players and friends, we share the same musical tastes and we've gone on to do a lot of stuff together since with the Sack Trick albums. And to have Bruce Dickinson singing in the band? That's more than most people could hope for.

"We went through a lot together on tour in Europe, the States, South America and Japan – mostly fun – but the weirdest and strangest story was the Bosnian tour we did. We were the only western band to play in Sarajevo during the war while it was still under siege. Words can't describe the feelings we experienced, meeting the soldiers on the front line, orphans, refugees and UN workers with the distant sound of gunfire. It was awful and inspiring. I've never seen anything like it."

"*Skunkworks* wasn't a waste of time," is Bruce's conclusion. "I learned a huge amount about myself on that album. I had a lot of fun, I also almost gave up music as a career. *Skunkworks* was a low point in terms of career, commercial success and yet I remember it very fondly, and I still like the record a lot."

For Bruce it was time for a rebirth, or an accident of birth if you will. Only his teaming up with Roy Z and Adrian Smith for 1997's *Accident Of Birth* album was no fluke. The album would see Dickinson place himself fully back into the metal fold, and he did it with some style. Finally, he used the opportunity to release some of his acoustic work but it is ironic that in doing so he also produced his heaviest solo material to date. Quite simply, the album is fantastic from start to finish and was a clear indication the ex-Iron Maiden singer had now truly found his solo feet.

"I think Bruce was even contemplating retirement," says Roy Z now, "but then I called him one day and said, 'hey, man, if you ever feel like doing a metal record – I've got these songs.' Next thing I know Bruce is on a plane out to LA and we wrote most of *Accident Of Birth* on the spot. And then Adrian came into the picture and brought in a couple of songs he'd written and that was it."

Perhaps because of this, *Accident Of Birth* doesn't even seem like a solo record. It has more of a band feel than any of Bruce's work in Maiden post-1990 and certainly more coherent and undeniably 'Bruce' than his previous ventures alone. There is everything here that one had come to expect and love about the vocalist – full-on, overblown, heavy metal epics (the title track and 'Welcome To The Pit'), melancholy warblings ('Arc Of Space'), intelligent, thought-provoking lyrics throughout and catchy duelling guitar battles such as on 'Road To Hell.' For a little reminiscence Dickinson hired Derek Riggs for the artwork, which turned out to be a strange and not remotely pleasant looking Punch (of Punch and Judy fame) bursting out of a pregnant human (presumably) with baseball bat in hand. "Bruce had the idea and I just executed it," says Riggs. "I actually preferred the single (sleeve) to the album. That was Bruce's idea as well." The single was a similar take on the Punch theme and the cover image also appeared on the album version at the back of the CD tray.

"I really wanted to make a kick ass metal record with Bruce at the time," says Roy Z of his return to the Dickinson line-up, "and so did Bruce once he heard the musical ideas I had. I think we accomplished that – a lot of people commented that *Accident Of Birth* was the type of record they wished Maiden had made but couldn't. We definitely tapped into the Maiden vibe but at the same time it wasn't a retro trip. It sounded classic yet fresh and it still holds up well ten years later."

Credit must certainly go to Roy Z not only for co-writing most of the songs with Bruce, but also for overseeing production duties and creating a giant metal hybrid which sounded as if it could attack you from behind the speakers at any moment. Perhaps a return to the Bruce of old was helped along by the acutely 'metal' lyrics, and none were more metal than the title track. "'Accident Of Birth' is about a family from Hell," Bruce mused. "Except they're in hell and one of them has accidentally been born, and they want him back and he doesn't want to go. For all the same reasons that you wouldn't want to go back to your family if they're a pain in the ass so he doesn't want to go back to his family. Ok, so they're in Hell that makes a little difference too." And he turned to familiar inspiration for the emotional 'Man Of Sorrows', citing Aleister Crowley as the subject: "It's about the young Aleister Crowley, Aleister Crowley as a boy. And what kind of feelings turn a 12-year-old boy into, basically what inspires a boy to make a life choice: 'Hey what do you want to be when you grow up?' 'I want to be the Antichrist.'"

Interestingly, Bruce was hardly optimistic about his chances of being successful with *Accident Of Birth*, saying, "As far as I was concerned, *Accident...* might be the last record I ever made, so I might as well do what I was good at." It was indeed a stellar record, but its follow up was mightier still. With a concept in mind and a heavier desire working into his head, Bruce set to work on his widely considered masterwork, *The Chemical Wedding*. Lyrically the inspiration came from works by the classic English poet, William Blake.

In all honesty, although the musings of the allegedly schizophrenic Blake are an interesting sideline and certainly well tackled by Dickinson, he could have been singing about a strawberry cheesecake and it wouldn't have mattered. Some felt this was how Maiden could or even should sound, and perhaps they might have had Bruce still been in the band. There are the kind of catchy short and sharp tunes Maiden had belted out in the past, such as the opener 'King In Crimson' and the title track. There are long concept riddled epics like 'The Alchemist' and 'Book Of Thel.' The imagery is alluring, capturing some of Blake's own paintings to accompany the lyrical theme. Indeed, Blake is widely viewed as a superb artist as well as poet and the man himself felt the two disciplines should not be separated. It seems Bruce was well aware of this and thus did well in gaining permission to use Blake's paintings.

As he had done before, Bruce was successfully merging varying pieces into one. Though Blake was the inspiration and at times the source, it seems almost as if Bruce took on the poet's spirit while creating the album. Who knows, if Blake had been alive in the late twentieth century he might well have been a heavy metal fan.

But *The Chemical Wedding* is not all serious, and its aura was not entirely created by Blake and Dickinson. The song 'Machine Men' features some low voices in the first section of the song; this was actually Bruce reading randomly from the *Yellow Pages*!

The album sold around 40,000 units in America which, given that it pre-dated the re-emergence of the heavy metal scene on a worldwide scale, was a very respectable figure. It helped that Bruce's work received rave reviews in varying types of metal magazines and websites, from extreme metal publications to those that were more hard rock oriented.

It is undoubtedly a phenomenal album with broad consequences for the ex-Maiden singer. Not since he was at his peak with the band had the media taken him so seriously or given him the credit he richly deserved. Hitting the globe with an album rooted in deep, dark and intellectual metal was just about perfect at the time of release since for the next few years metal would receive a makeover, with bands like Hammerfall helping to re-establish the popularity of the genre.

It was tough for Bruce to follow his acclaimed 'best' solo work, so instead he followed it up with a real Best Of collection, where those who had come to his solo material belatedly could hear his past accomplishments. The double set was lovingly compiled, featuring two new (and brilliant) tracks as well as plenty of material which had previously been either hard to find or unavailable.

Bruce, understandably pleased with the new respect shown him as a solo performer, realised a compilation was the best thing for his career at that moment.

Afterwards Bruce continued to keep his name in the public arena with a special yet somewhat low-key release titled *Scream For Me Brazil*. The title was obviously a play on the singer's famous catchphrase, but this was no Iron Maiden cover band. Rather, it was an opportunity for Bruce to release songs most recently performed, from *The Chemical Wedding* release.

"It was amazing," Bruce said of his time in Brazil. "I think we played to 20,000 people in six days. We did five shows in six days. We couldn't go outside our hotel because there were kids out there. It was insane! We had a fantastic time."

By 2004 the perennially busy Dickinson was back in Maiden, busily bringing them back to the fore. But this time he was more comfortable in being able to record a solo album as and when he felt like it. It's a shame it took so long for Bruce to update his solo career, but thankfully when he was ready, the resultant album was worth waiting for.

Tyranny Of Souls consists of a clever merging of most of Dickinson's back catalogue, with melody, heaviness and dark imagery aplenty.

Speaking of the recording process between himself and Bruce, Roy Z explained, "I usually come up with the music and then we get together and arrange and tweak it and Bruce comes up with most of the words and melodies. At least that's how it worked on *Tyranny Of Souls*. I had demoed ten songs and played them to Bruce over the phone. This sounds crazy but he literally came up with melody ideas and song titles on the spot and started singing to me over the phone. So I sent him roughs of those ten and he started working on melodies and lyrics whenever and wherever, even while on tour with Maiden. He had a couple of windows where he was able to stop by in LA and we did the vocals at my place. I took care of the rest, got the bass, drums and keyboard tracks from all the different guys and then Bruce came out to LA again for part of the final mix."

And Z was in no doubt as to Dickinson's prowess as a premier world heavy metal singer. "Bruce is the ultimate pro as a singer," he thinks. "When you get to work with someone like him you realise why he is where he is and what separates the men from the boys, so to speak. Take *Tyranny Of Souls* for example. Bruce was scheduled to come in for a vocal session but had a nasty spill on stage with Maiden and cracked his ribs. He was in a lot of pain, so much so that he had to lie down to be able to sing at all. But he pulled it off and came through with flying colours. His vocals on *Tyranny…* are amazing! On a personal level, Bruce is like a big brother who watches over me and makes sure I'm OK. There is never a formula to what we do, everything happens in every possible way. That is why it is a lot of fun working with Bruce. The heavens pour out these tunes and we just catch them."

Like the best professionals in any walk of life, when the time comes for Bruce to leave the world of metal he will do so with grace and dignity, not that it will end his association with music. As he once said, "I'll be in music probably until I croak. I think even if I'd quit music completely, for any reason, I would only have stopped playing the commercial music game. I wouldn't stop singing, in actual fact, I'd probably just be learning to play the acoustic guitar better and just be doing acoustic on my own, It'd be fun."

NAIL THAT FOKKER!

"I've got a large house with a massive garden. I have two dogs. In the house, I love this little room, a kind of library where I have some six or seven hundred books. I love reading, my sources of inspiration are quite diverse, and I use old books, like the one I recently acquired – published in

1890, it deals with fantasy and imaginary subjects. I like magical treatises, occult stuff. I'm less interested these days, though, as I found out that a large number of those books are pure bullshit." Bruce Dickinson

What follows is an examination of the other pursuits Bruce has involved himself with as well as some lesser-known facts about the man himself.

AIR RAID RECORDS

In February 1997 Bruce Dickinson formed his own label, Air Raid Records, which would see him put out tons of reissued and previously 'impossible to find' rock records, as well as a selection of carefully compiled albums featuring extra tracks, etc. As the official website spiel states, "We are an independent label specialising in rock and pop music from the 60s to the 21st century on CD and DVD. We focus on two distinct areas: reissues of historic classic albums and issues of never-before-available albums by some familiar artists. All our CDs and DVDs are created with the full co-operation of the artists, and include extensive liner notes and photographs. The addition of bonus tracks and digital remastering ensures the highest quality."

FENCING

"Last year, for instance, I took with me – like I usually do – my fencing kit. You can't imagine the problems I had with the customs! I'd learned how to say 'fencing' in ten different languages! And every time, I was asked the same question, 'Oh I see, you're a professional fencer!' And my answer was always the same, 'No, I'm a singer!' They'd look at me pretty suspiciously!" Bruce Dickinson 1986

Many people know Bruce Dickinson likes to fence and indeed he is a past master at the sport. Here are some facts relating to the singer's preferred sporting activity.

• There was a rumour that Bruce turned down an offer to compete for the English National Fencing team in order to join Iron Maiden. However, this Bruce completely refutes, as he says: "No. That is someone getting very imaginative out there."

• Bruce was a professional fencer for many years, enjoying an international career. At one stage he was ranked the seventh best in men's foil discipline in Great Britain, and represented England in the European Cup in 1989.

• Bruce accidentally discovered he, like his father, is ambidextrous. Says the vocalist: "Knowing that he is ambidextrous and that I have some slight coordination problems with my movements, I switched to my right arm. I really progressed since! Much more evolution than in the previous seven years of practice and competition using my left hand. Who would have thought that I was ambidextrous too?"

• The singer keeps up with the world of fencing. Bruce formed a London-based company called Duellist in 1988, which he still presides over today. The official history states: "The Duellist story began on the 25th of July 1988 in Chiswick, London. Bruce started the company with the intention to provide the UK fencing population with products as good as those available on the continent but at an affordable cost. Enthusiastic reports about the quality of the equipment soon spread to far corners of the earth. Duellist's reputation for quality and excellence established us as one of the fastest growing companies in the market. The frequent launch of exciting and unpredictable products has helped us gain a world-class reputation."

• Both Alice Cooper and Bruce Dickinson were once named two of the Top Ten Sporting Rock Stars by the UK's *Sunday Times* newspaper. Cooper was included for his golfing pursuits while Bruce made it due to his Fencing expertise.

• *The Times* stated: 'It's not all drinking the blood of virgins on planet heavy metal, then. In 1989 public schoolboy and Iron Maiden vocalist Bruce Dickinson represented Britain in fencing's European championships. "Fencing is physical, mental and spiritual. It devours you," he says. The feature also mentioned Steve Harris' trials with West Ham United FC in 1972.

• The Top 10 Sporting Rock Stars, according to *The Sunday Times*:

   01. Rod Stewart
   02. Simon Le Bon
   03. Robbie Williams

04. Elton John
05. Mick Hucknall
06. Kenney Jones
07. Alice Cooper
08. The Gallagher brothers
09. Mick Jagger
10. Bruce Dickinson

• A typically humourless tribute from music channel VH1 put Dickinson's fencing interests (along with his two novels) at number 34 on their 'Top 40 Least Metal Moments' show. The programme included an interview with Twisted Sister's Dee Snider who discussed just how 'metal' Iron Maiden are, yet also how Bruce changed his metal image and began wearing white tights in order to fence. The show followed an earlier programme entitled '100 Most Metal Moments'.

EXTERMINATE!

If you have come to the conclusion throughout this book, and more specifically this chapter, that the real Bruce Dickinson is a few sandwiches short of a picnic, or just a touch eccentric, then the realisation that the man is obsessed with science fiction and especially *Dr Who* might come as no surprise. Even more disturbingly, Bruce has a real full size Dalek prop in his house. The singer stores the *Dr Who* 'star' in his hallway after he bought it from a second hand magazine. He once claimed it was embarrassing how much he had to pay for it.

"I remember talking to Martin Birch about it and going 'I am really sad and embarrassed about this, but I am going to pay this for a Dalek'", says the singer. "And he turned around and went 'A Dalek? A real Dalek? You have got to do it!' So I went and got the money out of the cash point and went and paid the guy cash for this Dalek. It is absolutely awesome. It is a real full size Dalek and you can get into it. You have to be a real midget to get into it, but my oldest kid can do it and he walks around and operates it. The head moves and the little eye moves and he goes: 'EX-TERMINATE ALL TEACHERS!!!'"

The most stressful part of the transaction came when Bruce had to transport the Dalek to his home, as he explains, "I had to stuff it in three sections in the back of a car and you should have seen the looks! I was driving and all of a sudden people would see this Dalek staring at them out of the back of this 4 X 4!'"

DISCOGRAPHY

More than most hard rock or heavy metal singers, Bruce has a varied range of material. Thus, it is not the most consistent set of albums by a vocalist, but it sure is entertaining. What follows is the album discography for Bruce, with a score out of ten for each. The score for the Best Of compilation shows that, were Bruce to release an album of studio material as consistent as this, he could not be denied full marks. Elsewhere there are always one or two filler tracks on most of the albums.

TATTOOED MILLIONAIRE (7.5) *Son Of A Gun / Tattooed Millionaire / Born In '58 / Hell On Wheels / Gypsy Road / Dive! Dive! Dive! / All The Young Dudes / Lickin' The Gun / Zulu Lulu / No Lies*
(CD, LP, cassette – EMI 1990)

BALLS TO PICASSO (8) *Cyclops / Hell No / Gods Of War / 1000 Points Of Light / Laughing In The Hiding Bush / Change Of Heart / Shoot All The Clowns / Fire / Sacred Cowboys / Tears Of The Dragon*
(CD, LP, cassette – EMI 1994)

ALIVE IN STUDIO A (8) *Cyclops / Shoot All The Clowns / Son Of A Gun / Tears Of The Dragon / 1000 Points Of Light / Sacred Cowboys / Tattooed Millionaire / Born In '58 / Fire / Change Of Heart / Hell No / Laughing In The Hiding Bush*
(CD, LP, cassette – EMI 1995)

ALIVE AT THE MARQUEE (8) *Cyclops / 1000 Points Of Light / Born In '58 / Gods Of War / Change Of Heart / Laughing In The Hiding Bush / Hell No / Tears Of The Dragon / Shoot All The Clowns / Sacred Cowboys / Son Of A Gun / Tattooed Millionaire*
(2-CD, 2-LP, double cassette – Raw Power 1995)

SKUNKWORKS (8) *Space Race / Back From The Edge / Inertia / Faith / Solar Confinement / Dreamstate / I Will Not Accept The Truth / Inside The Machine / Headswitch / Meltdown / Octavia / Innerspace / Strange Death In Paradise*
(CD, LP, cassette – Raw Power 1996)

ACCIDENT OF BIRTH (9) *The Freak / Toltec 7 Arrival / Star Children / Taking The Queen / Darkside Of Aquarius / Road To Hell / Man Of Sor-*

rows / Accident Of Birth / Magician / Welcome To The Pit / Omega / Arc Of Space
(CD, LP, cassette – Raw Power 1997)

THE CHEMICAL WEDDING (9) *King In Crimson / Chemical Wedding / The Tower / Killing Floor / Book Of Thel / Gates Of Urizen / Jerusalem / Trumpets Of Jericho / Machine Men / The Alchemist / Return Of The King*
(CD, LP, cassette – Air Raid 1998)

SCREAM FOR ME BRAZIL (7) *Trumpets Of Jericho / King In Crimson / Chemical Wedding / Gates Of Urizen / Killing Floor / Book Of Thel / Tears Of The Dragon / Laughing In The Hiding Bush / Accident Of Birth / The Tower / Dark Side Of Aquarius / Road To Hell*
(CD, LP, cassette – Air Raid 1999)

THE BEST OF (10) *Broken / Tattooed Millionaire / Laughing In The Hiding Bush / Tears Of The Dragon / The Tower / Born In '58 / Accident Of Birth / Silver Wings / Dark Side Of Aquarius / Chemical Wedding / Back From The Edge / Road To Hell / Book Of Thel (Live) / Bring Your Daughter To The Slaughter / Darkness Be My Friend / Wicker Man / Real World / Acoustic Son / No Way Out / Midnight Jam / Man Of Sorrows / Ballad Of Mutt / Re-Entry / I'm In A Band With An Italian Drummer / Jerusalem (Live) / Dracula*
(CD, LP, cassette – Metal-Is/Sanctuary 2001)

TYRANNY OF SOULS (8) *Mars Within / Abduction / Soul Intruders / Kill Devil Hill / Navigate The Seas Of The Sun / River Of No Return / Power Of The Sun / Devil On A Hog / Believil / A Tyranny Of Souls*
(CD, LP, Cassette – Sanctuary 2005)

In 2005 the entire Bruce Dickinson catalogue was reissued with bonus tracks for each album. The following list shows the extra tracks available for each album, which incidentally are well worth purchasing for the first time, or simply for an upgrade!

Tattooed Millionaire Bonus Tracks

1) Bring Your Daughter... To The Slaughter (original soundtrack version)
2) Ballad Of Mutt

3) Winds Of Change
4) Darkness Be My Friend
5) Sin City
6) Dive! Dive! Dive! (live)
7) Riding With The Angels (live)
8) Sin City (live)
9) Black Night (live)
10) Son Of A Gun (live)
11) Tattooed Millionaire (live)

Balls To Picasso Bonus Tracks

1) Fire Child
2) Elvis Has Left The Building
3) The Breeding House
4) No Way Out... To Be Continued
5) Tears Of The Dragon (acoustic chillout)
6) Winds Of Change
7) Spirit Of Joy
8) Over And Out
9) Shoot All The Clowns (12" extended remix)
10) Laughing In The Hiding Bush (live)
11) The Post Alternative Seattle Fall Out (live)
12) Shoot All The Clowns (7" remix)
13) Tibet
14) Tears Of The Dragon (First Bit, Long Bit, Last Bit)
15) Cadillac Gas Mask
16) No Way Out... Continued

Skunkworks Bonus Tracks

1) I'm In A Band With An Italian Drummer
2) Rescue Day
3) God's Not Coming Back
4) Armchair Hero
5) R101
6) Re-Entry
7) Americans Are Behind
8) Inertia (live)
9) Faith (live)

10) Innerspace (live)
11) The Prisoner (live)

Accident Of Birth Bonus Tracks

1) The Ghost Of Cain
2) Accident Of Birth (demo)
3) Starchildren (demo)
4) Taking The Queen (demo)
5) Man Of Sorrows (radio edit)
6) Man Of Sorrows (orchestral version)
7) Man Of Sorrows (Spanish version)
8) Darkside Of Aquarius (demo)
9) Arc Of Space (demo)

The Chemical Wedding Bonus Tracks

1) Return Of The King
2) Real World
3) Confeos

AN INTERVIEW WITH CHRIS DALE

Though Atom Seed were a different style to the Dickinson material and indeed the Iron Maiden albums, both their recordings are highly recommended for open-minded listeners who enjoy catchy hooks and expert musicianship.

The releases did just about make it on to compact disc, though they are both now deleted. However, there is a site put together by Chris Dale which explores his other work and includes MP3s of both Atom Seed and Sack Trick (his current band) www.sacktrick.com.

I spoke to Chris at length about his time with Bruce. Here follow the parts of the interview, which were too long or out of context to be included in the body of this chapter.

PAUL STENNING: **What did you have to play at the audition for Bruce's band?**

CHRIS DALE: "We got given an advance tape of the *Balls To Picasso* album and had to learn four songs off it ('Tears Of The Dragon', 'Shoot

All The Clowns' and a couple of others). But we learned the whole album. I think that impressed Bruce a bit. We had a day jamming with him and Alex. We did all the songs, plus we fooled around with a couple of Deep Purple riffs. Bruce asked a lot of questions like 'do you sing?' and 'are you scared of flying?' (typical Bruce!). Then at the end of the day we went for a drink together and he dropped me off at home and said, 'we'll be in touch'. Then a couple of weeks later we were told to learn a few more songs ('Sin City', 'Black Night', 'Wishing Well' and 'Tattooed Million-aire') and come for another jam. At the end of that second audition he told us we'd got the job. We were over the moon!"

PS: Was this the first time you had met Alex Dickson? It's nice you've maintained your working relationship after *Skunkworks*...

CD: "Yes, I'd seen him play before but never met him. He's an incredibly shy person; I didn't really get to know him until we went on tour. Since then we've been very good friends, we've got a lot of similar tastes. He's a really talented musician and singer, he taught me a lot and inspired me to work much harder... and party harder! After *Skunkworks* split we sat around and chatted about the type of album we'd like to make and ended up making three very silly Sack Trick albums together, including a Kiss tribute album called *Sheep In Kiss Make Up* that we got Bruce to sing on too."

PS: So how was it, suddenly being in Bruce's band?

CD: "For the first couple of days after the audition, it was kind of weird. Nothing changed, I was still living in the same house doing the same things, signing on the dole but in the back of my head I kept thinking 'Shit, I'm in Bruce Dickinson's band!' Nothing happened for a couple of months while a tour was being booked, then it all kicked off..."

PS: Did you feel part of it in terms of contributions, or was everything decided by Bruce?

CD: "It was quite a good arrangement. Everybody was allowed their say, but at the end of the day Bruce was making the decision. That was fair, it was his solo career after all and it stopped any arguments. I don't think we had an argument in the whole time in the band really. I'd say 'I think we should do this...' and Alex would say 'No, I think it should be like that...' then Bruce would say 'No actually we're doing this...' End of argument!

247

You had to respect Bruce's opinion too, after all he'd been in the business a while and knew what he was talking about."

PS: **It seems quite strange that your earlier work was quite upbeat and bubbly (just like your subsequent work in fact) yet** *Skunkworks* **was a really dark, introspective album, especially for Bruce. Did it come easily to just jump in the groove of the material and were you surprised at how different it was for him?**

CD: "It wasn't too contrived. Alex Dickson recorded a load of instrumental demos (probably about 30), and then me and Alex Elena would jam them with him while Bruce got some lyrical ideas. Then we picked the best 20 or so. The only conscious decision was to try different things and not to sound like Maiden, so we avoided galloping bass lines, twin harmony guitars and the like. Yes, it does sound very dark, although we were having great fun with it."

PS: **Of course it doesn't go unnoticed that for the b-sides, you were having a good laugh together too. It seemed like you all got on really well?**

CD: "Yes, we did have good fun. Me and the two Alexs bonded really well as musicians and friends. Even when we weren't on tour we hung out together all the time. Bruce had his own schedule a lot of the time with press interviews, flying planes and being a sensible family man, but whenever he was around it was very relaxed. I'd kind of forget who he was, then every now and then in rehearsal or something I'd freeze for a second thinking 'shit that's the bloke out of Iron Maiden!'"

PS: **I read an interview where you said Sack Trick had played at Bruce's son Austin's eleventh birthday party in 2001. You said then you kept in touch with Bruce but that was five years ago, so are you still in touch with him? If so, how often and what kind of relationship do you have?**

CD: "Yes, we're still good friends, probably better friends now than back then. Back then I always felt slightly like he was my boss. Now we're just two friends who meet up down the pub for a pint every now and then. He really likes Sack Trick and often pops down to a gig we're playing. I quite like Maiden so I often pop down to a gig he's playing!"

PS: **Do you think either you, Alex or Alessandro would play with Bruce again?**

CD: "Yes. We still play together every now and then. Bruce got up and sang at a Sack Trick gig at a pub in London. Then a couple of years ago, he did some solo European Festival gigs and we played as his band again. Alex Elena lives in New York now so we got Sack Trick's drummer, Robin Guy to play. They were really good fun gigs, headlining massive festivals. Bruce's *Best Of* album was out at the time so we did songs from all his solo albums and a few Maiden tracks too.

Me and Bruce also guested on the Brazilian artist, Tribuzy's *Execution* album that came out last year. Then we went out to do some gigs over in Brazil with him. Most of the gig was Tribuzy songs then at the end me, Bruce and Roy Z did 'Tears Of The Dragon' and a few Maiden songs. Bruce's main priority right now is of course Iron Maiden, but I wouldn't be surprised if we did some more of his solo gigs with him in future.

PS: **Have you listened to his subsequent solo stuff?**

CD: "It's really good. Roy is a very talented guy who knows how to get the best out of Bruce, they work well together. Albums such as *Accident Of Birth*, *The Chemical Wedding* and *Tyranny Of Souls* aren't as experimental as *Skunkworks*, but not all experiments are meant to be repeated!

PS: **Even at the time I personally thought *Skunkworks* was brilliant, and with hindsight you can kind of see the material was quite ahead of its time for most metal heads anyway. Do you think it's one of those albums that will be recognised as a classic somewhere down the line?**

CD: "It's funny I read recently on the Iron Maiden forum that people were rediscovering the album, now it's been re-released with bonus tracks. I don't think it'll ever be seen as a classic next to things like *The Number Of The Beast*, but I think it was important that Bruce tried something new at the time. Looking back, I'm still proud of it, there's some really strong songs there and a side of Bruce's singing that you won't hear anywhere else.

PS: **How would you describe the way he was then and the way he is now, or the last time you saw him – especially since rejoining Maiden?**

CD: "He's not changed much. Same old Bruce, good bloke who happens to be a very talented singer!"

PS: Do you know any other of the Maiden members?

CD: "Yes, I've met a few... Janick used to sign on at the same dole office as me before he joined Maiden. He was one of the guys who recommended me to Bruce. I still see him around every now and then. Nicko and Adrian I've met a couple of times, always very friendly. Paul Di'anno I knew from years ago. I used to bump into him at rock clubs in London. A lot of people (including himself) say he's got a really nasty streak, but I've only ever seen the fun side of him. After the *Skunkworks* split I got asked to join his band at one point, I had other things in my schedule at the time so couldn't do it. Maybe then I would have seen the other side of him.
Blaze I've also known for years. As you may know, Atom Seed supported Wolfsbane quite a lot back in the early '90s. We all crashed over at his place one night and drank Newcastle Brown until the early hours. He's a very intense guy with quite an articulate and serious side to him.
But I've never met Steve Harris. I've occasionally been at the same party as him but always been too nervous to go and say hello!
Oh! And best of all, I'm mates with Eddie! Jeff Williams was the drum tech on the *Skunkworks* tour (he's a hilarious bloke), then went on to drum tech for Nicko in Maiden and to be Eddie in costume and stilts every night... how cool is that?"

MORE WORDS WITH ROY

Here are some more excerpts of my absorbing interview with guitarist Roy Z.

PAUL STENNING: I remember Bruce playing the Downset album that you produced on a radio show... did you turn him on to that band and also other music?

ROY Z: "Yeah, Bruce got turned onto Downset through me and the fact that I was recording them at the same studio we did a lot of the Tribe stuff and also bits of 'Shoot All The Clowns' (and later on *Accident Of Birth* and *The Chemical Wedding*), which was a late addition to the *Balls To Picasso* album, at the request of Mercury. So there was this circle of bands and people in and out of Silver Cloud, Joe Floyd's now defunct studio in

Burbank, and Downset, Tribe and Bruce was all part of that. Bruce is an open-minded dude and into new music and he liked Downset – he even adapted a bit of that vibe with the rap part in 'Shoot All The Clowns.'"

PS: Were you or are you a Maiden fan? If so what is your favourite album?

RZ: "Of course I'm a Maiden fan. I was at Long Beach Arena as a kid when *Live After Death* was recorded! Maiden was the shit back then and they're still awesome in concert. I'm definitely partial to the early albums because that's what I grew up on. *Iron Maiden, Killers, The Number Of The Beast* and *Piece Of Mind* – you can't beat that stuff. Classics all the way."

PS: With Bruce rejoining the band and taking Adrian with him, was there ever a discussion about you going with him? Would you have done so if it were possible?

RZ: "Nah, there was never any discussion about me joining Maiden. They don't need four guitar players and I don't think Steve would let anyone who isn't English join his band anyway. I love Maiden but I'm not too sure they love me. I really wanted to produce their reunion album."

PS: Have you met any of the other Maiden members, other than Adrian of course?

RZ: "Yeah, I've met all of the Maiden guys. The first time was when I was in London in '93 with my band doing the *Balls To Picasso* album and Bruce was doing his farewell show with Maiden. We've crossed paths a few more times over the years but the only guys I know well are Bruce and Adrian. Other than Bruce, the only time I get to see the Maiden guys is when they play LA and then it's usually just a quick hello."

PS: How would you describe Adrian Smith professionally and personally?

RZ: "Adrian is a cool, down-to-earth guy – there's no rock star bullshit or anything like that with him. We've always gotten along great and respected each other both personally and musically. I've pretty much always been the only guitar player in the bands I've been in, but I had no problems

251

working with Adrian when he joined us for *Accident Of Birth*. Adrian is a very easy going guy and great to work with. He brought his sound and his style, which complimented my way of playing very well. We had good chemistry both on a personal and musical level and I think that comes through on those albums. Adrian is not a flashy guitar player but he's got a great sense of melody and a unique sound and style. He's also written some damn good songs."

PS: What is your favourite era of the Bruce solo material?

RZ: "My favourite is *The Chemical Wedding* because it has it's own sound and energy. I believe it has stood and will stand the test of time."

PS: Favourite song you and Bruce have written?

RZ: "That is a hard question but if I had to go with one I would say 'The Alchemist'."

PS: Was there ever a point – or is there now even – where you would want to just work with Bruce full-time instead of him doing Maiden and you doing your own thing?

RZ: "No, I need the freedom to do different things and if I ever committed to something exclusively it would be my own band, Tribe Of Gypsies. I want for the Tribe to get to the point where it is a full-time thing that earns all of us a living. That's the goal and that's the dream. And I'm sure Bruce has no plans to pursue a solo career full-time. He's got Maiden, he's got his airline gig, he's a DJ, and he's got a family – being a solo artist probably ranks about fourth on his list of priorities at this stage in his life."

PS: How did the sales for *Tyranny Of Souls* go? It is a very strong album but I worried it was not too well promoted and may have slipped by more unnoticed than say, *Chemical Wedding*?

RZ: "I don't know what the sales are on *Tyranny Of Souls*. It's not really that the album wasn't promoted well but it wasn't supported with a tour – or gigs, period. Obviously touring would've extended the life of the record but it isn't my call and Bruce is a busy guy between his work with Maiden and being an airline pilot, which is something he really enjoys. I can see why he wouldn't want to sacrifice what little time he has left busting his tail as a solo artist. When we did *Balls...*, *Accident...*, and ...*Wed-*

ding, Bruce was focusing all his energies on his solo career because that's all he had on his plate. It's different now that he's back in Maiden."

PS: Was it always Bruce's intention to continue with his solo stuff even after rejoining Maiden?

RZ: "I'm not sure but he rejoined Maiden with the understanding that he could continue doing solo records if he wanted to. There are four other writers in Maiden besides Bruce so there's only so much input you can have in a situation like that. When he's doing a solo album it's just him and me and Bruce can do whatever he feels like doing. I think he really values that creative freedom being a solo artist affords him so he'll probably always be doing stuff on the side, whether it's with me or someone else."

PS: Will there be another solo album at some point and will you work with Bruce?

RZ: "Yeah, we've talked about doing another album. When exactly that might be, I don't know but I'd imagine it won't be another seven years between records. It's all about juggling schedules and finding the time to write and put it all together."

PS: Particular people have also described Maiden as difficult to work with, though this is the minority – from your perspective and observations is there a big ego in camp Bruce or Maiden, or are other people just being difficult?

RZ: "I've never worked with Maiden so I can't comment on the dynamics in that group. Obviously Steve and Bruce have had their differences in the past but they're all older now and give each other enough space to make it work. The bottom line is – Maiden is Steve's baby all the way and at the end of the day he's the one who guides the ship the way he sees fit. Being a band leader myself I can relate."

PS: I know for certain Bruce has an ego, but perhaps it's a necessary one, 'the lead singer has to be confident' syndrome – is he more quietly confident than brash and arrogant?

RZ: "A lead singer definitely has to have a lot of confidence and a certain arrogance can't hurt as long as it doesn't carry over once you're off the stage. That's when LSD (lead singer's disease) becomes a problem. Bruce can be brash because he is opinionated, as anyone that's ever gone to a Maiden show would know. But as far as he and I go - we get along great and work together extremely well. He's come to be like a big brother to me, a musical soul brother."

PS: What are your current projects?

RZ: "Well, I'm happy to say that there will be a new Tribe Of Gypsies record in the very near future. We are mixing the album as we speak and should have everything wrapped up in the next couple of weeks. It took us a long time to put this thing together but it's coming out awesome. We're all really happy with it. Other than that I'm working on a couple of other projects I don't want to get specific about right now."

PS: What is most important to you in your life?

RZ: "My music, my girl, my family, my friends – and my health. Being a producer and working in a studio for months on end can be a very taxing thing. It's pretty easy to develop some bad habits that can affect your life negatively if you're not careful. The last couple of years have been pretty stressful for me and I'm trying to take it a bit easier this year."

Sources:

www.sacktrick.com
The Sunday Times (www.timesonline.co.uk)
VH1 (www.vh1.com/shows/dyn/the_greatest/86676/episode.jhtml)
Ram Samudrala (www.ram.org)
Seriah Azkath.
www.geocities.com/sunsetstrip/club/5619/
World Wide Web Multi Media Magazine.
www.oundleschool.org.uk/
Costa Zoulio, 5 February 1999 (Triple JJJ FM Radio).
www.geocities.com/sunsetstrip/club/5619/interviews/as1097.html.
www.issues2000.org/Celeb/George_Bush_Sr__Welfare_&_Poverty.htm
www.darklyrics.com/b/brucedickinson.html
*http://www.nando.myacen.com/brucefans/index.php?option=com_*
frontpage&Itemid=1
http://www.bookofhours.net/samson/
Q Magazine

Publishing Credits courtesy of Duellist Enterprises, EMI and Air Raid Records.
The Adventures Of Lord Iffy Boatrace, *First published in May 1990 by Sidgwick & Jackson Limited*

Chapter 18
Devilish Ravings

A DEREK RIGGS INTERROGATION

He is the artist responsible for some of the most eye-catching, glorious and popular heavy metal album sleeves of all time. Perhaps the unsung hero of the Maiden success story, Derek Riggs worked solely for the band from the early days up until 2000. His designs provided Iron Maiden with a clear identity, and they also gave the band Eddie. Many Maiden fans may love Derek's work, yet for such an important piece of the jigsaw, Riggs was certainly a behind-the-scenes kind of guy. I got in touch with him through his website and asked permission for a very rare interview. He was extremely approachable and affable, and answered virtually everything I threw at him. His answers may surprise you, giving an alternative view of life in the Maiden camp. Ladies and gentlemen, I present a Q & A with Mr Derek Riggs.

PAUL STENNING: **I would like to know how the process develops for designing a record cover. Do you personally draw it first or do the full painting in colour? What kind of material do you submit the painting on?**

DEREK RIGGS: "For the ideas, there is no set process. Some people come to me with ideas and I paint that, other people have no idea and more or less leave it up to me. Mostly I prefer people to have at least an idea of the direction they want to go in, otherwise we can waste a lot of time trying to work it out between us."

As for the pictures, the early ones were done in designers gauche, or acrylic paint on illustration board (cardboard with a nice surface), then they are photographed and a printing plate is made from that. Then they're given to the printer. Because of all these steps, the colours were never right. They always got lost or changed somewhere in the process.

The later pictures are done on a computer, then they go straight to the printers. The colours on these later pictures are far better than on the older ones. Mostly because all the middlemen, who used to mess things up, have gone.

Sometimes I start with a sketch, other times I just get on with making the picture. Often a sketch is not necessary for me but it is necessary for the client to see what I am thinking about. Often there are substantial differences between the sketch and the finished artwork.

PS: I'm not sure if there's ever been an interview where you were able to explain about your life a little bit more. Would you be able to say a bit about yourself: how old you are, what age you began drawing/painting ?

DR: "I am 47 years old, I have been a professional illustrator since the late 1970s. I was freelance until the early 1980s when Iron Maiden put me under a contract to just work for them and no one else. This lasted until the mid-1990s when I went freelance again.

"I began drawing and painting as early as I can remember. I prefer painting; drawing to me is like doing half a picture. I need something more substantial to be able to get into it properly, I can't really get interested in drawing very much. To me it is just a prelude to making a painting. Although painting itself isn't really of much interest either, the thing I am actually doing is making an image. The paint is just a means to an end. This is why I took to computers so quickly. I don't care about the medium; I often use photocomposition to make a background and 3D modelling to make the figures. It's the image that is important; the paint just gets in the way."

PS: Is it true you barely make a living from the Maiden paintings? I've read that initially you got paid and then also a small portion of each record?

DR: "No that's rubbish, it's completely wrong, it must have been a misquote. I got paid an average amount for the covers and then I got paid a royalty from the merchandise, which was sold through the shops. I didn't get rich or anything but it was a pretty decent living.

"I do not currently receive royalties from any Maiden merchandise. Eventually royalties fall to the point where it costs more to administer them than to pay them, so they did a cash buyout of the remaining rights."

PS: You've done a lot of work with other rock/metal artists. Is there more scope for originality?

DR: "No, not really. People often come to me with an idea, so I am often just painting someone else's idea. Sometimes I have turned down commissions because I just thought the idea sucked so badly. Rock stars often have very fixed ideas about what might sell, that's why you get so many muscled men in armour and dragons. The public don't care; they just like a good picture. Basically the chance to be original and do something I like is pretty scarce."

PS: You were originally responsible for Eddie. At some points did you wish you'd never created him, given you had to draw him for every Maiden cover?

DR: "Yes, I got sick of painting him. That's why on the *Seventh Son...* album there wasn't much of him left. I just started chopping bits off him so that I wouldn't have to paint him. He became a bit like my very own Frankenstein's monster. I made him but he will pursue me to my death in the Antarctic."

PS: It seems you've never really been given your due. Without your covers everything from how the sleeves looked to what kind of merchandise they could develop would have been different. Does it bother you or do you think many fans know it was more down to you than the band?

DR: "I did what I did, and it worked. The band was the biggest metal band in the world, they had the coolest covers and the merchandise outsold everyone. Then one day the band decided that everything was due to them being utterly brilliant and all the ideas were theirs. So then I let them take over and I started to move on.

Then what happened was this: Maiden decided it would be a really great idea to tag Eddie onto the tail end of a football team, so they did an album about football, Big 11, or something I think it was called. You get a merchandise figure that literally sells more than Mickey Mouse and you make him an add-on to a football team... great idea.

From there the covers went from horror to kitsch and then into camp, and the fans lost interest. It was no longer unique, it was run-of-the-mill camp and they became so unpopular that they lost their recording contract and had to move to Sony records. You decide who was doing the work. From the emails I get, I think the fans know already."

PS: I read you say you were making a lot up as you went along and therefore the band were claiming credit for an idea which couldn't

possibly have been theirs… who did you mainly work within Maiden, was it more Rod, or Steve, or a combination of everyone?

DR: "Mostly I worked with Rod. That is, if there was a definite idea I would hear about it through Rod and the management, I hardly ever had contact with the band, as they were off touring. I went to a couple of meetings and stuff but those were never very constructive. Usually everyone ended up talking about something other than the covers. I was at one meeting, which was supposed to be about the album concept, and Bruce went on and on about making the stage five feet wider so he could run about more. We never did get to talk about the album; I ended up talking to Rod over the phone about it."

PS: **I know you don't care so much about them anymore but presumably you get a lot of new people coming along and looking at your work because of your old designs. Do you mind, or do you feel like you're restricted in terms of ability because the old covers are all of a certain type?**

DR: "No I don't feel restricted. When I did the Maiden covers I used a particular style of working. Once I had started in that style I was more or less forced to continue with it. As for my own private pictures, I never really settled on any one style, my pictures tend to vary from one to the other both in style and in quality.

"I recently got a large number of the Maiden pictures together and put them on my site. I thought that fans might like to see them. Because they are all on CD covers now, this may be the biggest size some people have ever seen them."

PS: **What is your personal favourite Maiden cover you designed?**

DR: "I don't really have a favourite."

PS: **Which album or single was the quickest and conversely the longest to do?** *Somewhere In Time* **and** *Powerslave* **seem the two most detailed on the surface…**

DR: "All of the early covers, both albums and singles, were done in a hell of a rush. The deadlines were crippling. They would phone me up on Thursday night and want the picture finished by Monday morning. All of the album covers and single covers up until *Piece Of Mind* were done at this rate. By way of comparison, book cover artists were getting two to three weeks to do a cover. So I was working bloody fast. The fastest album cover was probably *The Number Of The Beast*, which was done over a weekend. It was originally done for the single but it got used for the album instead. It was never really finished because the level of detail needed prohibited me from working on the figures for very long.

"*Somewhere In Time* was the slowest to do. It took two and a half months. The original picture was 15 inches by 32 inches, which is only a little bit bigger than the printed size of the record. If you look at the version on my website on a seventeen inch monitor, that is about the actual size of the painting."

PS: Why did that the first album have quite a simple design, followed by a clutch of intricate covers, before *No Prayer For The Dying/Fear Of The Dark* which went back to being relatively simple? Was it down to the band being more picky?

DR: "No, nothing like that. Some pictures lend themselves to being very complicated and others don't. Some pictures just won't support a high level of detail; you get a better image if you leave it out. I am not obsessed with the detail; I just try to make pictures that I think the fans will like. Sometimes that includes a lot of details, and sometimes not."

PS: There are a lot of pieces that evoke Roger Dean. Is he an artist you admire? Do you enjoy the prog rock style/fantasy artwork?

DR: "Yes, I always enjoyed looking at his latest piece of work. He was a very imaginative artist and created many pictorial innovations. I even made a picture, which was deliberately like his style. It's on my website, and it's called 'Yes, Definitely' because it looks a bit like the early Yes covers. I am fond of that style of cover. Sometimes my work tends to veer into that direction; perhaps a bit too much for heavy metal covers."

PS: What generally inspires you – do you tend to look at books, TV, the internet for inspiration or do you literally sit with a blank sheet and imagine from the start?

DR: "I watch movies; I read books about natural history, science fiction, horror, science, UFOs. I watch documentaries; I read *New Scientist* and scientific American magazines. Basically I try to soak up as much as I can. I am not influenced by other artists very much though. I don't often look at art books or go to art galleries and I don't really pay any attention to other illustrators' work. I follow my own nose and look for things that interest me."

PS: You have a section for the unpublished illustrations on your site... are these pieces ones you've submitted to anyone or just for your own amusement?

DR: "I did them because I got ideas for pictures and so I made them. They were not commissioned and have not been submitted to anyone for publication. I did them for the fun of it. Or sometimes to see if a particular idea or technique would work. Often when I do my own pictures I do them to a format shape like a book cover or a CD cover, but that is just a habit, and you never know if someone will take a liking to one of them, I might even get to sell one..."

PS: How is your health these days? Do you draw/paint every day for pleasure or are you constantly working?

DR: "Health is a bit crap, has been since the 1980s. I don't make pictures every day. I started a couple of sci-fi novels but lost interest in them. My current effort is a horror story. I wrote some music but it was a bit odd... Maybe I will put some of it on my site sometime, but it will have to be tarted up a bit first. I am making an ambient synth album at the moment. I don't have a record deal or anything; I just want to write a longer piece of music."

PS: You cited health (M.E.) as the reason you stayed with Maiden, was this because you had only one or two sleeves to design over a long period, i.e. you could take your time?

DR: "I couldn't take my time, things were done in a big hurry. But when I had finished I could stop and recover. The Chronic Fatigue syndrome wipes you out if you keep going too long without a break. I would work for a few months quite hard and then it would take me the rest of the year to get my health back together again. Then it would start all over again."

PS: What's the general time frame you have to design a cover these days?

DR: "With Maiden it was all very rush, rush. These days I take three to four weeks to do a cover, because I'm not going to suffer like that again just for a CD cover. It's not worth the pain."

PS: **What's your view of MP3s making the idea of an album cover redundant? It seems the newer generation is not so obsessed with artwork...**

DR: "Firstly, a band's first contact with the public is the picture on the front of the cover. This is what is on the magazine advertising, the tour posters, the street posters, and the point of sale advertising. Without a strong image you can just disappear into the crowd.

"A 12" record used to be treated as a cultural event. It was a big format and had a big picture to go with it. The covers used to open out into a gatefold cover; you could put art on the outer and inner surfaces and on the inner sleeve as well. That all ended with the CD crystal case. In marketing terms the crystal case was just a complete disaster. The covers went from being impressive objects to practically insignificant additions.

"The rise of MP3 downloads has simply finished the job off nicely. Now there is practically no avenue for you to advertise your new album and link it with a certain image or style. Your music has no covers. There is no way to link merchandise with the product; this is an important source of revenue for all bands. The customer cannot identify the product by the image or link himself to that product with a certain style. If you are a musician, you now have less to sell. If you are a customer, you get less for your money. No cover art, no T-shirts, no tour merchandise and hence smaller tours. All you get is a compressed version of a song, which is not half as good as if you bought the CD version. But if you buy ten downloads then you have paid as much as you would for a CD even though it's not such good quality.

"It's the record business shooting itself in the foot again and also sabotaging the youth culture, making it uniformly bland and faceless by denying it a visual style to call it's own. On the other hand, the musicians will now have to rely entirely on the quality of their music. This may not be the benefit they probably think it will. With no way of advertising a product, the record companies will no longer be willing to front huge sums of money to produce new bands. So they will concentrate on things they know will sell to the teenage girls like Britney Spears and her ilk. The result may well be a preponderance of bland soul/pop. I think we are seeing the beginnings of this already with all the boy and girl bands who are all so unique and original (NOT). So you pay your money and you make your choice. You get the music you deserve. The choice is there, so choose it."

PS: Are there any artists you particularly like? Can you direct some metalheads to *real* art?

DR: "No, I don't like real art. Well... ok then... go look at Joan Miro, Max Ernst, Mondrian, Picasso, Dali, John Martin, Rene Magritte, Jean Tinguey, Bruce Pennington, Eddie Jones, Jack Kirby, Josh Kirby... oops, I slipped a couple of illustrators in there by mistake... never mind."

PS: Any more you could tell readers, for instance are you married, do you live in London still, pets, whatever!?

DR: "No, no, no. Not married. I don't live in London, I don't have any pets. I don't have a life, I just make pictures and write music and stories."

Chapter 19
Did You Know?

Iron Maiden is such a long-standing band with a fervent set of fans and highly knowledgeable followers, but hopefully this section contains facts and figures even the most well informed admirer may not have previously known. Here, in this easy to read chapter, I present an in-depth fact guide to the Irons.

ARTWORK

For many Maiden devotees part of the magic of every new Iron Maiden sleeve, be it single or album, lies in discovering where the mysterious symbol appears. Because on every official release where Derek Riggs has been responsible for cover art, the following symbol appears: http://derekriggs.ballconsultinggroup.com/Pages/maiden.dir/31.html

Far from being a secret symbol associated with the band, this is actually Riggs' signature. If you look closely, the symbol is actually his initials (with the D mirrored). Riggs is a fierce believer in symbolism, so it is no coincidence his signature is so intriguing.

Regarding his trademark, Riggs explains: "The first symbol I used had some meanings which are outlined below. The little gold one I use now is just a back to front letter D, and a letter R side by side inside a circle and has no meaning beyond that (I got fed up with the bullshit and felt like a change). The original symbol comes from the Jewish mystical path called the holy Qabalah (cabalah). They are from a diagram called the tree of life, which consists of ten such circles representing different concepts or states of being called sephirot. The big circle at the top represents god, or the fundamental generative power of the universe, the two beneath represent opposing forces or concepts. In one instance they can represent male and female (archetypal male and female as two aspects of the creative force – one is energy and the other is structure. Energy without structure just evaporates, structure without energy is too restrictive to do anything) and therefore represent the balance of opposites. The arrow is the direction of the flow of energy from god to earth, or the flow of inspiration from the unmanifest world (subconscious mind) to the material world. Also, the arrow points to the chasm or barrier between god and the world or between the unmanifest and manifest aspects of reality, which cannot be crossed.

(For a better understanding of this refer to the book *The Mystical Qabalah* by Eliphas Levi.)"

    The following is a list of all the Maiden albums or singles where Derek's work appears, and a pointer as to where to find his trademark symbol:

- *Iron Maiden*: Check the second brick from the left, six rows down.
- *Killers*: In the window at the bottom on the right.
- *The Number Of The Beast*: Just to the right of the Devil's ankle.
- *Piece Of Mind*: On the back cover, as part of a necklace held within a Skeletal hand. (The signature is not on the CD version, as part of the picture was cut off).
- *Powerslave*: At the pyramid's entrance, where Eddie's genitals would be.
- *Live After Death*: Open up the CD case and follow the stone path back through the centre of the cemetery. There is a tombstone in the middle with the symbol on it. There is also another tombstone behind the cat and the red rose which has 'Here Lies Derek Riggs' inscribed.
- *Somewhere In Time*: Eddie's breastplate.
- *Seventh Son Of A Seventh Son*: In the water.
- *No Prayer For The Dying*: The dot over the 'i' in Dying appears to be the signature.
- *Fear Of The Dark*: (This cover credited to Melvyn Grant, see note at bottom).
- *A Real Dead One*: On the outside corner of Eddie's right eye.
- *A Real Live One*: On the inside of Eddie's right thigh.
- 'Running Free' single: On the cardboard box to the right of the uncovered rubbish bin.
- 'Sanctuary' single: On the folded section of the Iron Maiden poster.
- 'Women In Uniform': On the stone wall just right of the rubbish bin, beneath Margaret Thatcher's right elbow.
- 'Purgatory' single: Left of Satan's throat.
- 'The Trooper' single: On the ground beneath Eddie's legs.
- 'Aces High': On the front of the plane, just below the cockpit, on the left hand side.
- 'The Judge' (*First Ten Years*) - It appears to be sideways on the right-hand corner of the book in front of Eddie.
- 'The Prophet' (inner sleeve of *Seventh Son Of A Seventh Son*): On the right hand corner of the book that Eddie is writing in.
- *Maiden Japan*: Between Eddie's ankle and the 81.

• *Maiden England* video: At the corner of the Union Jack flag nearest to Eddie.
• *A Real Live One*: On the head of the bass guitar.
• *A Real Dead One*: On the wrist of the hand that is pulling down on Eddie's mouth.

Note: The *Fear Of The Dark* illustration is by Melvyn Grant. According to an interview with Bruce Dickinson on MTV shortly after the album was released, they picked three different artists to do a cover for the album, and chose the best one out of the three submitted. He also stated that Derek would still be involved with future artwork and that he wasn't fired.

Riggs' take on the album artwork is rather different: "The band and management were just being such assholes that I put down my pencils and refused to do any work for them, I just got so fucking fed up with being messed about and given the run around. They just couldn't make their minds up about anything. In the end they had to use a sketch that they got from someone else, that's why one side of the picture is black, it was never done as a finished picture. But after they had finished changing their minds every five minutes and fucking me about they didn't have time to do anything else.

"Oh dear, how sad, never mind…"

BANDS WHO HAVE OPENED FOR IRON MAIDEN

This list is by no means complete but here are some of the most interesting groups who supported the boys. Some went on to huge success following their shows with Maiden, others faded into obscurity.

Blitz Fish (18/11/76)
Praying Mantis (numerous dates 1979-1980)
Urchin (08/10/79)
Trust (w/ Nicko McBrain on drums) (15/03/80)
Humble Pie (Jun '81)
Whitesnake (Jul '81)
Blackfoot (Mar-Apr '82)
Girlschool (Jul '82)
Vandale (09/06/83)
Rock Goddess (June '84)

Fastway (Jun-Jul '83)
Saxon (Jun-Jul '83)
Coney Hatch (Jul-Aug '83)
Quiet Riot (Sep-Oct '83)
Michael Schenker (Nov '83)
Waysted (11/09/84)
Twisted Sister (28/01/85)
W.A.S.P. (World Slavery Tour)
Accept (World Slavery Tour)
Motley Crue (World Slavery Tour)
Queensryche (World Slavery Tour)
Warrior (World Slavery Tour)
Ratt (World Slavery Tour)
Mamas Boys (World Slavery Tour)
Yngwie Malmsteen (08/01/87)
Vinnie Vincent Invasion (27/02/87)
Waysted (07/04/87)
Killer Dwarfs (07/08/88)
Ace Frehley's Comet (07/08/88)
Wolfsbane Intercity Express Tour 1990 (a series of roughly 30 UK shows)
Helloween (7th Tour Of A 7th Tour)
Guns N' Roses (7th Tour Of A 7th Tour)
Megadeth (7th Tour Of A 7th Tour)
L.A. Guns (7th Tour Of A 7th Tour)
King's X, Anthrax (21/12/90)
Anthrax (Feb-Mar '91)
Dream Theater (May/June '92)
Testament (27/08/92)
Warrant (02/09/92)
The Almighty (09/04/93, 17/05/93)
Corrosion of Conformity (11/07/92)

30 AMAZING FACTS

1.   Nicko McBrain once played in a band with Pat Travers, but does
not remember the experience fondly. When asked about Travers in 1988,
Nicko replied, "I wouldn't stop to PISS on him!"
2.   Bruce Dickinson and Janick Gers have a fondness for ten-pin bowling. Their favourite bowling alley is in Harrow, London.

3.   Steve Harris' first bass guitar was a copy of a Fender Telecaster which cost him £40.

4.   Bruce's nickname of Air Raid Siren supposedly comes from the sound of his voice but he actually received the honour after shattering a huge glass globe with one scream, at Chelsea College whilst in Samson.

5.   Whether by chance or design, titles of the first six Maiden studio albums are in alphabetical order: *Iron Maiden, Killers, (The) Number Of The Beast, Piece Of Mind, Powerslave,* and *Somewhere In Time.* The following set of studio recordings, however, can be placed in reverse alphabetical order: *Seventh Son Of A Seventh Son, No Prayer For The Dying,* and *Fear Of The Dark.*

6.   The opening song on *Seventh Son Of A Seventh Son,* 'Moonchild', was recorded in just one take.

7.   Maiden is one of just three bands to have made more than one appearance at the Castle Donington Monsters Of Rock Festival. The others are Whitesnake (twice), AC/DC (three times) and Metallica (three times).

8.   During the Fear Of The Dark tour Maiden visited Russia for the first time. In celebration the Maiden back catalogue was officially released in the country on vinyl, also a first.

9.   Bruce was arrested once, in Lubbock, Texas. An over zealous security guard was hurting fans as they came over the barrier. It was alleged Bruce looped his microphone lead around the guard's neck and tried to strangle him.

10.   'Purgatory' is the only Maiden single which failed to reach the UK top 40. All the early hits reached respectable positions. 'Sanctuary' was the highest chart hit with a peak position of 29. Sadly, 'Purgatory' only reached number 52.

11.   When Bruce was in Samson the band wrote a song/improvisation called 'The Pig In Lipstick' (this was never released). The song is about one of their groupies who apparently had a weight problem. Or at least Bruce had a problem with her weight... Bruce later used the lyrics for 'Nodding Donkey Blues'.

12.   Steve Harris has played football alongside the following ex-professionals: Glenn Hoddle, Steve Coppell, Frank Worthington, Archie Gemmill, Gerd Muller, Nayim, Paul Allen, Frank McAvennie and Rene and Willie Van Der Kirkhoff.

13.   Other 'famous ex footballer' fans of Maiden include Terry Butcher and Paul Mariner.

14.   A dedicated fan of the band had his name changed by deed poll to Iron Maiden. Steve recalls, "At first I didn't think anybody was that crazy to do that, but he loved the band that much... I talked to him and he didn't seem to be a nutter or stupid, he seemed like a nice, quiet, normal bloke."

15. While the band was in Nassau in '83 they ran out of money. The cash they tried to wire from England was taking too long and so Rod Smallwood took matters into his own hands. He took his last $50 and walked down to the local casino. For the next six nights in a row he won $300!

16. One of Dave Murray's guitars used to belong to the late Free guitarist, Paul Kossoff.

17. During Maiden's World Slavery tour, Bruce was nicknamed 'Fyffes' (as in the banana company) due to his penchant for yellow coloured spandex trousers.

18. Nicko McBrain played drums on 'Nice One Cyril' by The Cockerel Chorus.

19. 'Bring Your Daughter... To The Slaughter' is loosely based on the poem 'Too Coy His Mistress' by Andrew Marvell.

20. In the introduction to the *Real Dead One* album Bruce introduces 'Where Eagles Dare' by saying, "Whatever the problem, Clint Eastwood's gonna fix it!" This is a reference to the movie of the same name in which Eastwood starred.

21. In the movie *Dead Man Walking* starring Sean Penn as a convicted murderer on Death Row, Penn is seen sporting a *Piece Of Mind* tattoo on his arm. Proof then that anyone who is supposed to be crazy must listen to heavy metal.

22. In the movie *Morons From Outer Space* Eddie also makes an appearance. In one particular scene where a character is acting crazy, a person holds up the *Number Of The Beast* album cover and points to it as if to say "You're insane!"

23. During a show at The Palladium in New York one idiotic 'fan' threw a firework, which hit Dave Murray's guitar roadie, Bill, in the face, almost blinding him. The band later heard that justice had been dished out by fans after the gig, when the culprit was beaten up. Thankfully Bill recovered after a few days in hospital.

24. There is no love lost between Paul Di'Anno and Dennis Stratton, but did you know that (as Di'Anno describes) "Even now Dennis Stratton spends his weekends playing covers of Oasis or Robbie Williams in pubs in the East End of London. Not really Metal, is it?"

25. During the 80s 'Phantom Of The Opera' accompanied an advert for Lucozade and featured English athlete Daley Thompson sprinting down a running track!

26. Steve says, "I've got audio tapes that go right back from '76, not right from the first gigs, but from the days when we used to play places like the Bridge House. They're a bit dodgy. The tapes exist, but I never play 'em to anyone!"

27. During the early part of 1983 when the band was in Nassau, Bahamas everyone was designated a nickname. Adrian Smith became known as Melvin, Dave was Nobby, Nicko was Boomer (due to his very loud farts) and Bruce was Conan The Librarian.

28. Also in 1983, during the World Piece tour, Bruce travelled back to his hotel alone and decided to purchase fifty pints of beer in preparation for the large number of guests he expected to come any second. Ozzy Osbourne walked in first. At the time Ozzy was shunning alcohol so when he rejected Bruce's offer of a pint Bruce asked him if he would like to steal a taxi! Before Ozzy could agree Sharon took him off to bed. One wonders if this incident played some part in the Ozzfest debacle more recently.

29. During a very early show in 1979, Maiden played the very tiny UMIST venue in Manchester, England. Though the reason is not clear, Dave Murray apparently hit on one particular girl who was already taken. The following week after the gig there was a letter published in *Sounds* that read, "I would just like to warn Dave Murray the lead guitarist of Iron Maiden that if he steps foot inside Manchester again I will personally pummel his brains in, cos he's ruined what I thought was an ace relationship with my girlfriend. And may I point out that no matter how much she rubs his name in my face I still think Deb Brown of Wythenshawe is the best yet. Jealous Dave."

30. Before a gig in Edinburgh, Scotland during the summer of 1980, Clive Burr was taken ill with food poisoning. Rather than cancel the gig, Vic Vella persuaded the drummer to play in the face of adversity. Burr did so and promptly fainted at the end of the show.

ENTER THE HARLOT

Following a concert on August 15th, 1983 on the *Piece Of Mind* tour at Memorial Stadium in Buffalo, NY, Iron Maiden was hit with a lawsuit. A female audience member had joined the band onstage dancing provocatively. The original article reads:

'MODEL FILES LAWSUIT AGAINST ROCK GROUP'

A 22-year-old Buffalo model who claims a member of the heavy-metal rock group Iron Maiden ripped off the top of her bathing suit when she appeared on stage at a recent concert, filed a $350,000 lawsuit Wednesday against the band, its singer and its management firm.

Attorney Arnold Lieberman, who filed the suit on behalf of model Suzette Kolaga, said the incident occurred during Iron Maiden's concert before 7,000 fans in Memorial Auditorium on Aug. 15. He said legal papers will be served on the band when it appears in Rochester today (09/01/83) for a scheduled concert.

The suit, filed in State Supreme Court, seeks $150,000 in general damages against the English band, singer Bruce Dickinson (sic) and the management firm, American Talent International of New York, plus $200,000 in punitive damages against Dickinson.

Ms. Kolaga, a professional fashion model, won a local "Ms. Heavy Metal" contest, and because of that was invited onstage during the performance to crack a whip and dance around Dickinson.

The suit alleges that Dickonson, without consent, warning or provocation, pushed and assaulted her and tore the top off her bathing suit. Dickinson 'willfully, wantonly and shamelessly' exposed her to the crowd attending the concert, the suit contends, thereby holding her up to 'scorn, shame and extreme embarrassment' and seriously damaging her 'personal and professional reputation'.

Ms. Kolaga wore a one-piece bathing suit with a plunging neckline, thigh-high leather boots and leather gloves, with a chain and handcuffs dangling from a leather belt.

Mr. Lieberman said she has asked not to talk to reporters because she is "still mildly hysterical" over the incident. Mr. Lieberman said she is "only working part-time because she is still upset."

(Note: The matter was eventually dismissed).

BAR ROOM PURSUITS

Steve has a public house in his private house! Named Harry's Bar, the bass player explains: "It's exactly like having my own pub. My mate Vic Vella actually looks after my place for me when the band are working, and he was the one who built the bar for me. Fans of ours would know Vic's name from our album sleeves and also from years ago when he used to come out on the road with us. He's been with me for about twelve years now, and he's married with five children, and he decided a few years ago he wanted to come off the road. So Vic actually takes care of the place full-time and he's brilliant at that sort of work. He and a mate of his built the bar. They completely converted this large room, put loads of beams hanging from the ceiling, proper bar with pumps that serve Ruddles and ESB bitters. And the best thing of all is there's never any worry about driving home, just stumble upstairs and straight into bed!"

Steve also owns Eddie's Bar in the Algarve, Portugal. This is a small, dark and cosy pub with tons of Maiden memorabilia on the walls, ceiling and behind the bar. Should you wish to visit, the address is: 59 Rue de Loule Santa Barbara de Nexe Algarve, Portugal.

WHERE ARE THEY NOW?

In the interest of readers I made sure of catching up with everyone who's been mentioned in this book to see what they have been doing with themselves.

NEAL KAY

Neal is now retired but keeps himself busy and still occasionally dons the decks for a spot of DJing.

KEITH WILFORT

"I live in the South Bay Area, by Los Angeles. Right now I am between jobs. I was working for Bravado USA in Los Angeles whom Sanctuary bought out in 1994. I got laid off in October 2005, due to budgetary problems, and have been temping since then. I still see Maiden when they play out this way and keep in touch whenever possibble."

STEVE 'LOOPY' NEWHOUSE

"I work for Royal Mail, based in Romford, Essex. I've been doing the job for eleven years, and it's nice to know I have a guaranteed income for once in my life. After I left the Iron Maiden thing, I hooked up with a company called Stage Miracles, a stage crew outfit that supply people to do pretty much the same thing I was doing for Maiden, but on a far grander scale. We went all over Europe setting up and taking down shows, scaffolding as well. It was a good life, and I have few regrets."

TONY MOORE

(From his official website, www.tony-moore.com) "In 1986 Tony was invited to play keyboards with a new band called Cutting Crew who then went on to have a massive worldwide hit with 'I Just Died In Your Arms Tonight'. For two more years he toured the world and recorded with the band until it was time to move on, at which point he signed a solo deal with a small independent label in London. He released one single to critical acclaim, before joining forces with Argentine singer/songwriter Marie Claire D'ubaldo. He co-wrote and co-produced tracks for her debut album on Polydor that sold over 250,000 worldwide.

In 1997 Tony established the legendary Kashmir Klub in London. The formula of providing an incredible sound system, sourcing the best of emerging and established artists, hosting the show as if it were live TV, and getting everyone to perform in an acoustic and 'back to basics' format, quickly made the Klub into one of the most important and compelling venues in London. Over its seven year history Tony introduced debut London performances from Damien Rice and KT Tunstall, as well as unannounced sets from Sheryl Crow, Dave Stewart, Fleetwood Mac and many more. The Kashmir closed in 2003 after the building was re-developed.

In July that year he took over running and booking all the music at The Bedford in Balham. The venue, under his musical stewardship, has grown into an award-winning location. In 2004 it won Best Pub in the country, it has twice won the best pub and club award, as well as the *Evening Standard* pub of the year.

For the last eighteen months Tony has also co-presented an overnight show on BBC London 94.9fm, where he has brought live music guests into the studio and championed the cause of new talent to an ever growing audience, establishing a persuasive platform to experience the very best musical creativity around.

In 2004 Tony was made the sole Inductee into the MMF (Music Managers Forum) Roll of Honour for outstanding contribution to the British Music Industry."

MAURICE COYNE (URCHIN)

"I retired from guitar playing in the late 80s and never thought I'd play again, but in about 1995 I picked up the guitar again for fun. The following year some old buddies organised a jam and out of that we formed Rewind, a classic rock covers band. We gigged all over London and at loads of biker events all over the country. In 2002 we called it a day because our drummer was moving to the North East. I kept up the playing and about 18 months ago put another covers band together called Pinnacle Of Decline (it's a Roger Daltrey quote) and we're trying to get some gigs at the moment. I teach guitar two nights a week from home and still plan to record a solo album on my PC (I've been saying 'I'll start next week!' for the past three years!)"

CHRIS AYLMER (SAMSON)

"After Samson I teamed up with Niki Buzz, an American singer/ guitarist who already had two albums out as M80. Despite some good reviews and storming gigs, management problems forced Niki back to the States. I then joined an all-girl band where I met singer Sheila James. The gigs were average but it was fun in the dressing room! Since I've immersed myself in Doctor Ice – playing devastating heavy rock with a sprinkling of updated Samson tracks."

BILL LEISEGANG (SHOTS/XERO)

"I released two solo albums (working with Glenn Hughes on three songs on my first album *No Strings Attached*), John Wetton also sings on two tracks. I did a live TV gig with Glenn Hughes and Mel Galley. I played guitar on Rod Stewart's number one single 'Downtown Train'. Lemmy sang on my song 'Where's the Party?' on Nina Hagen's album (I also toured with Nina for ten years). Then I made an album with Midge Ure called *Kingdom Come*, as well as an EP with Zodiac Mindwarp."

JASE EDWARDS (WOLFSBANE)

"Over the last ten years I've been having a family which I am very proud of and love very much. My daughter is eight now. I co-wrote a musical called *The Pearl,* based on a novel by John Steinbeck. I started driving trucks and teaching myself music engineering/production. I have produced *The Wildhearts Strike Back,* engineered and mixed *Valor Del Corazon* by Ginger (ex-Wildhearts) and I am now playing guitar for Ginger & The Sonic Circus. We have just finished a UK tour and played a couple of shows in New York. We are headlining the third stage at Download in 2006 and I am lined up to produce the follow up to *Valor...* soon. I am also working with Conny Bloom (The Electric Boys and Hanoi Rocks) and CJ from The Wildhearts solo projects, both very exciting. And there are many more projects in the planning stage."

JEFF HATELEY (WOLFSBANE)

"I'm living in the Tamworth area, happily married and doing a 'normal' job. I still love music and enjoy playing and writing songs. I am not in a regular band at the moment, but I'm sure it won't be too long before

I am gigging again. I think I have done my bit for rock'n'roll and should leave it to younger ones to try and 'make it'."

STEVE 'DANGER' ELLETT (WOLFSBANE)

"I was a scuba diving instructor for five years, that was a doss. I've also had a go at management but I don't have the capital – a lot of graft for very little reward. I like travelling. And my new venture: tour bus driver."

Sources:

Derek Riggs interviews conducted by Paul Stenning, George Matsagouras and Enough Magazine (2001).
Steve Harris quotes from Somewhere On Tour programme.
www.geocities.com/sunsetstrip/club/5619/
http://www.geocities.com/sunsetstrip/club/5619/interviews/as1097.html
www.maidenfans.com
http://perso.wanadoo.fr/fredouille/sakkath/eddiesbar/english/main.html

Chapter 20
The Ultimate Best Of Album

There have been many Iron Maiden compilations, both live and studio. Naturally, as the band has progressed and produced new material, they are consistently changing their live set around.

But let's not kid ourselves here, the so called *Best Of* collections have been anything but. So here's an experiment to find the ultimate Iron Maiden album.

Taking every studio album and rating each song (marks out of ten, half points can be used) we will discover not only which is the best album, but also the songs which should really be used on a *Greatest Hits* compilation. I have tried to be objective and analyse the songs according to their worth, and their impact at the time. Otherwise, it would be possible certain songs, which have permeated the brain too much and are pretty much 'overkill' Maiden tracks such as 'Wrathchild', 'Run To The Hills', 'Iron Maiden' etc, would receive fewer marks than they really deserve.

Everyone has an opinion, of course, and Maiden fans are among the most vociferous in their views, but that is the beauty of this little exercise. You may or may not agree with me, but try the system yourself to discover which album is really the most consistent! Enjoy…

IRON MAIDEN

Prowler (8)
Remember Tomorrow (7.5)
Running Free (8)
The Phantom Of The Opera (8)
Transylvania (6)
Strange World (6)
Charlotte The Harlot (7)
Iron Maiden (7.5)
TOTAL 58
AVERAGE MARK 58/8 songs = **7.25**

KILLERS

The Ides Of March (6)
Wrathchild (8)

Murders In The Rue Morgue (9)
Another Life (6)
Genghis Khan (6)
Innocent Exile (7.5)
Killers (8)
Prodigal Son (6)
Purgatory (8)
Drifter (6)
TOTAL 70.5
AVERAGE MARK 70.5/10 songs = **7.05**

THE NUMBER OF THE BEAST

Invaders (7)
Children Of The Damned (10)
The Prisoner (8)
22 Acacia Avenue (7.5)
The Number Of The Beast (8)
Run To The Hills (7)
Gangland (6.5)
Hallowed Be Thy Name (10)
TOTAL 64
AVERAGE MARK 64/8 songs = **8**

PIECE OF MIND

Where Eagles Dare (8)
Revelations (10)
Flight Of Icarus (8)
Die With Your Boots On (9)
The Trooper (9)
Still Life (6)
Quest For Fire (6.5)
Sun And Steel (6.5)
To Tame A Land (7)
TOTAL 70
AVERAGE MARK 64/9 songs = **7.7**

POWERSLAVE

Aces High (9)
2 Minutes To Midnight (9)
Losfer Words (Big 'Orra) (4)
Flash Of The Blade (8.5)
The Duellists (6.5)
Back In The Village (7.5)
Powerslave (10)
Rime Of The Ancient Mariner (10)
TOTAL 64.5
AVERAGE MARK 64/8 songs = **8.06**

SOMEWHERE IN TIME

Caught Somewhere In Time (7)
Wasted Years (6)
Sea Of Madness (5)
Heaven Can Wait (8.5)
The Loneliness Of The Long Distance Runner (5.5)
Stranger In A Strange Land (6)
Déjà Vu (7.5)
Alexander The Great (10)
TOTAL 55.5
AVERAGE MARK 55.5/8 songs = **6.93**

SEVENTH SON OF A SEVENTH SON

Moonchild (8)
Infinite Dreams (8)
Can I Play With Madness? (8)
The Evil That Men Do (8.5)
Seventh Son Of A Seventh Son (7.5)
The Prophecy (6.5)
The Clairvoyant (7.5)
Only The Good Die Young (7)
TOTAL 61
AVERAGE MARK 61/8 songs = **7.62**

NO PRAYER FOR THE DYING

Tailgunner (8)
Holy Smoke (9.5)
No Prayer For The Dying (9)
Public Enema Number One (6)
Fates Warning (6)
The Assassin (7.5)
Run Silent Run Deep (6.5)
Hooks In You (5)
Bring Your Daughter To The Slaughter (6)
Mother Russia (6)
TOTAL 69.5
AVERAGE MARK 69.5/10 songs = **6.95**

FEAR OF THE DARK

Be Quick Or Be Dead (9)
From Here To Eternity (6)
Afraid To Shoot Strangers (6)
Fear Is The Key (6)
Childhood's End (7)
Wasting Love (8)
The Fugitive (6.5)
Chains Of Misery (7)
The Apparition (5)
Judas Be My Guide (7.5)
Weekend Warrior (4)
Fear Of The Dark (9)
TOTAL 81
AVERAGE MARK 81/12 songs = **6.75**

THE X FACTOR

Sign Of The Cross (5.5)
Lord Of The Flies (5.5)
Man On The Edge (7)
Fortunes Of War (3)
Look For The Truth (4)
The Aftermath (4)

Judgement Of Heaven (4)
Blood On The World's Hands (4)
The Edge Of Darkness (5.5)
2 AM (6)
The Unbeliever (7.5)
TOTAL 56
AVERAGE MARK 56/11 songs = **5.09**

VIRTUAL XI

Futureal (8)
The Angel And The Gambler (5)
Lightning Strikes Twice (5.5)
The Clansman (8.5)
When Two Worlds Collide (4)
The Educated Fool (4.5)
Don't Look To The Eyes Of A Stranger (5)
Como Estais Amigos (4.5)
TOTAL 45
AVERAGE MARK 74.5/11 songs = **5.62**

BRAVE NEW WORLD

The Wicker Man (8.5)
Ghost Of The Navigator (9.5)
Brave New World (7)
Blood Brothers (9)
The Mercenary (6)
Dream Of Mirrors (6)
The Fallen Angel (5.5)
The Nomad (7)
Out Of The Silent Planet (7.5)
The Thin Line Between Love And Hate (6)
TOTAL 72
AVERAGE MARK 72/10 songs = **7.2**

DANCE OF DEATH

Wildest Dreams (6)
Rainmaker (9)

No More Lies (6)
Montsegur (8.5)
Dance Of Death (7)
Gates Of Tomorrow (6)
New Frontier (7)
Paschendale (6.5)
Face In The Sand (6)
Age Of Innocence (6)
Journeyman (6.5)
TOTAL 74.5
AVERAGE MARK 74.5/11 songs = **6.77**

The final album chart looks like this:

POWERSLAVE **8.06**
THE NUMBER OF THE BEAST **8**
PIECE OF MIND **7.7**
SEVENTH SON OF A SEVENTH SON **7.62**
IRON MAIDEN **7.25**
BRAVE NEW WORLD **7.2**
KILLERS **7.05**
NO PRAYER FOR THE DYING **6.95**
SOMEWHERE IN TIME **6.93**
DANCE OF DEATH **6.77**
FEAR OF THE DARK **6.75**
VIRTUAL XI **5.62**
THE X FACTOR **5.09**

It's hard to argue with the top three, although many might contend a different order. My guess is it's the rest of the chart that might provoke argument. Though the first two Paul Di'Anno-fronted albums chart very high, this actually reflects the quality of the material rather than the singing. The albums I thought would be higher, such as *Somewhere In Time* or *Fear Of The Dark* are actually fairly low down.

I personally enjoy listening to those two albums, probably a lot more than the first two, but looking at the material objectively, both *Iron Maiden* and *Killers* are stronger and more consistent than *Somewhere In Time* or *Fear Of The Dark*.

No surprise to see the Blaze-era albums at the bottom. They simply do not compare to the other Maiden material and Blaze put in a weak performance for much of the two records. I'd like to have seen *No Prayer For The Dying* higher up as I think it is a very underrated album, but taking into account the merely average songs that make up half of the order, perhaps it's more understandable.

I'm also quite surprised *Piece Of Mind* is not number one or two as I have often believed it is my favourite Maiden album, but then *The Number Of The Beast* and *Powerslave* were certainly in contention. And being fair, if *Powerslave* did not contain a pointless instrumental track it would have scored even higher. In my view, Iron Maiden was at its most consistent for this album and it rightly warrants top billing.

Now let's look at the ultimate *Best Of* based on the Top 20 Maiden songs from the list.

Children Of The Damned (10)
Hallowed Be Thy Name (10)
Revelations (10)
Powerslave (10)
Rime Of The Ancient Mariner (10)
Alexander The Great (10)
Holy Smoke (9.5)
Ghost Of The Navigator (9.5)
Murders In The Rue Morgue (9)
Die With Your Boots On (9)
The Trooper (9)
Aces High (9)
No Prayer For The Dying (9)
Be Quick Or Be Dead (9)
Fear Of The Dark (9)
Blood Brothers (9)
Rainmaker (9)
2 Minutes To Midnight (9)
Flash Of The Blade (8.5)
Heaven Can Wait (8.5)
The Evil That Men Do (8.5)
The Clansman (8.5)
The Wicker Man (8.5)
Montsegur (8.5)

It looks rather different from the popularly believed *Best Of*, doesn't it?! I would be proud to put this compilation into the world and slap the Maiden logo on it, and I don't mind saying I think this is far more representative of the band's career and *should* be the sort of compilation they put out. Now it's your turn...

Iron Maiden Discography

ALBUMS

IRON MAIDEN
Prowler / Remember Tomorrow / Running Free / Transylvania / Phantom
Of The Opera / Strange World / Charlotte The Harlot / Iron Maiden
(LP, CD, Cassette – EMI 1980)

IRON MAIDEN (ENHANCED)
Prowler / Remember Tomorrow / Running Free / Transylvania / Phan-
tom Of The Opera / Strange World / Charlotte The Harlot / Iron Maiden /
Sanctuary
(LP – EMI 1980, CD – EMI 1988)

KILLERS
The Ides Of March / Wrathchild / Murders In The Rue Morgue / Another
Life / Genghis Khan / Innocent Exile / Killers / Prodigal Son / Purgatory /
Twilight Zone / Drifter
(LP, CD, Cassette – EMI 1981)

KILLERS (ENHANCED)
The Ides Of March / Wrathchild / Murders In The Rue Morgue / Another
Life / Genghis Khan / Innocent Exile / Killers / Prodigal Son / Purgatory /
Twilight Zone / Drifter / Twilight Zone
(LP – EMI 1981, CD – EMI 1988)

THE NUMBER OF THE BEAST
Invaders / Children Of The Damned / The Prisoner / 22 Acacia Avenue /
The Number Of The Beast / Run To The Hills / Gangland / Total Eclipse /
Hallowed Be Thy Name
(LP, CD, Cassette – EMI 1982)

THE NUMBER OF THE BEAST (ENHANCED)
Invaders / Children Of The Damned / The Prisoner / 22 Acacia Avenue /
The Number Of The Beast / Run To The Hills / Gangland / Total Eclipse /
Hallowed Be Thy Name / Total Eclipse
(CD – EMI 1998)

PIECE OF MIND
Where Eagles Dare / Revelations / Flight Of Icarus / Die With Your Boots On / The Trooper / Still Life / Quest For Fire / Sun And Steel / To Tame A Land
(LP, CD, Cassette – EMI 1983)

PIECE OF MIND (ENHANCED)
Where Eagles Dare / Revelations / Flight Of Icarus / Die With Your Boots On / The Trooper / Still Life / Quest For Fire / Sun And Steel / To Tame A Land / Cross-Eyed Mary
(LP – EMI 1983, CD – EMI 1998)

POWERSLAVE
Aces High / 2 Minutes To Midnight / Losfer Words / Flash Of The Blade / The Duellists / Back In The Village / Powerslave / Rime Of The Ancient Mariner
(LP, CD, Cassette – EMI 1984)

POWERSLAVE (ENHANCED)
Aces High / 2 Minutes To Midnight / Losfer Words / Flash Of The Blade / The Duellists / Back In The Village / Powerslave / Rime Of The Ancient Mariner / Bonus Tracks - Rainbow's Gold / King Of The Twilight / I've Got The Fire / Cross Eyed Mary / Still Live (Live)
(CD, Cassette – EMI 2000)

LIVE AFTER DEATH
Intro: Churchill's Speech / Aces High / 2 Minutes To Midnight / The Trooper / Revelations / Flight Of Icarus / Rime Of The Ancient Mariner / Powerslave / The Number Of The Beast / Hallowed Be Thy Name / Iron Maiden / Run To The Hills / Running Free / Wrathchild / 22 Acacia Avenue / Children Of The Damned / Die With Your Boots On / Phantom Of The Opera
(LP, CD, Cassette – EMI 1985)

SOMEWHERE IN TIME
Caught Somewhere In Time / Wasted Years / Sea Of Madness / Heaven Can Wait / The Loneliness Of The Long Distance Runner / Stranger In A Strange Land / Deja-Vu / Alexander The Great
(LP, CD, Cassette – EMI 1986)

SOMEWHERE IN TIME (ENHANCED)
Caught Somewhere In Time / Wasted Years / Sea Of Madness / Heaven
Can Wait / The Loneliness Of The Long Distance Runner / Stranger In
A Strange Land / Deja-Vu / Alexander The Great / Reach Out / Juanita /
Sheriff Of Huddersfield / That Girl / Total Eclipse / Remember Tomorrow
(Live)
(CD – EMI 1995)

SEVENTH SON OF A SEVENTH SON
Moonchild / Infinite Dreams / Can I Play With Madness? / The Evil That
Men Do / Seventh Son Of A Seventh Son / The Prophecy / The Clairvoy-
ant / Only The Good Die Young
(LP, CD, Cassette – EMI 1988)

SEVENTH SON OF A SEVENTH SON (ENHANCED)
Moonchild / Infinite Dreams / Can I Play With Madness? / The Evil That
Men Do / Seventh Son Of A Seventh Son / The Prophecy / The Clairvoy-
ant / Only The Good Die Young / Black Bart Blues / Massacre / Prowler
'88 / Charlotte The Harlot '88 / The Clairvoyant (Live) / The Prisoner
(Live) / Infinite Dreams (Live) / Killers (Live) / Still Life (Live)
(CD – EMI 1995)

NO PRAYER FOR THE DYING
Tailgunner / Holy Smoke / No Prayer For The Dying / Public Enema
Number One / Fates Warning / The Assassin / Run Silent Run Deep /
Hooks In You / Bring Your Daughter To The Slaughter / Mother Russia
(LP, CD, Cassette – EMI 1990)

NO PRAYER FOR THE DYING (ENHANCED)
Tailgunner / Holy Smoke / No Prayer For The Dying / Public Enema
Number One / Fates Warning / The Assassin / Run Silent Run Deep /
Hooks In You / Bring Your Daughter To The Slaughter / Mother Russia
/ All In Your Mind / Kill Me Ce Soir / I'm A Mover / Communication
Breakdown / Nodding Donkey Blues / Number Of The Beast (Live) / The
Prisoner (Live)
(CD – EMI 1995)

FEAR OF THE DARK
Be Quick Or Be Dead / From Here To Eternity / Afraid To Shoot Strangers / Fear Is The Key / Childhood's End / Wasting Love / The Fugitive /

Chains Of Misery / The Apparition / Judas Be My Guide / Weekend Warrior / Fear Of The Dark
(LP, CD, Cassette – EMI 1992)

FEAR OF THE DARK (ENHANCED)
Be Quick Or Be Dead / From Here To Eternity / Afraid To Shoot Stran-
gers / Fear Is The Key / Childhood's End / Wasting Love / The Fugitive /
Chains Of Misery / The Apparition / Judas Be My Guide / Weekend War-
rior / Fear Of The Dark / Tailgunner / Holy Smoke / The Assassin
(CD – EMI 1992)

A REAL DEAD ONE
The Number Of The Beast / The Trooper / Prowler / Transylvania / Re-
member Tomorrow / Where Eagles Dare / Sanctuary / Running Free / Run
To The Hills / 2 Minutes To Midnight / Iron Maiden / Hallowed Be Thy
Name
(LP, CD, Cassette – EMI 1993)

A REAL LIVE ONE
Be Quick Or Be Dead / From Here To Eternity / Can I Play With Madness?
/ Wasting Love / Tailgunner / The Evil That Men Can Do / Afraid To Shoot
Strangers / Bring Your Daughter To The Slaughter / Heaven Can Wait /
The Clairvoyant / Fear Of The Dark
(LP, CD, Cassette – EMI 1993)

LIVE AT DONINGTON
Be Quick Or Be Dead / The Number Of The Beast / Wrathchild / From
Here To Eternity / Can I Play With Madness? / Wasting Love / Tailgunner
/ The Evil That Men Do / Afraid To Shoot Strangers / Fear Of The Dark
/ Bring Your Daughter To The Slaughter / The Clairvoyant / Heaven Can
Wait / Run To The Hills / 2 Minutes To Midnight / Iron Maiden / Hallowed
Be Thy Name / The Trooper / Sanctuary / Running Free
(3-LP, 2-CD, Cassette – EMI 1993)

THE X FACTOR
Sign Of The Cross / Lord Of The Flies / Man On The Edge / Fortunes
Of War / Look For The Truth / The Aftermath / Judgement Of Heaven
/ Blood On The World's Hands / The Edge Of Darkness / 2 A.M. / The
Unbeliever
(LP, CD, Cassette – EMI 1995)

THE X FACTOR (ENHANCED)

Sign Of The Cross / Lord Of The Flies / Man On The Edge / Fortunes Of War / Look For The Truth / The Aftermath / Judgement Of Heaven / Blood On The World's Hands / The Edge Of Darkness / 2 A.M. / The Unbeliever
Bonus CD – Justice Of The Peace / I Live My Way / Judgement Day
(CD – EMI 1995)

BEST OF THE BEAST

Virus / Sign Of The Cross / Afraid To Shoot Strangers / Man On The Edge / Be Quick Or Be Dead / Fear Of The Dark / Holy Smoke / Bring Your Daughter To The Slaughter / Seventh Son Of A Seventh Son / Can I Play With Madness? / The Evil That Men Do / The Clairvoyant / Heaven Can Wait / Wasted Years / 2 Minutes To Midnight / Running Free / Rime Of The Ancient Mariner / Aces High / Where Eagles Dare / The Trooper / The Number Of The Beast / Revelations / The Prisoner / Run To The Hills / Hallowed Be Thy Name / Wrathchild / Killers / Remember Tomorrow / Phantom Of The Opera / Sanctuary / Prowler / Invasion / Strange World / Iron Maiden
(4-LP, 2-CD, MiniDisc, Cassette – EMI 1996)

VIRTUAL XI

Futureal / The Angel And The Gambler / Lightning Strikes Twice / The Clansman / When Two Worlds Collide / The Educated Fool / Don't Look To The Eyes Of A Stranger / Como Estais Amigos
(LP, CD, Cassette – EMI 1998)

VIRTUAL XI (ENHANCED)

Futureal / The Angel And The Gambler / Lightning Strikes Twice / The Clansman / When Two Worlds Collide / The Educated Fool / Don't Look To The Eyes Of A Stranger / Como Estais Amigos
Bonus CD – Blood On The World's Hand / The Aftermath
(CD – EMI 1998)

ED HUNTER

Iron Maiden (Live) / The Trooper / The Number Of The Beast / Wrathchild / Futureal / Fear Of The Dark / Be Quick Or Be Dead / 2 Minutes To Midnight / Man On The Edge / Aces High / The Evil That Men Do / Wasted Years / Powerslave / Hallowed Be Thy Name / Run To The Hills

/ The Clansman / Phantom Of The Opera / Killers / Stranger In A Strange Land / Tailgunner
Disc 3 Contains a PC game
(3-CD – EMI 1999)

BRAVE NEW WORLD
The Wicker Man / Ghost Of The Navigator / Brave New World / Blood Brothers / The Mercenary / Dream Of Mirrors / The Fallen Angels / The Nomad / Out Of The Silent Planet / The Thin Line Between Love And Hate
(2-LP, CD, MiniDisc, Cassette – EMI 2000)

ROCK IN RIO
Intro / The Wicker Man / Ghost Of The Navigator / Brave New World / Wrathchild / Two Minutes To Midnight / Blood Brothers / Sign Of The Cross / The Mercenary / The Trooper / Brave New World (Video)/Dream Of Mirrors / The Clansman / The Evil That Men Do / Fear Of The Dark / Iron Maiden / The Number Of The Beast / Hallowed By Thy Name / Sanctuary / Run To The Hills / A Day In The Life (Video)
(3-LP, 2-CD, double cassette – EMI 2002)

EDWARD THE GREAT
Run To The Hills / The Number Of The Beast / Flight Of Icarus / The Trooper / 2 Minutes To Midnight / Wasted Years / Can I Play With Madness? / The Evil That Men Do / The Clairvoyant / Infinite Dreams / Holy Smoke / Bring Your Daughter To The Slaughter / Man On The Edge / Futureal / The Wicker Man / Fear Of The Dark (Live At Rock In Rio)
(LP, CD – EMI 2002)

DANCE OF DEATH
Wildest Dreams / Rainmaker / No More Lies / Montsegur / Dance Of Death / Gates Of Tomorrow / New Frontier / Paschendale / Face In The Sand / Age Of Innocence / Journeyman
(LP, CD – EMI 2003)

SINGLES

The Soundhouse Tapes EP
Iron Maiden / Invasion / Prowler
(7" – Rock Hard 1979)

Running Free / Burning Ambition
(7" – EMI 1980)

Sanctuary / Drifter (Live) / I've Got The Fire (Live)
(7", Cassette – EMI 1980)

Sanctuary / Drifter (Live) / I've Got The Fire (Live) / Prowler
(12", CD – EMI 1980)

Prowler / Running Free
(7" – EMI 1980)

Women In Uniform / Invasion / Phantom Of The Opera (Live)
(12" – EMI 1980)

Women In Uniform / Invasion
(7" – EMI 1980)

Twilight Zone / Wrathchild
(7", 12", Cassette – EMI 1981)

Wrathchild / Genghis Khan
(7" – EMI 1981)

Purgatory / Genghis Khan
(7" – EMI 1981)

Maiden Japan EP
Running Free / Remember Tomorrow / Killers / Innocent Exile
(12" – EMI 1981)

Maiden Japan EP (Enhanced)
Running Free / Remember Tomorrow / Wrathchild / Killers / Innocent
Exile
(12" – EMI 1981)

Run To The Hills / Total Eclipse
(7", 12" – EMI 1982)

The Number Of The Beast / Remember Tomorrow (Live)
(7", 12", Cassette – EMI 1982)

Flight Of Icarus / I've Got The Fire
(7", 12", Cassette – EMI 1983)

The Trooper / Cross-Eyed Mary
(7", 12", Cassette – EMI 1983)

2 Minutes To Midnight / Rainbow's Gold
(7", Cassette – EMI 1984)

2 Minutes To Midnight / Rainbow's Gold / Mission From 'Arry
(12", CD – EMI 1984)

Aces High / King Of Twilight
(7", Cassette – EMI 1984)

**Aces High / The Number Of The Beast (Live) / King Of Twilight /
Rainbow's Gold / Cross-Eyed Mary**
(12" – EMI 1984)

Aces High / King Of Twilight / The Number Of The Beast (Live)
(12", CD – EMI 1984)

Running Free (Live) / Sanctuary (Live)
(7", Cassette – EMI 1985)

**Running Free (Live) / Sanctuary (Live) / Murders In The Rue
Morgue**
(12", CD – EMI 1985)

Run To The Hills (Live) / Phantom Of The Opera (Live)
(7", Cassette – EMI 1985)

Run To The Hills (Live) / Phantom Of The Opera (Live) / Losfer Words (Live)
(12", CD – EMI 1985)

Wasted Years / Reach Out
(7", Cassette – EMI 1986)

Wasted Years / Reach Out / Sheriff Of Huddersfield
(12", CD – EMI 1986)

Stranger In A Strange Land / That Girl
(7", Cassette – EMI 1986)

Stranger In A Strange Land / That Girl / Juanita
(12", CD – EMI 1986)

Can I Play With Madness? (Promo)
(7" – EMI 1988)

Can I Play With Madness? / Black Bart Blues
(7", Cassette – EMI 1988)

Can I Play With Madness? / Black Bart Blues / Massacre
(12", CD – EMI 1988)

The Evil That Men Do / Prowler '88
(7", Cassette – EMI 1988)

The Evil That Men Do / Prowler '88 / Charlotte The Harlot '88
(12", CD – EMI 1988)

The Clairvoyant / The Prisoner (Live) / Heaven Can Wait (Live)
(12", CD –EMI 1988)

The Clairvoyant / The Prisoner (Live)
(7", Cassette – EMI 1988)

Infinite Dreams (Live) / Killers (Live)
(7", Cassette – EMI 1989)

Infinite Dreams (Live) / Killers (Live) / Still Life (Live)
(12", CD – EMI 1989)

Holy Smoke / All In Your Mind
(7", Cassette – EMI 1990)

Holy Smoke / All In Your Mind / Kill Me Ce Soir
(12", CD – EMI 1990)

Bring Your Daughter To The Slaughter / I'm A Mover
(7", Cassette – EMI 1990)

Bring Your Daughter To The Slaughter / I'm A Mover / Communication Breakdown
(12", CD – EMI 1990)

Be Quick Or Be Dead / Nodding Donkey Blues
(7", Cassette – EMI 1992)

Be Quick Or Be Dead / Nodding Donkey Blues / Space Station No. 5
(12" – EMI 1992)

Be Quick Or Be Dead / Nodding Donkey Blues / Space Station No. 5 / The French Message From Bruce Dickinson
(CD – EMI 1992)

From Here To Eternity / Roll Over Vic Vella
(7", Cassette – EMI 1992)

From Here To Eternity / Roll Over Vic Vella / No Prayer For The Dying (Live)
(12", CD – EMI 1992)

From Here To Eternity / Roll Over Vic Vella / Public Enema Number One / No Prayer For The Dying (Live)
(CD – EMI 1992)

Wasting Love (Promo)
(7" – EMI 1992)

Wasting Love / Tailgunner (Live) / Holy Smoke (Live) / The Assassin (Live)
(CD – EMI 1992)

Fear Of The Dark (Live) / Tailgunner (Live)
(7" – EMI 1993)

Fear Of The Dark (Live) / Hooks In You (Live)
(7" – EMI 1993)

Fear Of The Dark (Live) / Tailgunner (Live) / Hooks In You (Live) / Bring Your Daughter To The Slaughter (Live)
(CD – EMI 1993)

Fear Of The Dark (Live) / Be Quick Or Be Dead / Hooks In You (Live)
(12" CD – EMI 1993)

Fear Of The Dark (Live) / Bring Your Daughter To The Slaughter / Hooks In You (Live)
(CD – EMI 1993)

Hallowed Be Thy Name (Live) / Wrathchild (Live)
(7", CD – EMI 1993)

Hallowed Be Thy Name (Live) / The Trooper (Live) / Wasted Years (Live)
(12"– EMI 1993)

Hallowed Be Thy Name (Live) / Wrathchild / Wasted Years (Live) / The Trooper (Live)
(CD – EMI 1993)

Man On The Edge / The Edge Of Darkness / Judgement Day
(CD – EMI 1995)

Man On The Edge / The Edge Of Darkness / I Live My Way
(12" – EMI 1995)

Man On The Edge / The Edge Of Darkness / Judgement Day / Blaze Bayley Interview Pt. 1
(12" – EMI 1995)

Man On The Edge / The Edge Of Darkness / Justice Of The Piece / Blaze Bayley Interview Pt. 2
(12" – EMI 1995)

Lord Of The Flies / Doctor, Doctor / My Generation
(CD – EMI 1995)

Virus / Sanctuary (Metal For Muthas Version) / Wrathchild (Metal For Muthas Version)
(12", CD – EMI 1996)

Virus / Man On The Edge / Afraid To Shoot Strangers (Live) / 2 Minutes To Midnight / The Trooper / The Number Of The Beast / Wrathchild / Strange World / Iron Maiden.
(CD – EMI 1996)

Virus / Man On The Edge / Afraid To Shoot Strangers (Live) / 2 Minutes To Midnight / The Trooper / The Number Of The Beast / Strange World / Iron Maiden.
(CD – EMI 1996)

Virus / Doctor, Doctor / My Generation
(CD – EMI 1996)

Virus / Prowler (*Soundhouse Tapes* Version) / Invasion (*Soundhouse Tapes* Version)
(12", CD – EMI 1996)

The Angel And The Gambler / Blood On The World's Hands (Live) / The Aftermath (Live) / Man On The Edge (Enhanced Video)
(7", CD – EMI 1998)

The Angel And The Gambler / Blood On The World's Hands (Live) / Afraid To Shoot Strangers (Live) / Man On The Edge (Enhanced Video)
(CD – EMI 1998)

Futureal / The Angel And The Gambler / The Evil That Men Do (Live) / Man On The Edge (Live)
(CD – EMI 1998)

The Wicker Man / Futureal (Live) / Man On The Edge (Live) / The Wicker Man (Enhanced Video)
(CD – EMI 2000)

The Wicker Man / Powerslave (Live) / Man On The Edge (Live) / The Wicker Man (Enhanced Video)
(CD – EMI 2000)

The Wicker Man / Powerslave (Live) / Killers (Live)
(12" – EMI 2000)

The Wicker Man / Futureal (Live) / Killers (Live) / Futureal (Enhanced Video)
(CD – EMI 2000)

Out Of The Silent Planet / Aces High (Live)
(7", CD – EMI 2000)

Out Of The Silent Planet / Aces High (Live) / Wasted Years (Live) / Out Of The Silent Planet (Enhanced Video)
(CD – EMI 2000)

Out Of The Silent Planet / Aces High (Live) / Wasted Years (Live)
(12" – EMI 2000)

The Wicker Man / Ghost Of The Navigator / Brave New World / Dream Of Mirrors / The Fallen Angel (Promo)
(CD – EMI 2000)

Run To The Hills / Total Eclipse
(7" – EMI 2002)

Run To The Hills (Live) / Children Of The Damned (Live) / Total Eclipse (Live) / Run To The Hills (Live Video)
(CD – EMI 2002)

Run To The Hills (Original Single Version) / 22 Acacia Avenue (Live) / The Prisoner (Live) / Run To The Hills (Camp Chaos Video)
(CD – EMI 2002)

Run To The Hills (Live From Rock In Rio 2001) / Run To The Hills (Original Single Version) / 22 Acacia Avenue (Live '82) / Children Of The Damned (Live '82) / Total Eclipse (Live '82) / Prisoner (Live '82) / Run To The Hills (Video) / Run To The Hills (Video)
(CD – EMI 2002)

Run To The Hills (Original 1982 Version) / Run To The Hills (Live from Rock In Rio 2001)
(CD – EMI 2002)

Edward The Great – The Greatest Hits Sampler EP (Promo)
The Number Of The Beast / Can I Play With Madness / The Trooper / Bring Your Daughter To The Slaughter / The Wicker Man
(CD – EMI 2002)

Eddie's Archive Sampler EP (Promo)
BBC Archives - Iron Maiden (BBC Friday Rock Show '79) / Prowler (Reading Festival '80) / The Prisoner (Reading Festival '82) / Wrathchild (Donington Monsters Of Rock Festival '88) / Beast Over Hammersmith - Children Of The Damned / 22 Acacia Avenue / Best Of The B-sides - Drifter (Live) / All In Your Mind
(CD – EMI 2002)

Wildest Dreams / Pass The Jam / Blood Brothers (Orchestral Version)
(CD – EMI 2003)

Wildest Dreams / Pass The Jam
(7", CD – EMI 2003)

Wildest Dreams / The Nomad (Rock Mix) / Blood Brothers (Rock Mix) / Clip Of 2003 EPK
(DVD – EMI 2003)

Wildest Dreams (Promo)
(7" – EMI 2003)

Rainmaker / Dance Of Death (Orchestral Version) / More Tea Vicar
(CD – EMI 2003)

Rainmaker (Video) / The Wicker Man (Live) / Children Of The Damned (Live) / Video Stills Slide Show
(DVD – EMI 2003)

Rainmaker (Promo)
7" – EMI 2003

***Dance Of Death* Sampler EP** (Promo)
Wildest Dreams / Rainmaker / No More Lies / Paschendale / Journeyman
(CD – EMI 2003)

BOOTLEGS

This is not an exhaustive list of all the Maiden bootlegs available. In fact, there are roughly five times more products available worldwide than listed here. However, many of those are of poor quality, so instead, the ones listed here are either of great significance historically, or sound top notch.

MAIDEN MUSIC MACHINE
London Music Machine, England, 10th September 1979 (CD/LP)
Wrathchild / Sanctuary / Prowler / Remember Tomorrow / Another Life / Running Free / Transylvania / Invasion / Charlotte The Harlot / Phantom Of The Opera / Iron Maiden / Guitar Solo Dave Murray / Drifter

RUSKIN ARMS '79
Ruskin Arms, England, Friday 5th October 1979 (CD/LP)
The Ides Of March / Wrathchild / Sanctuary / Prowler / Remember Tomorrow / Running Free / Another Life / Transylvania / Strange World / Invasion / Charlotte The Harlot / Phantom Of The Opera / Iron Maiden / Innocent Exile / Tony Parsons Solo / Dave Murray Solo / Drifter / I've Got The Fire

LIVE AT TIFFANY'S
Tiffany's Club, Scotland, 4th February 1980 (CD/LP)
Wrathchild / Sanctuary / Prowler / Remember Tomorrow / Running Free / Transylvania / Strange World (Cut) / Strange World / Charlotte The Harlot / Phantom Of The Opera / Iron Maiden / Transylvania / Bonus - Sabbath Bloody Sabbath (Bruce Dickinson) / Bonus Track - Living In A Fuckin Timewarp (Gogmagog)

KILLING TIME
De Vereeniging Nijmegen, Holland, 24th April 1981 (CD/LP)
Genghis Khan / Killers / Purgatory / Sanctuary / Remember Tomorrow / Twilight Zone / Phantom Of The Opera / Iron Maiden / Transylvania / Drifter

ANOTHER LIVE
Kosei Nenkin Hall, Japan, 23rd May 1981 (CD/LP)

Wrathchild / Purgatory / Sanctuary / Remember Tomorrow / Another Life / Twilight Zone / Strange World / Murders In The Rue Morgue / Iron Maiden / Transylvania / Drifter

LUND – PAUL'S LAST GIG
Olympean, Sweden, 10th September 1981 (CD/2-LP)
Ides Of March / Sanctuary / Purgatory / Wrathchild / Twilight Zone / Remember Tomorrow / Genghis Khan / Killers / Another Life / Drum Solo / Innocent Exile / Running Free / Murders In The Rue Morgue / Phantom Of The Opera / Iron Maiden / Transylvania / Guitar Solo / Drifter / Prowler

TOTAL ECLIPSE
The New Theatre, Oxford, England, 9th March 1982 *(CD/2-LP)*
Murders In The Rue Morgue / Wrathchild / Run To The Hills / Children Of The Damned / The Number Of The Beast / Another Life / Killers / 22 Acacia Avenue / Total Eclipse / Running Free / Drum Solo / Transylvania / Guitar Solo / Prisoner / Hallowed Be Thy Name / Phantom Of The Opera / Iron Maiden / Sanctuary / Drifter / Prowler

DRAMMEN 83 (WORLD PIECE TOUR)
Drammenshallen, Norway, 4th June 1983 *(CD/2-LP)*
Intro / Where Eagles Dare / Wrathchild / The Trooper / Revelations / Flight Of Icarus / Die With Your Boots On / 22 Acacia Avenue / The Number Of The Beast / Still Life / To Tame A Land (Cut) / To Tame A Land (Continues) / Phantom Of The Opera / Hallowed Be Thy Name / Iron Maiden / Run To The Hills / Sanctuary / Drifter / Prowler

LAST PRAYER (WORLD PIECE TOUR)
Sporthalle, Germany, Tuesday 16th October 1984 *(CD/2-LP)*
Intro / Aces High / 2 Minutes To Midnight / The Trooper / Revelations / Flight Of Icarus / Rime Of The Ancient Mariner / Losfer Words / Powerslave / Guitar Solo / The Number Of The Beast / Hallowed Be Thy Name / Iron Maiden / Run To The Hills / Running Free / Sanctuary

LIVE IN QUEBEC CITY 1984 (WORLD SLAVERY TOUR)
Coliseum, Canada, 26th November 1984 *(CD/2-LP)*
Intro / Aces High / 2 Minutes To Midnight / The Trooper / Revelations / Flight Of Icarus / Rime Of The Ancient Mariner / Bruce Dickinson Introduces Next Song / Losfer Words / Powerslave / Guitar Solo / The Number Of The Beast / Hallowed Be Thy Name / 22 Acacia Avenue / Iron Maiden / Run To The Hills / Running Free / Sanctuary

DOIN' MY JOB (WORLD SLAVERY TOUR)
Arma Di Taggia, Italy, 22nd August 1984 *(CD/LP)*
Intro / Aces High / 2 Minutes To Midnight / The Trooper / Revelations
/ Flight Of Icarus / Rime Of The Ancient Mariner / The Number Of The
Beast / Hallowed Be Thy Name / 22 Acacia Avenue / Iron Maiden / Run
To The Hills / Running Free

ROCK IN RIO (WORLD SLAVERY TOUR)
Rock In Rio Festival, Brazil, 11th January 1985 *(CD/LP)*
2 Minutes To Midnight / The Trooper / Revelations / Flight Of Icarus /
Rime Of The Ancient Mariner / Powerslave / The Number Of The Beast /
Hallowed Be Thy Name / Iron Maiden / Run To The Hills / Running Free

MONSTERS OF ROCK (SEVENTH TOUR)
Donington Festival, UK, 20 August 1988 *(CD/LP)*
Moonchild / The Prisoner / Wrathchild / Infinite Dreams / The Trooper /
Heaven Can Wait / The Clairvoyant / Seventh Son Of A Seventh Son / The
Number Of The Beast / Hallowed Be Thy Name / Iron Maiden

MONSTERS OF ROCK FESTIVAL (FEAR OF THE DARK TOUR)
Donington, UK, 22 August 1992 *(2-CD/2-LP)*
Be Quick Or Be Dead / The Number Of The Beast / Wrathchild / From
Here To Eternity / Can I Play With Madness / Wasting Love / Tailgunner
/ The Evil That Men Do / Afraid To Shoot Strangers / Fear Of The Dark
/ Bring Your Daughter To The Slaughter / The Clairvoyant / Heaven Can
Wait / Run To The Hills / 2 Minutes To Midnight / Iron Maiden / Hallowed
Be Thy Name / The Trooper / Sanctuary / Running Free / Public Enema
Number One

LOS ANGELES 2000 (BRAVE NEW TOUR)
Universal Amphitheater, USA, 13th September 2000 *(2-CD)*
The Wicker Man / Ghost Of The Navigator / Brave New World / Wrath-
child / 2 Minutes To Midnight / Bruce's Speech / Blood Brothers / Sign Of
The Cross / The Mercenary / The Trooper / Dream Of Mirrors / The Clans-
man / The Evil That Men Do / Fear Of The Dark / Iron Maiden / Number
Of The Beast / Hallowed Be Thy Name / Sanctuary

HEADBANGER'S FEST 2001 (BRAVE NEW TOUR)
Foro Sol, Mexico City, Mexico, 9th January 2001 (2-CD)
Intro / The Wicker Man / Ghost Of The Navigator / Brave New World
/ Wrathchild / 2 Minutes To Midnight / Blood Brothers / Sign Of The

Cross / The Mercenary / The Trooper / Dream Of Mirrors / The Clansman / The Evil That Men Do / Fear Of The Dark / Iron Maiden / The Number Of The Beast / Hallowed Be Thy Name / Sanctuary / The Fallen Angel / Out Of The Silent Planet

CHILE 2001 (BRAVE NEW TOUR)
Estadio Chile, Santiago, Chile, 9th January 2001 *(2-CD)*
The Wicker Man / Ghost Of The Navigator / Brave New World / Wrathchild / 2 Minutes To Midnight / Blood Brothers / The Mercenary / The Trooper / Dream Of Mirrors / The Clansman / The Evil That Men Do / Fear Of The Dark / Iron Maiden / The Number Of The Beast / Hallowed Be Thy Name / Sanctuary / Run To The Hills

LIVE ONLINE – CLIVE BURR BENEFIT GIG
Brixton Academy, London, 21st March 2002 *(2-CD)*
The Wicker Man / Ghost Of The Navigator / Brave New World / Wrathchild / 2 Minutes To Midnight / Blood Brothers / The Clansman / The Mercenary / The Trooper / Dream Of Mirrors / The Evil That Men Do / Fear Of The Dark / Iron Maiden / The Number Of The Beast / Children Of The Damned / Hallowed Be Thy Name / Run To The Hills

CHILLED BONES IN MILANO 2003 (DANCE OF DEATH TOUR)
Milan Filaforum, Italy, 27th October 2003 (CD)
Wildest Dreams / Wrathchild / Can I Play With Madness / The Trooper / Dance Of Death / Rainmaker / Brave New World / Paschendale / Lord Of The Flies / No More Lies / Hallowed Be Thy Name / Fear Of The Dark / Iron Maiden / Journeyman / The Number Of The Beast / Run To The Hills

BOX SETS

THE FIRST TEN YEARS (10-LP/10-CD – EMI 2004)
Running Free / Burning Ambition / Sanctuary / Drifter / I've Got The
Fire / Listen With Nicko Part 1 /
Women In Uniform / Wrathchild / Listen With Nicko Part 2 / Twilight
Zone / Invasion / Phantom Of The Opera / Purgatory / Genghis Khan /
Maiden Japan / Running Free / Remember Tomorrow / Killers / Innocent
Exile / Listen With Nicko Part 3
Run To The Hills / Total Eclipse / The Number Of The Beast / Remember Tomorrow / Listen With Nicko Part 4
Flight Of Icarus / I've Got The Fire / The Trooper / Cross Eyed Mary /
Listen With Nicko Part 5
2 Minutes To Midnight / Rainbow's Gold / Mission From 'Arry / Aces
High / King Of Twilight / Number Of The Beast / Listen With Nicko Part
6
Running Free / Sanctuary / Murders In The Rue Morgue / Run To The
Hills / Phantom Of The Opera / Losfer Words(Big 'Orra) / Listen With
Nicko Part 7
Wasted Years / Reach Out / Sheriff Of Huddersfield / Stranger In A
Strange Land / That Girl / Juanita / Listen With Nicko Part
Can I Play With Madness? / Black Bart Blues / Massacre / The Evil That
Men Do / Prowler '88 / Charlotte The Harlot '88 / Listen With Nicko
Part 9
The Clairvoyant / The Prisoner / Heaven Can Wait / Infinite Dreams /
Killers / Still Life / Listen With Nicko Part 10

EDDIE'S HEAD (CD – EMI 1998)
Contains all Iron Maiden's studio albums.

EDDIE'S ARCHIVE (6-CD – EMI 2002)
Disc 1: Iron Maiden / Running Free / Transylvania / Sanctuary / Wrathchild / Run To The Hills / Children Of The Damned / Number Of The
Beast / 22 Acacia Ave / Iron Maiden / Transylvania / The Prisoner / Hallowed Be Thy Name / Phantom Of The Opera
Disc 2: Prowler / Remember Tomorrow / Killers / Running Free / Transylvania / Iron Maiden / Moonchild / Wrathchild / Infinite Dreams / The
Trooper / Seventh Son of a Seventh Son / The Number Of The Beast /
Hallowed Be Thy Name / Iron Maiden

Disc 3: Murders In The Rue Morgue / Wrathchild / Run To The Hills / Children Of The Damned / The Number Of The Beast / Another Life / Killers / 22 Acacia Ave / Total Eclipse

Disc 4: Transylvania / The Prisoner / Hallowed Be Thy Name / Phantom Of The Opera / Iron Maiden / Sanctuary / Drifter / Running Free / Prowler

Disc 5: 1. Burning / Drifter / Invasion / Remember Tomorrow / I've Got The Fire / Cross-Eyed Mary / Rainbow's Gold / King Of Twilight / Reach Out / That Girl / Juanita / Sheriff Of Huddersfield / Black Bart Blues / Prowler '88 / Charlotte The Harlot '88

Disc 6: All In Your Mind / Kill Me Ce Soir / I'm A Mover / Communication Breakdown / Nodding Donkey Blues / Space Station No. 5 / I Can't See My Feelings / Roll Over Vic Vella / Justice Of The Peace / Judgement Day / My Generation / Doctor, Doctor / Blood On The World's Hands / The Aftermath / Futureal / Wasted Years

BOOKS

IRON MAIDEN: Running Free (Garry Bushell, Ross Halfin, Zomba, UK, 1985)

IRON MAIDEN: A Photographic History (Ross Halfin, Zomba, UK, 1988)

IRON MAIDEN: Infinite Dreams (Dave Bowler, Bryan Dray, Music Book Services, UK, 1996)

RUN TO THE HILLS: The Authorised Biography (Mick Wall, Sanctuary, UK, 1998)

THE IRON MAIDEN COMPANION (Marco Gamba, Italy, 2000)

IRON MAIDEN (Ross Halfin, Omnibus, UK, 2006)

INTERVIEWS

CDs
Playing With Madness (Baktabak, 1991)
Maximum Iron Maiden Biography (Chrome Dreams, 2001)
Iron Maiden X-Posed (Chrome Dreams, 2003)

12"s
Interview (Picture disc, Baktabak, 1987)
Conversation (AVI, 1988)
Playing With Madness (Baktabak 1991)

DVDS

Raising Hell (BMG Special Products, 2000)
Classic Albums: Number Of The Beast (Eagle Rock, 2001)
Rock In Rio (EMI, 2002)
Visions Of The Beast (EMI, 2003)
The History Of Iron Maiden: Part 1, The Early Days (EMI, 2004)
Iron Maiden: The Legacy Of The Beast (Chrome Dreams, 2004)
Death On The Road (EMI, 2005)

VHS

Live At The Rainbow (Video Collection Int., 1980)
Video Pieces (EMI, 1981)
Behind The Iron Curtain (Video Collection Int., 1984)
Live After Death (Video Collection Int., 1985
The First Ten Years: The Videos (EMI, 1990)
12 Wasted Years (Picture Music Int., 1987)
Maiden England (EMI, 1988)
Live At Donington (Picture Music Int., 1992)
Raising Hell (Picture Music Int. 1993)
Classic Albums: Number Of The Beast (Eagle Rock, 2001)
Rock In Rio (Sanctuary, 2002)
Visions Of The Beast (EMI, 2003)

WEBSITES

www.ironmaiden.com
www.maidenfans.com
www.eddiesbar.fr.st/
www.eddiethegreat.free.fr/
www.home.arcor.de/alexander-g/
www.ironmaidenchopper.com/
www.perso.wanadoo.fr/ironmaiden/
www.ironmaidenbrasil.com
www.rockaxis.com/~maiden/
www.ironmaiden-planet.de/
www.ironmaidenbooks.com
www.ironmaidenheaven.com
www.ironmaidenfan.de.vu/
www.maidenitalia.com/ironmaiden
www.ironmaiden.sk/
www.iron-maiden.startkabel.nl/
www.ironmaidensweden.se/
www.maidencentral.com/
www.maidenzone.com/
www.webironmaiden.com/

ALSO AVAILABLE FROM CHROME DREAMS

Maximum Maiden
The Unauthorised Biography Of Iron Maiden
Cat: ABCD050

Iron Maiden are a household name the world over. With album sales over 50 million, the band are now rightly regarded as the 'classic' British rock band in every sense of the word. 'Maximum Maiden' presents the full unauthorised audio-biography of the group from their origins as a bar band in the mid-70s, trying to keep rock alive in spite of the onslaught of punk, through the mega hits of the 80s to the present day. Essential listening for any metal fan.

**Available from all good record stores,
online at Amazon and other good sites and from
www.chromedreams.co.uk**

ALSO AVAILABLE FROM CHROME DREAMS

Iron Maiden X-Posed
Unpublished And Rare Interviews Set
Cat: CTCD7035

Iron Maiden X-Posed provides yet more insight into this most metal of groups with interviews with band members from different stages in their career. Presented in a collectors' slipcase with poster, the set details what the band really think about their fans and their massive worldwide fame – in their own words.

Available from all good record stores, online at Amazon and other good sites and from www.chromedreams.co.uk